Open Systems: The Reality

T.A. Critchley and K.C. Batty
IBM (UK) Ltd

Prentice Hall
New York   London   Toronto   Sydney   Tokyo   Singapore

First published 1993 by
Prentice Hall International (UK) Limited
Campus 400, Maylands Avenue
Hemel Hempstead
Hertfordshire, HP2 7EZ
A division of
Simon & Schuster International Group

Printed and bound in Great Britain by
Redwood Books Ltd, Trowbridge, Wiltshire

Library of Congress Cataloging-in-Publication Data

Critchley, T. A.
  Open systems, the reality / T. A. Critchley and K. C. Batty.
    p.   cm. — (BSC practitioner series)
  Includes index.
  ISBN 0-13-030735-1
  1. Operating systems (Computers) 2. Open system interconnection.
I. Batty, K. C. II. Title. III. Series.
QA76.76.063C735   1993
004'.36—dc20   93-7961
                                                         CIP

British Library Cataloguing in Publication Data

A catalogue record for this book is available from
the British Library

ISBN 0-13-030735-1

  2   3   4   5   97   96   95   94

Open Systems: The Reality

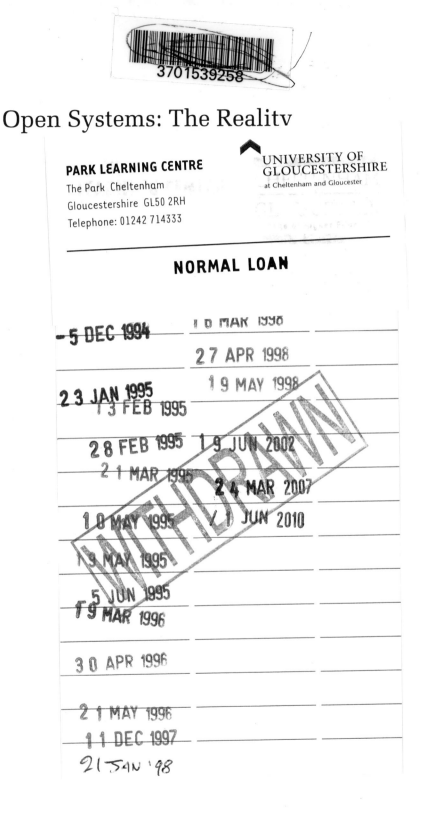

PARK LEARNING CENTRE
The Park Cheltenham
Gloucestershire GL50 2RH
Telephone: 01242 714333

UNIVERSITY OF
GLOUCESTERSHIRE
at Cheltenham and Gloucester

NORMAL LOAN

BCS Practitioner Series

Series editor: Ray Welland

TO

Robert Batty and Albert Critchley,
our late fathers.

Contents

Foreword by Peter Cunningham

For more than a decade, companies and users committed to open systems have been changing the way in which organizations use Information Technology. The rapid product life cycle of computer hardware platforms is making it more and more difficult for MIS directors and corporate IT systems designers to keep abreast of the latest developments. Fortunately, open systems has permitted those same people to rely upon a stable suite of interfaces, services and protocols that function on even the latest platforms. This ability, even in the face of rapid change, has in turn permitted application developers to ensure that their applications continue to be compatible, both past and present, even as the supporting hardware and basic systems software changes around them.

Unfortunately, this stability comes with a high cost. The definition of open systems is difficult. Throughout this book, the authors describe the ways in which open systems have evolved. That evolution, and the industry-wide agreement that the definition of each open systems component represents, can take years to complete. Each hardware vendor, application developer and end-user participating in the development of an open system specification has his own interests and reconciling the various points of view can often be difficult. As a result, it is often necessary for certain suppliers and end-users to lead and evangelize certain technologies, thus pioneering the way forward for others.

In the last couple of years, companies have increasingly moved to a model of competitive tender procurement and are now moving towards multi-vendor open systems at a fast rate. The definition of an open systems platform is today complete enough that it is possible to construct an environment that will carry an organization forward into the next century. As many of the largest corporations and institutions consider the alternatives for 'downsizing' or 'rightsizing' their legacy systems, and for integrating their departmental islands of computing into an Enterprise-wide solution, they can rely upon the foundation of open systems that has been laid. With the help of this book, and others like it, it will be easier for companies to plan their MIS procurements and deployment of open systems and to start the transition.

In the end, it is the vote of the buyer that helps us on the supply side of the industry to understand if we have the technology mix right. We believe we now have all the pieces in place for buyers to move forward with confidence. We shall see if the next phase of the computing industry's evolution is as exciting as the last.

Peter Cunningham, President and CEO, UNIX International.

Foreword by Geoffrey E. Morris

The biggest phenomenon of the 90s has been the consumers' demand for information - the very lifeblood of successful business and government.

It has also not escaped the notice of the business man that for years the computer industry has been driven by designer collections of unintelligible technology, waltzed down the catwalk to the applause of computer scientists the world over. Those designers, who were themselves once the prime market for their own products, designed proprietary solutions for the same problems year after year. The result was a shrinking demand for large scale computers and a rising demand for individual computers. Enter information confusion and chaos, stage left.

The economics of market competition, however, result in the inevitable broadening of product appeal and expansion in the market, to the point where demand for homogeneity takes over. Enter open systems, stage right.

The essence of an open systems strategy is that the buyer will benefit from a much simpler application of information technology - a much simpler method of integrating all the information management systems. The reality is, that by making technology interoperate more easily, and enabling information to be more portable, those of us who are in information-critical jobs will buy more. Such is the role of open systems: to expand the use of computers to manage and manipulate information. To date, the open systems segment of the computer industry is expanding the fastest at 30% per annum and has grown from almost nothing in 1985 to a $70 billion market in 1992.

At the very heart of open systems are several basic needs. A computing architecture of standard interfaces, or 'plugs and sockets', which allow the consumer a wide choice of products that interoperate, knowledge and information that will provide a business case for action and a safe method of choosing suppliers who make and market systems that are truly open.

The authors of this book you have started to read are treating you to a most comprehensive and enlightening assessment of the structure and quality of open systems. You will be guided by industry knowledge and insights from the early perceptions of open systems, through the history of computing to the present day value of open systems.

X/Open's role has been twofold. Firstly, to stimulate the suppliers of computer systems to standardize their interfaces, or 'plugs and sockets', and to publicly declare the extent of standardization by obtaining certification through the X/Open branding scheme. To date, the reality is 35 branded suppliers and over 600 branded products. Secondly, to provide the buyer with a business case methodology to procure open systems. To date, the X/Open brand has been used by government and business in purchases totalling $7 billion.

By reading this book, you will obtain huge benefit from the industrial experiences of the authors Dr. Terry Critchley and Mr. Ken Batty, their analysis of the growth of a new phenomenon in computing and the practical benefits of the application of open systems. Read on, and keep an open mind.

Geoffrey Morris, President and CEO, X/Open Company.

Foreword by David Tory

The book you are about to read will tell you about the computing phenomenon known as open systems. Open systems have been promoted, one might say 'hyped', aggressively and broadly. Even a casual perusal of a computer publication will yield a number of articles on the subject. Yet two things will be missing: a single, sensible definition, and a good reason to join the crowds who claim to be moving to openness.

The Open Software Foundation has a vested interest in open systems, not as they are being promoted to the IT world, but rather as they are being implemented in commercial computing installations. We agree with authors Dr. Critchley and Mr. Batty: the only good reason to move to open systems is a business reason.

It would be difficult to find two people who agree on a definition for open systems, much less a business rationale. In fact, in this book, a number of individuals, involved one way or another with the industry, are asked for their definitions; none agrees with another. OSF defines open systems as application portability and interoperability across and between incompatible systems. Portability and interoperability are concepts which can be tied directly to your business, because they relate to preservation of investment, preservation of data and applications, and preservation of the skill sets of that most important asset: your employees.

Since 1988, the year we were founded, OSF has been saying that no one technology, or class of technology, equals 'open systems'. The only thing that makes a system open is the user's ability to do his or her work, without worrying about which operating system or graphical user interface is running, and without having to know too much about where the data is stored or how. What counts is portability - being able to move and use data where it is convenient to the user; and interoperability - the capability of tying together machines of all makes and classes, in different physical locations, as it is convenient to the user.

At OSF, we also look at open systems as freedom of choice. The bonds of history, the limits of strict single-vendor control of your business's computing assets, has been broken. More than ever before, users of Information Technology are free to choose computing solutions that meet the needs of their businesses.

In an admirable way, this book describes the history of open systems, explores the reality as we know it today, and proposes a path to an even better model. By de-mystifying the subject, and returning always to the bottom line: *is there a business reason for moving to open systems?* the authors make clear the risks and rewards of open systems. In doing so, they have performed a service for all who have a vital interest in managing information to best serve the needs of their businesses. They are to be congratulated for writing a really excellent and comprehensive reference book on the subject.

David Tory, President and CEO, Open Software Foundation.

Editorial Preface

The aim of the BCS Practitioner Series is to produce books which are relevant for practising computer professionals across the whole spectrum of Information Technology activities. We want to encourage practitioners to share their practical experience of methods and applications with fellow professionals. We also seek to disseminate information in a form that is suitable for the practitioner who often has only limited time to read widely within a new subject area or to assimilate research findings.

The role of the BCS is to provide advice on the suitability of books for the Series, via the Editorial Panel, and to provide a pool of potential authors upon which we can draw. Our objective is that this Series will reinforce the drive within the BCS to increase professional standards in IT. The other partners in this venture, Prentice Hall, provide the publishing expertise and international marketing capabilities of a leading publisher in the computing field.

The response when we set up the series was extremely encouraging. However, the success of the Series depends on there being practitioners who want to learn, as well as those who feel they have something to offer! The Series is under continual development and we are always looking for ideas for new topics and feedback on how to further improve the usefulness of the series. If you are interested in writing for the Series then please contact us.

Open systems is a subject which is currently getting a great deal of media coverage and many extravagant claims are being made for this technology. If, like me, you don't know much about open systems and are mystified by all the different standards, then this book will be useful to you. It is written in provocative style, challenging the reader to think about the problems and potential benefits of open systems, and presents a clear overview of concepts, terminology and technology.

Ray Welland Computing Science Department, University of Glasgow

Editorial Panel Members

Frank Bott (UCW, Aberystwyth), Dermot Browne (KPMG Management Consulting), Nic Holt (ICL), Trevor King (Praxis Systems plc), Tom Lake (GLOSSA), Kathy Spurr (Analysis and Design Consultants), Mario Wolczko (University of Manchester).

Preface

This book is about the emotive subject of 'open systems'. In most disciplines, the author (or authors) of a book would be expected to outline their credentials and long experience in that particular discipline. This is a difficult thing to do in the emerging arena of 'open systems' since there are no veterans in the subject, in the same way as there are no veteran children. There will be cries from those people who have been involved with OSI or UNIX for years but, as we shall see, open systems is much more than the individual elements. People often retrofit open systems history onto the history of UNIX or OSI but only with hindsight, equating long experience in UNIX or OSI to long experience in open systems.

We, the authors, hope to establish our credentials via this book and in addressing the key question: 'If open systems is the solution, what was the problem?'

There are probably as many definitions and ideas as to what an open system is (although a single open system, like the first telephone, isn't a great deal of use) as there are pages in this book. Therefore it is important at the outset that we lay out our terms of reference and terminology before discussing the subject in any depth. This will hopefully avoid antagonizing the reader (or reviewer!) whose paradigm or model of open systems is different from ours. Our paradigm will be explained, convincingly we trust, in Chapter 2 but suffice it to say here, for those familiar with open systems, that it generally agrees with the IEEE definition and its implications.

Adopting or migrating to 'open systems' is not a single act, like buying a packet of recycled envelopes. It is more of a journey towards some goal, like the green movement so popular today. Moreover, this goal is more often than not specific to the organization making the move and warrants careful planning and implementation to yield any business or financial benefits. Going open because it is seen to be the thing to do can be a sterile and risky business. There is really only one good reason for making major changes to the IT structure of a company and that is business benefit. If it does not have such a benefit, be it increased sales, competitive advantage or whatever, then it is merely a cosmetic exercise (maybe) or pandering to an open systems whim. To put this in context, a typical large organization might spend 1.5% of its turnover on IT. Saving, say, 20% of that, although desirable, might have less effect than taking 3% off the salary bill or increasing sales by 5%. Indeed, the latter business benefits might even require extra IT spend to achieve.

Such a migration does not necessarily mean using UNIX or a UNIX-like operating system since choosing an open system is much more than the selection of an operating system or a type of hardware. In this book, we will illustrate this point by exploring the 'open' aspirations of some major computer vendors such as Digital Equipment Corporation, IBM and ICL involving their own, non-UNIX, operating systems.

It would be untrue to say that there is presently a stampede towards 'open systems' since probably 80% of the systems installed today do not meet any generally agreed definition of openness. Romtec estimate that organizations which have adopted UNIX systems still run 90% of their IT workload on proprietary systems.

There is, however, a drift towards open systems but with a broad spectrum of commitment and understanding. The commitment ranges from organizations with a defined policy of only installing open systems to those who are totally bemused by the whole issue. This book is aimed at people who would like to bypass the 'hype' about open systems, but want to understand the concepts and the reality. This sort of understanding may help them realize that open systems and Utopia are not necessarily synonymous, and that any benefits accruing are not necessarily immediate, nor are they guaranteed. Open systems pundits say that the full reality of open systems will not be with us for periods varying between five and twenty years.

It would be equally untrue to say there are opposing camps in the form of open and proprietary vendors. Rather, there are people who have been happy in the world of 'proprietary' systems who are venturing into open systems, while there are others watching to see how they fare. The former is often referred to as 'downsizing' or, more recently, 'rightsizing' and we will discuss this phenomenon in the book. There are, however, opposing factions within the open systems movement suggesting, perhaps, that there are several open systems! We will attempt to show that while there may be several definitions and implementations of open systems, there can only be ONE ultimate open system environment. This fact is the absolute crux of understanding open systems and it is this 'proof' which will remove the UNIX operating system in its many forms as mandatory for openness, though not its right to be classed as open.

The reader will have deduced by now that 'open systems' is not a mature or well-defined subject like the C language is, for example. There are no standards for open systems - only standards for the elements with which people try to construct open systems. There are many elements which guide and comprise implementations of open systems. The major ones we explain in this book. For example, there are the standards bodies (IEEE, ISO, ANSI and so on) which define the rules for portability and interoperability; communications and distributed processing (NFS, NCS, TCP/IP and so on) and the major suppliers of today's UNIX implementations - Unix System Laboratories (USL) and the Open Software Foundation (OSF). We will examine in some depth the X/Open organization and its work in consolidating standards into practical, working environments. Although these elements are mainly associated with UNIX in its various forms, they are not exclusive to that environment as we shall see.

Like marriage, the reality of open systems can be very different from the picture painted by the media. It behoves us all to try to understand the subject of 'open systems' so that in considering migration from proprietary (or vendor-specific) systems to open systems, the baby is not thrown out along with the bath water! Open systems and closed minds make strange bedfellows.

We are confident that this book will prove as useful and enjoyable in five years time as it is (hopefully) today as the open journey progresses. There will, of course, be major changes in the specific products and ideas which make up an open systems implementation, but we trust that the ideas and philosopy outlined in this book will remain valid. It is this philosophy which will permit such advances because it dispenses with the dogma of mandating specific hardware and operating systems as prerequisites for open systems.

Finally, although we are employed by IBM, any opinions expressed in this book are solely our responsibility and are in no way meant to suggest that these are, or are not, official IBM positions.

T.A. Critchley
K.C. Batty
Manchester

List of Figures

Acknowledgements

People

Thanks are due to personnel from ICL, DEC and several third party software suppliers. In true open systems fashion, they supplied information about their companies' products when asked and we hope our use of that information in this book is fair. In particular, Nic Holt of ICL and Richard Briggs of DEC were most helpful in supplying data about openness in their non-Unix systems. UNIX International (Graham Wilson and Nick Price), Open Software Foundation (Colin Scaiffe) and the X/Open Company also gave freely of information and relevant documents.

Finally, we would like to thank the many IBM personnel who have reviewed the manuscript, made comments, offered material to work on and given us ideas from their presentations and in discussions. In particular, we would single out Ken Griffiths (without whom this book would have been published earlier), Peter Idoine, Jay Ashford, John Fetvedt, Horst Truestedt, Steve Bateman, Ping Lin, Robert Youngjohns, Mel Zimowski, Carys Davies, Marcella Arnow, Pete Meier, Keith Barlow, Simcha Gralla, Martin King, Steve Ford, Nick Kraven, Sue Littler and Tony Robbins.

We are most grateful to Peter Cunningham, Geoff Morris and David Tory for reviewing and commenting on the material as well as writing forewords with uncannily similar sentiments about open systems. They were actually written without collusion.

Finally, thanks must go to Sally Farr and her team at the IBM Manchester Publishing Centre, especially to Rachel Wetherill and Peter Wright for their help with the diagrams. Together we discovered the lack of standards in the publishing world!

Trademarks

- AIX, IBM, OS/2, OS/400, and Systems Application Architecture are registered trademarks of International Business Machines Corporation. AIX/6000, AS/400, ES/3090, graPHIGS, Presentation Manager, RISC System/6000, SAA, System/370, System/390, and VM/XA are trademarks of International Business Machines

- Apollo is a registered trademark of Apollo Computer, Inc. Network Computing System and NCS are trademarks of Apollo Computer, Inc.

- AT&T is a registered trademark of American Telephone & Telegraph

- DEC is a registered trademark of Digital Equipment Corporation

- Encina and Transarc are registered trademarks of Transarc Corporation.

- GL is a trademark and Silicon Graphics is a registered trademark of Silicon Graphics, Inc.

- HP is a trademark of Hewlett Packard Inc.

- INGRES is a registered trademark of the Ingres Corporation, Inc.

- Intel is a registered trademark of the Intel Corporation. 386 and 486 are trademarks of Intel.

- Microsoft is a registered trademark of Microsoft Corporation, Windows is a trademark of Microsoft Corporation.

- Motorola is a registered trademark of Motorola Corporation. 68000, 68020 and 68030 are trademarks of Motorola.

- OSF, Open Software Foundation, OSF/1, OSF/Motif and Motif are trademarks of the Open Software Foundation, Inc.

- PEX is a trademark of Massachusetts Institute of Technology

- PostScript is a trademark of Adobe Systems, Inc.

- SPECmark is a trademark of Standard Performance Evaluation Corporation.

- Sun is a registered trademark and Network File System, NFS, ONC, PC-NFS, SunOS, and SPARC are trademarks of Sun Microsystems, Inc.

- TPC is trademark of Transaction Processing Performance Council

- UNIX is a registered trademark of UNIX System Laboratories, Inc.

- UI-ATLAS is a trademark of UNIX International, Inc.

- USL is a registered trademark of UNIX System Laboratories, Inc.

- VAX is a trademark of Digital Equipment Corporation.

- XENIX is a registered trademark of Microsoft Corporation

- X Window System is a trademark of the Massachusetts Institute of Technology.

- X/Open is a trademark of X/Open Company, Ltd. in the U.K. and other countries.
- /usr/group is a trademark of UniForum.

Part 1
Setting the Scene

Chapter 1 Introduction

Theirs not to reason why, theirs but to do or die ... [1]

1.1 How to Use This Book

This book is meant for managers who make IT decisions, and for technical people at the strategic and tactical levels in an IT infrastructure. This includes technical planners, systems architects and designers as well as people whose jobs are centred around IT standards. However, anyone who is interested in IT and open systems might find it useful too. The reason for trying to satisfy the needs of different people in a single book is the nature of open systems information, particularly that on standards.

We were asked the classic author's question 'Who is this book written for?', to which we replied 'Anyone interested in open systems but with little knowledge'. There is a continuous spectrum of knowledge about open systems and trying to categorize one or two sets is difficult. We might have opted to address senior user or IT management with overviews, requirements and justifications but this has been done in other books and in numerous articles. What we felt was needed in a book was a balanced view of the subject with enough detail to show that the subject of open systems is as wide as it is deep. It is not a trivial subject.

For every senior manager who issues an open systems edict, there are probably twenty people who need to carry it out. The knowledge which helped the manager make his decision will not help those down the line who need to plan and implement that edict. We have therefore decided to address the audience of $20x$ people rather than x, although the latter are not excluded by any means.

For people interested in open systems, available sources of standards information present two extremes to the unwary. There are magazine articles and sales

---

[1] Alfred Lord Tennyson, 'The Charge of the Light Brigade'.

presentations at one end and the impenetrable volumes of definitive standards at the other - making it difficult to get a clear, reasonably technical grasp of open systems. The poor IT person whose 'need to know' falls between these two extremes is sadly neglected, having either to believe what the open systems zealot or antagonist says or to read the source documents in order to make his or her own mind up. This assumes, of course, that he or she can afford to buy the definitive works. Either way, such a person could be in what Americans call a 'no-win' situation in trying to learn enough about the subject to make decisions.

A glance at the table of contents should be enough to guide the reader to the sections of interest to them. The book can be read from beginning to end or dipped into at any point. If the latter mode of reading is used, the reader may have to refer to the glossary, index or earlier sections for information to allow him or her to understand the section chosen.

The book has been reviewed not only for technical accuracy but also by people with some IT knowledge with an eye on its usability by non-experts. It appeared to satisfy them. The favourite *modus operandi* seems to be to take a quick first pass and increase the level of understanding in a second pass through the book or when using it in reference mode.

1.2 Our Objectives

If you asked the question 'What is the capital of England?', you would more than likely get the answer 'London'. Ask the question 'What is beauty?' and you will have dozens of ideas and definitions from a large enough sample of people. Everyone has an intuitive feeling they know what beauty is but would find it difficult to define what it is or to explain to someone how one might migrate to being a beautiful person! The idea of open systems is very similar: maddeningly familiar yet difficult to define so as to cover the many IT situations in which organizations find themselves.

People often sidestep the definition issue by declaring what *they* mean by an open system and then there can be no argument - it is Unix or OSI or perhaps DOS PCs! For such individuals, this book possibly has no message since it is not a textbook on those subjects. For those who are not sure just what open systems are, this book should give enough information and references to work out what open systems mean to them and their organization. We have tried not to imply, as some texts and articles do, that everyone must go open as soon as possible irrespective of the consequences.

We wrote this book about open systems with the following intentions:
Overall,

- to give people sufficient knowledge, background and grasp of the open systems environment (OSE) and its terminology to feel comfortable in a discussion about open systems. There will be people who find sections of this book elementary and others who find sections quite technical. We have had to assume some IT knowledge on the part of most readers but do explain many terms in a glossary to avoid constant explanatory interruptions to the flow of the book. Some of the analogies can be skipped by experienced readers if they understand the topic being discussed. Conversely, people new to the topic can skip technical sections if they feel they add no value.

- to outline the scope of open systems issues by presenting perceptions of what open systems are and how they relate to the requirements of open systems users and prospective users.

Specifically,

- to describe the basic concepts of distributed and client/server computing systems, and interoperability. These often form the core of open systems computing
- to explain the standards which are fundamental to the timely achievement of open systems goals
- to describe the major standards bodies, their work and the relationships between them
- to classify the different types of IT organization which aspire to open systems computing, and the issues they face, particularly those with 'legacy' systems[2]
- to outline the open systems approaches of major IT vendors
- to try to present a balanced view of the offerings of the competing factions in the open systems arena, as far as our knowledge and access to information allow
- to make it self-contained enough that a grasp of the subject can be attained without frequent recourse by the reader to other books
- to differentiate clearly between concepts/architectures and resulting implementations.

To achieve these objectives, the book is divided into five parts:

1. Part 1 sets the scene for the discussion of open systems by looking at what people mean by open systems and what requirements are placed upon such systems.
2. Part 2 traces the history and development of IT systems and how the need for open systems arose.

---

[2] An open systems term for existing, traditional IT systems such as mainframes.

3. Part 3 is concerned with standards which are the basis for the open systems environment (OSE).

4. Part 4 looks at the ways of achieving 'openness'.

5. Part 5 presents a series of technical appendices to supplement Parts 1 to 4 and provide a reference base.

The book is split into nineteen chapters and these are structured as follows:

- Chapter 1 is what you are reading now.

- Chapter 2 looks at the ideas people have about what the words 'open system' actually mean and examines how they address the needs for openness as expressed by a wide range of IT users.

- Chapters 3, 4 and 5 trace the history of proprietary systems and networks and the Unix counterparts, culminating in a look at Open Systems Interconnection (OSI) in Chapter 6.

- Chapter 7 presents an overview of distributed computing, which forms the basis of much open systems computing.

- Chapter 8 reviews the areas of portability and interoperability which were the two areas where the ideas in Chapter 2 reached a consensus. The text briefly describes each relevant topic and points out why standards are needed to achieve openness.

- Chapter 9 sets out the details of the bodies and consortia who specify standards while Chapter 10 describes the organizations which implement these standards.

- Chapters 11 and 12 take a pragmatic look at the 'paths to openness' by looking at the types of IT organization which aspire to open systems and why they cannot all use the same methods. In particular, the hot topic of downsizing and rightsizing is dealt with in Chapter 12.

- Chapters 13, 14, 15 and 16 look at the standards developed and implemented in the following areas:

  - portability
  - user interfaces
  - interoperability, both pragmatic and standards-based.

  Chapter 16 focuses very much on online transaction processing (OLTP) and relational databases, both local and distributed. They have a heavy influence on what is and is not possible in open systems today. In the main, these chapters complement Chapter 8 in attempting to answer the questions posed there.

- Chapter 17 outlines the efforts of the major vendors to add 'open' features to their previously proprietary operating systems, for example, VMS and VME. It also contains a brief discussion of mainframe Unix.

- Chapter 18 examines in some depth the major interoperability technologies from the Open Software Foundation (OSF) and UNIX International (UI) and its sister body UNIX System Laboratories (USL). These technologies include the OSF's DCE and DME plus the UI-ATLAS framework from UI.

- In Chapter 19 we try to summarize what has gone before and position the opposing views of 'stay mainframe' and 'distribute everything' in the move to open systems.

The book was never intended to be the lazy man's guide to (open systems) riches. Each organization has its own starting point and its own open systems destination and we would be foolish to proffer a simple route map for everyone to follow. All we can hope to achieve is to educate, explain the issues and considerations and make suggestions where appropriate.

After all, no one has actually climbed a very big open systems mountain and returned to tell us all how it is done. If they had, this book would be superfluous.

1.3 Key Things to Consider

If your organization is involved in, or considering, an open systems strategy, then there are some key questions you should ask yourself as a representative of that organization:

- Why are you making or considering the move to 'open systems'?

  1. demonstrable business benefit

  2. obsolete equipment or applications

  3. reduced IT costs

  4. hype or the 'bandwagon' syndrome

  5. because someone has ordered you to do so

  6. don't know.

If the answer is 1 then the move is probably well justified. If the answer is 3 then be prepared to offer, or ask for, detailed objective proof of savings to be made without sacrificing business benefit, integrity, security or systems management functions. If the answer is 4, 5, or 6 then you may have problems of project direction and motivation.

- If you choose particular 'open' vendors to supply your hardware, application, data base, communications, OLTP or whatever, ask yourself what would happen to your company if any or all those vendors ceased trading. Could you simply call in other, solvent vendors and carry on as before?

- If your supplier says his product is 'open', test that assertion against your perception of openness, or perhaps against that outlined in this book. In particular, challenge the statement 'It runs on platform X, and everyone knows platform X is open' or 'We are fully open'. Depending on what products are on offer, you should ask pertinent questions about conformance to the standards we address in this book.

- The discussion of portability and interoperability centres around layers of functions from the application to the machine hardware or telephone wires in the case of communications. There are standards in place and being developed at each level in this hierarchy. Adopting standards higher up the standards hierarchy affords better isolation from changes in the lower levels of that hierarchy. It also offers a wider choice of IT options and vendors.

  You will need to decide at which level in the hierarchy of portability and interoperability layers your company will adopt its standards. We will cover this in Chapter 4 after the discussion of layered architectures and application programming interfaces (APIs). Suffice it to say here, the lower down the layers you select, and insist upon, a particular standard, the less room you have for manoeuvre - unless of course you select several as options. An example of this is the choice between TCP/IP, OSI, IPX, SNA and so on.

If these key areas do not concern you overly, then you are in a very good position to move into an OSE - if they do, you have added incentive to read this book.

Chapter 2 Perceptions of Open Systems

I declare this thing open - whatever it is.[1]

There are a number of reasons put forward for open systems, some of which are discussed in this chapter in the context of what they actually are. Our feeling is that many of the reasons quoted come from the realization that IT is moving in that direction and we had better find out why. Peter Drucker has said: 'The center of gravity has shifted towards the knowledge worker'. This means that people who need information to do their job are now crucial to most businesses. A large amount of critical business data resides on computer systems and, as all IT people know, data needs to be accessed, then manipulated to provide information. Such data more often than not lives on a variety of computer systems - PCs, VAXes, Unix, mainframes and so on. In addition, programs needed by the knowledge worker are similarly dispersed in what are often called 'islands of IT'.

An example of the need for information and processing power is the design of a new car. In previous times, three or four years might be needed to bring out a new car. Nowadays, the increased competition (in all markets) has introduced a new dimension called 'time to market'. Car manufacturers faced with Japanese development methods no longer have the luxury of four years to design and build a new car - they may only have months. Pressures like these fuel the desire to merge an organization's disparate computer systems into a single, manageable entity so that data and processes are readily available to users. Short of standardizing on one system and throwing out the rest, the only feasible option for an organization is to get them to work together in IT harmony. Also, future IT purchases will be scrutinized for ability to partake in this harmonious environment,

---

[1] Prince Philip, on opening the annexe to Vancouver City Hall.

9

subsequently dubbed 'open systems environment' (OSE). This is a major 'why' in open systems - 'what' and 'who' are the subjects of later chapters.

We start with an examination of what is meant by 'open systems' and discuss the various understandings of the term. In particular, we shall try and see if the many differing definitions have any common themes. Secondly, we will review the requirements of IT users as expressed in a number of recent surveys, ending with a comparison of the common themes of open systems with these user requirements. This will show if the move towards open systems provides users with what they require.

2.1 Open Systems - Open Season on Definitions

In researching this book we discovered nearly one hundred definitions of 'open systems'. Whilst many had common themes and ideas, some were quite different and a few were contradictory.

Firstly, there were those who felt open systems could not be defined:

Michael O'Dell, Usenix Association: 'Open systems is a philosophy, not a thing.'

Secondly, there were those who felt any open systems definition was so clouded by the definer as to be worthless:

Network World 1991, anonymous: 'It took me a long time to understand what (the industry) meant by open vs. proprietary, but I finally figured it out. From the perspective of any one supplier, open meant "our products." Proprietary meant "everybody else's products." '

Thirdly, there were those who felt any definition was irrelevant because open systems were unachievable:

Jim Davis, Apple Corp: 'Open systems are popular fiction. To truly qualify as an open system a product must be so generic and standard that the user sacrifices the added value a product from a technology innovator such as (*here Mr. Davis names a vendor*) can offer.'

Esther Dyson, Editor and Publisher: 'Openness is vastly overrated and underachieved. It basically means that everything works on everything else. Today, the situation is that while a large number of companies offer what they call open systems, nobody wants to support their brand of openness.'

Most, however, were not as sanguine as these, though some would make the reader sanguine when read together:

'It is UNIX'

Arno Penzas, VP of Research, AT&T Bell Labs: 'In practical terms "Open Systems" is a code-phrase for UNIX-derived systems. When the phrase is used in advertising, UNIX is in fact meant because it is the only operating system that is specified by a standard.'

'It is not UNIX'

Bud Huber, User Alliance for Open Systems: 'UNIX is a proprietary operating system that incorporates several open system attributes. It is neither the definition nor the embodiment of open systems, because open systems is more than just an operating system.'

'It is the PC'

Bill Gates, Microsoft: 'There's nothing more open than the PC market. OS/2 and DOS users can choose the latest and greatest software.'

'It is UNIX and DOS'

Esther Dyson, Editor and Publisher: 'The UNIX people were the first to take on the mantle of open systems. I think DOS is an open system.'

'It is DOS, UNIX on SPARC and the IBM mainframe'

Scott McNealy, Sun Microsystems: 'There are three open systems on the market today; the IBM mainframe, the Intel/Microsoft-DOS environment and SPARC/UNIX/OpenLook/ONC.'[2]

'It is not any operating system'

Marc Schulman, formerly of UBS Securities: 'If application portability across multiple operating systems is the defining characteristic of open systems then, by definition no operating system can make a system open.'

UniForum UK: 'Open systems is an Information Technology interface strategy, not a product or products.'

'It is not an operating system, it is not a protocol'

Roger Stucke, Pacific Resources: '... what constitutes an "Open System" .... does not focus on specific operating systems and protocol stacks, but rather a set of functional requirements for accessing distributed data and applications in an enterprise network.'

'It is the OSI protocol'

CCTA OSI Product Guide: 'Open system is a term used to describe a computer system which implements OSI services and protocols in all seven layers; also used to describe concepts of portable software.'

'It is matching standards'

OSI Basic Reference Model (April 1982): 'The fact that a system is open does not imply any particular systems implementation, technology or means of connection but refers to the mutual recognition and support of the applicable standards.'

Ian Hugo, in his book *Practical Open Systems*: 'Open systems are those that conform to internationally agreed standards defining computing envi-

---

[2] Sun's Open Network Computing.

ronments that allow users to develop, run and interconnect applications and the hardware they run on, from whatever source, without significant conversion cost.'

Little wonder that many people have felt the need to point out that the term 'open systems' is not altogether clear.

> **Judith Hurwitz:** 'Open systems are not black or white. There is still a lot of gray.'

In saying open systems is not dependent on operating system both Marc Schulman and UniForum go on to state that it is a standards-based interface that is important.

> **Marc Schulman, when at UBS Securities:** 'A system can be made open only by the presence of an additional layer of software that acts as an interface between operating systems and applications. What users need are standards that define the interface between operating systems and applications. Interface-defining standards, not standardized products, are the foundation of open systems.'

> **UniForum UK:** 'Open systems is an Information Technology interface strategy, not a product or products: by conforming to internationally adopted and publically owned standards and specifications, it allows computer-based systems to work together irrespective of their ownership, source of supply or location of any system component - be it hardware processor, peripheral or ancillary, packaged or custom written software, or human skill.'

This can be demonstrated by examining further the quote from Scott McNealy. There is no doubt that, in environments where the machines are all either PCs, or IBM mainframes, or SPARC/UNIX systems, concepts like portability and interoperability are simply not issues. In that sense what McNealy says is absolutely right. However, try and port a PC application to either UNIX or MVS (IBM's mainframe operating system) and the lack of portability becomes apparent. Similarly try and set up a distributed database between the mainframe and either the DOS machine or the UNIX machine and the interoperability problem is all too apparent.

What resolves the problem is the adherence to standards. When the IBM mainframe and the PC become POSIX compliant it will be easier to port applications from them to the already compliant SPARC environment. Similarly, if all three environments are running software that makes them OSI compliant then interoperability is less of a problem. The thing that makes them open is the adherence to standards.

What is meant by 'standard' in this context is fairly clear.

> **European Commission IT Department:** 'Open systems are those systems and components that can be specified and multisourced in a competitive marketplace. Open systems specifications must be controlled by

international standardization bodies (*de jure* standards) or at least by as independent as possible a specifier with a sufficiently great market acceptance (*de facto* standards). An open system specification must not be owned by any single vendor and must be freely available.'

X/Open Company: 'Open systems are computers and communications environments based on formal and *de facto* interface standards. These interfaces must not be owned by any single vendor and must be freely available.'

Furthermore the process that makes these standards 'open' is clear.

Speaker at Interop '90 (paraphrased and maybe apocryphal):   'If you ask to gain access to a technology and the response you get back is a price list, then that technology is "open". If what you get back is a letter from a lawyer, then it's not "open".'

Gartner Group: 'An open system is a compliant implementation of an evolving set of vendor-neutral specifications for interfaces, services, protocols and formats designed to effectively enable the configuration, operations and substitution of the entire system, its application and/or its components with equally compliant implementations preferably available from many different vendors.'

However, once one accepts that open systems are derived from open standards it begs the question "What benefits do open systems confer?".

Many sources, either explicitly or implicitly, talk about interoperability.

Walter de Backer, in 1990 X/Open 'Open Systems Directive':   'Open systems incorporate supplier and product independent technology standards and allow information technology products to work together and share software so that customers can get the most value out of the information in their systems.'

Open Software Foundation: 'An open system environment enables users to mix and match software and hardware from several suppliers in a virtually seamless environment. The technologies enabling an open system environment should break down the barriers between diverse systems and give users the freedom to choose the systems and technologies that best meet their business needs.'

John Young, former CEO, Hewlett-Packard: 'An open system is a set of networked heterogeneous computers that can work together as if they were a single integrated whole - no matter where the systems are located, no matter how they express their information, no matter what supplier produced them, and no matter what operating system they use.'

Other sources suggest that portability is a benefit - though comparing Marc Schulman's quote from p. 12 with the one below demonstrates that there is confusion as to whether it is the application or the operating system that is portable.

Dennis Ritchie, AT & T Research Dept: 'The idea behind open systems is that it's now technically possible to have operating systems that are portable and run on a variety of platforms. In addition, those operating systems are also subject to standards that are independent of any particular manufacturer's products.'

Many sources talk about both interoperability and portability as benefits.

David Tory, Open Software Foundation: 'An open system is one that enables properly engineered applications software to:

- interact with users in a consistent style

- be ported across a wide range of platforms from multiple vendors

- interoperate with other open systems applications.'

UNIX International: 'Open systems provide interoperability of systems across a heterogeneous network, the portability of applications and the protection of investment.'

Some definitions add scalability as a benefit of an OSE.

X/Open Company: 'Open systems provide portability of software across industry standard platforms, interoperability between systems, much improved flexibility in the management of information resources and much greater choice in systems procurement.'

NIST: 'An Open Systems Environment encompasses the functionality needed to provide interoperability, portability, and scalability of computerized applications across networks of heterogeneous hardware/software platforms. The OSE forms an extensible framework that allows interfaces, services, protocols, and supporting data formats to be defined in terms of nonproprietary specifications that evolve through open (public), consensus-based forums.'

Pamela Gray, in *Open Systems - A Business Strategy for the 90s*: 'When the three characteristics: portability, scalability and interoperability, are taken together, and international standards set for them by an open process, and the results are available on equal terms to all, the result is to define that part of the computer industry known as "Open Systems".'

It was even possible to find those who talked of more than three benefits - though the additional ones were rarely the same. Perhaps the most interesting addition was 'compatibility'.

Peter Cunningham, UNIX International: 'Open system computing will exhibit four factors. The first is compatibility: applications running on a system should be able to run future releases. Next is portability. Applications running on a given hardware platform should be able to run on any vendor's computer based on that platform. Third is interoperability. Systems must be able to work together and share data. Finally there is scalability. Applications should be able to run on a full range of architectures, from laptops to mainframes.'

2.2 Making Sense of Open Systems

It would seem from all these quotes that openness is derived from standards adherence. Standards in this sense are clearly defined 'rules' relating to products and interfaces. Furthermore, to be truly open these standards must be publicly available and preferably defined by consensus.

This raises a number of issues.

- Where in the total system does openness reside? Must it be in a standard operating system or hardware standards or something else?
- Which of the many standards available confer openness?
- Are there degrees of openness or is it clear-cut?

2.2.1 Where Does Openness Reside?

Some say that for a system to be open it must run UNIX, others go further and say that it must be a particular UNIX implementation on a particular hardware platform. For them, openness resides in this particular operating system and hardware platform. We have tried to encapsulate several views of what open systems are in Figure 1 on page 16. The figure shows, on the left hand side, three 'views' of what a definition of an open system might contain. View 3, for example, includes a hardware specification, an operating system specification and reference to various open system standards. View 1 is operating system and hardware independent. The graph illustrates what happens to 'openness' and vendor choice as the definitions are refined to include first a named operating system, then a named hardware platform. The optimum point, we claim, lies at the intersection of the openness curve with the dotted line on the graph where operating system and hardware are excluded from the definition.

A definition of open systems that demands a particular operating system and a particular hardware base, does not differ in any significant respect from a definition of a proprietary system. It also creates exactly the situation which led to the 'need' for open systems. More importantly, it does not address the idea of openness bringing together mixed, or heterogeneous, environments. Heterogeneous, in the context of open systems, means *any* hardware platform and *any* operating system as long as they obey the agreed rules of 'open systems'. This in effect means that the 'openness' in open systems is based on those elements which give interoperability and portability, and not on the operating system or hardware platform. This is very useful for existing IT installations since some non-Unix operating systems, such as MVS and VMS, are superior to Unix in the functions and facilities needed to run complex or mission critical IT operations. It is also important to note that these systems will not disappear overnight, if ever.

Marc Schulman in his article 'Open Systems - Facts and Fallacies 1988' suggested:

> 'Unix and open systems are not synonymous. Open systems require applications portability, not operating system portability. The utilization of Unix does not ensure applications portability, and the employment of a proprietary operating system does not prevent applications portability.'

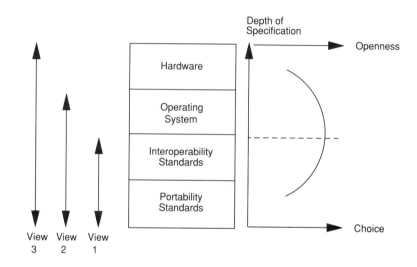

Figure 1. *Open Systems Viewpoints*

We agree with him. The openness lies in applying the standards which achieve the goal of openness and not in any particular hardware implementation or any particular operating system. As we shall see as we look at the different standards and different routes to openness, these standards usually apply to interfaces. The standard that makes an application portable from one operating system to another rests in the interface between the application and the operating system. If the application has the standard 'hooks' and the operating system the standard 'eyes' then the two will work together. Another operating system with standard 'eyes' in the same place will accept the application's 'hooks' without change - the application is portable from one to the other as a result of both operating systems and the application adhering to the standard interface. Openness therefore resides in standard interfaces, not in standard hardware or operating systems.

2.2.2 Which Standards Confer Openness?

There are literally hundreds of standards - the joke is often made that the nice thing about standards is there are so many to chose from. Which standards confer openness?

The simplest answer would be those that confer portability and interoperability. We have not included scalability, though some claim that as an open systems goal, as there is no accepted scalability standard to comply with. Whilst this is a simplistic answer we cannot find a better one. To limit the 'approved' standards to those that have, as an obvious example, ISO numbers, would remove many of the routes that are currently being taken to achieve portability and interoperability. Furthermore if something purporting to be a standard that brings openness is seen on examination to provide neither portability nor interoperability, then one can safely say that it is not an open system.

2.2.3 Are There Degrees of Openness?

The third issue we raised was whether there are degrees of openness or whether it is a black and white issue - are you open or are you not?

Imagine that there are only two standards in the world, called A and B. To use the 'hook and eye' analogy of earlier, A has a single central hook and eye whilst B has two hooks and eyes on the outside edge. As you can see from Figure 2, application A can be ported to any machine that has interface A, similarly B. But when application A is moved to a machine with the B interface it will not work. However, try and move it to a machine with an AB interface and it will. Indeed, either application A or application B will work.

Applications with the A interface consider machines 1 and 2 to be open. They match the agreed standard. Yet machines with the B interface consider these very same machines to be closed. Only machine 5, which matches both standards, is open to both applications. Given that in our analogy there are only two open system standards, machine 5 is the ultimate in open systems.

The other machines are open only in specific environments. Indeed, it may be said that it is the environment that is open if it matches standards and machines either can or cannot participate in that environment depending on whether they match those specific standards.

This is why the IEEE, in its POSIX standard, talks about the concept of an open systems environment rather than an open system. It says:

> **IEEE (POSIX 1003.0):** ' *Open Systems Environment (OSE)*: the comprehensive set of interfaces, services and supporting formats, plus user aspects, for interoperability or for portability of applications, data or people, as specified by information technology standards and profiles.'

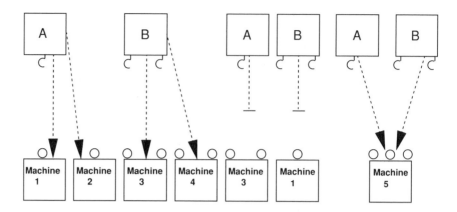

Figure 2. *Portability of Applications using Standards. Machine 5 is capable of dealing with more than one interface. This is important for proprietary systems supporting not only their standard interface but the POSIX interface as well.*

This definition is widely accepted - the European Workshop on Operating Systems (EWOS) has adopted it as has the International Standards Organization. Incidentally, it is also the one favoured by IBM.

The idea of an open systems environment makes it evident that openness is not clear-cut and an operating system that might take part in one open systems environment might not be able to take part in another. As a spokesman from one of the US standards bodies said:

Al Hankinson, NIST: 'Open systems is not a single-dimensional concept but multi-dimensional. There are degrees of openness.'

This leaves one further issue and rather than talk in abstract terms, let us take a real example. Consider an environment that has agreed on the widely used TCP/IP networking protocol. It would be commonly accepted that TCP/IP would make this environment open. However, a different environment which had standardized on the OSI protocols would also be described as open and yet the two would have nothing in common and would not connect. The idea that one open system could not interoperate with another open system is ridiculous.

The IEEE resolve this with their definition of an open system as:

'implementing sufficient open specifications for interfaces, services and supporting formats to enable properly engineered applications software:

- to be ported with minimal changes across a wide range of systems
- to interoperate with other applications on local and remote systems
- to interact with users in a style that facilitates user portability.'

So a system can take part in an open systems environment if it matches the standards that provide portability and interoperability already in that environment. This might be described as localized, or particular, openness. However, it can be described as an open system only if it matches such a range of standards that it would work in any open environment. This might be described as universal openness.

2.3 Definitions - Do They Match User Requirements?

It is all very well defining open systems and analyzing the resulting ideas, but do they reflect what IT users really want? Do the definitions take account of the wide variety of IT installations around today and address the users' concerns and issues about the OSE? Indeed, when were users first asked for their opinions and requirements? Probably only from 1990 onwards with the X/Open Xtra process (see Chapter 13). Let us examine the users' case.

2.3.1 IDC White Paper

This paper, entitled 'UNIX - Opening The Door To Business Solutions', identified five requirements of the IS manager - the first two perhaps the most relevant to our discussion. They were:

- the connection and management of distributed data resources
- the production of OLTP systems
- the development of mission-critical applications
- the increasing use of executive information systems and decision support
- the implementation of enterprise solutions and standards.

2.3.2 X/Open Xtra Survey

In 1991, a survey of the open systems requirements of the world's leading open systems users was conducted by X/Open via the Xtra requirements process (described in detail in Chapter 10).

The survey was sent to non-vendor group members across Europe, Japan and the USA. Over 230 responses were obtained from senior IT personnel in companies whose average revenues were $13 billion, with a combined IT outlay of $120 billion (of which $18 billion was on hardware). It should be noted that the companies which were invited to respond either had, or were considering, a policy of using IT technologies based on vendor-independent standards.

The results of the survey can be summarized as follows:

Customer Requirements

These are rated by importance within category:

- Communications - OSI, DCE, ONC, SNA and other
- DataBase - SQL, OO,[3] Non-SQL, hierarchical
- Application Development - CAE (Common Application Environment)
- User Interface - the choices are shown in Figure 3.

Figure 3. *Graphical User Interface Choices*	
Graphical User Interface	*%*
Character Based	32
Microsoft Windows	28
OSF/Motif	15
MAC	9
OpenLook	6
Presentation Manager	5
Internal GUI	5

Top Requirements

In order of importance, these were given as:

1. interoperability across heterogeneous systems and networks
2. architecture for enterprise-wide open systems
3. database access and management across heterogeneous networks
4. integrated open and proprietary network management
5. open systems access to proprietary mainframe applications
6. a single widely accepted GUI
7. a methodology for planning integration to an environment which incorporates vendor-independent standards
8. Single API to multiple GUIs.

---

[3] Object Orientation.

Perceived Inhibitors

Users view the main inhibitors to the total implementation of open systems environments as:

1. organizational readiness (training etc.)
2. plethora of new architectures
3. confusion about vendors, products and architectures
4. the gap between prioritized needs in open systems and the quality of available products
5. the risk open systems present to information assets.

Technical Requirements

In Figure 4, we reproduce the opinions of the responders assessing their priorities in various areas and the quality of delivery of products from vendors. In each case, marks are assigned out of 10. The differences indicate the gap between open systems requirements and what vendors and standards implementers can deliver in an OSE.

Figure 4. *User Technical Requirements*		
User Requirement	*Priority*	*Quality Delivered*
Client/server applications	8.2	4.6
Security of networked systems	8.1	3.8
Integrated system and network management	7.9	3.8
Electronic data interchange (EDI)	7.5	4.9
Interoperability among applications	7.4	3.7
Online transaction processing (OLTP)	7.4	4.3
Computer aided software engineering (CASE)	7.4	4.1
Distributed data with 2-phase commit (2PC)	7.4	4.2
Graphical user interface(s) (GUI)	7.4	5.7

2.3.3 Forrester Research - July 1991

In reply to the question 'Why does your company want OPEN SYSTEMS?', the Forrester Research survey of IT business priorities of selected *Fortune* 1000 companies yielded the results shown in Figure 5.

Figure 5. *Reasons for Wanting Open Systems*	
%	**Reason**
70	To integrate different systems/applications
26	To avoid being locked into one vendor
23	To gain access to as many applications as possible
20	To provide application portability
17	To make vendors compete on price

2.3.4 CSC-Index - January 1993

The consultancy CSC-Index published their sixth annual survey of IT directors' main concerns in their organizations. It emerges that their top business worries were:[4]

1. re-engineering business processes
2. cutting IT costs
3. aligning IT and company goals
4. building cross-functional systems
5. creating an information architecture
6. improving staff[5]
7. organizing and using data
8. integrating systems
9. changing platforms
10. moving to open systems.

---

[4] *Computing* 21 January 1993.

[5] We assume this means 'staff skills'.

Some of these items cover the same ground, in our opinion. For example, issue 10 covers several of the issues above it in terms of what we mean by 'moving to open systems'.

2.3.5 GUIDE 82 (1992)

GUIDE is an IBM user organization which makes representations to IBM stating IT requirements for IBM platforms. At a recent meeting, the GUIDE group presented IBM with a list of requirements. These requirements, although not specifically raised as 'open systems' issues, are very close to those we have outlined above. In essence, these are:

- open architecture with well-defined and well-documented interfaces
- transparent access to enterprise applications
- spread applications over two or more processors and complete in a timely, coordinated fashion
- integrity of data across the enterprise, process to process synchronization, and process recovery coordination
- transparent access to data anywhere, including ASCII to EBCDIC translation, data integrity via 2-Phase Commit (2PC) and standardized data packets
- utilization of network print facilities
- universal, active dictionary/directory which must be distributable
- single 'logon' with the option of distributed or central control and enterprise security
- facilities to develop cooperative applications, including an integrated development platform, online debugging, simulation testing and application modelling.

The GUIDE Cooperative Processing Strategy Paper also listed in its requirements section 'Conglomerate Management' under seven headings:

1. resource monitoring, the gathering of resource utilization data for processing that spans more than one system
2. performance monitoring across processors
3. workload balancing across processors
4. problem determination, including error logging, fault detection and diagnosis
5. configuration management, a simple operator interface for nondisruptive processor activation and deactivation, reconfiguration and monitoring
6. change management tools
7. system and application distribution, a secure software distribution facility that offers versioning, staging and integration.

2.4 Conclusions

The five surveys we have cited questioned entirely different user bases:

- GUIDE 82 is a user group whose members primarily use proprietary systems.

- X/Open members are drawn from both the proprietary and the Unix world - their membership of X/Open suggests their common interest is in standards.

- The Forrester Research, CSC-Index and IDC surveys drew on a wide cross-section of users.

However, the requirements of the users were remarkably consistent. The demands of users of proprietary systems do not differ markedly from the demands of users of UNIX and UNIX-like systems. All the surveys showed that interoperability and access to enterprise-wide applications was important. Similarly, all made mention of the desire for vendor neutrality, usually expressed as open systems standards. However, the Forrester report, which asked 'why do you want open systems', was the only one that mentioned portability. Most surveys also made some reference to manageability - which suggests that portability is not seen as very important whilst the latter is. Interestingly, none made mention of scalability as a requirement.

We would suggest that established users generally see interoperability as more important than portability for a simple reason. Portability suggests moving from one platform to another whilst interoperability suggests integrating existing platforms. Established users, who by definition have existing platforms, feel that portability is therefore a longer-term requirement. Their principle requirement in an OSE is interoperability. Included in interoperability is the seemingly obvious point that the system has to be made to work with existing systems. 'Companies like General Motors began to admit publicly that for every dollar spent on computerised equipment another dollar was spent on integration.'[6]

These established users also point to the importance of manageability - something not necessarily associated with open systems. It is our experience that the more vendors in the environment, the more open it is seen to be and more difficult to manage as a result. The delivery of interoperability, and indeed portability, without the delivery of manageability is very dangerous. It can be argued that a mixed, unmanaged, environment can eat into any savings made.

We talked in the preface about the need to show real business benefits before moving towards open systems. It is our strong belief that if the system adopted

---

[6] *Open Systems in Manufacturing - An Introduction to the Manufacturing Message Specification*, UK Department of Trade and Industry (DTI) publication.

lacks manageability the business benefits will be far outweighed by the cost and could potentially destroy the business altogether.

That does not mean we are against open systems. Rather we realize that proprietary users will not want their needs satisfied by jettisoning everything they have invested in over many years. They want these functions on the systems they have now, as well as on those they may acquire in the future. For such IT users, 'open systems' is something to evolve into rather than migrate to, the latter course of action suggesting leaving present investment behind.

There is no doubt that business and the IT world have decided that the next development in the industry will be the move towards open systems. It will be a pity if this move, which we believe is inevitable, produces a backward step in areas such as security, manageability and systems and network management. Accepting that it may, and then ensuring that it does not, is part of the reality of open systems.

Part 2
History and Development of IT Systems

Chapter 3 Information Technology - Ancestry and History

Our civilization ... has not yet recovered from the shock of its birth - the transition from the ... "closed society", with its submission to magical forces, to the "open society" which sets free the critical powers of men.[1]

Ancestry is not the same as history. Your own ancestry goes back a lot further than your history, which presumably began at conception. On IT timescales, the subject of open systems has a long ancestry but a relatively short history. To understand the implications of moving from where IT installations are today to 'open systems', it is useful to see how IT developed over the last 25 years and how the complex issues needing resolution arose. It is also very interesting!

To this end, we will describe in the next few chapters the chronological development of:

- the total computing environment
- proprietary operating systems and networks
- the UNIX operating system and TCP/IP networks
- the ISO OSI network model
- the modern open systems environment.

This should give you an understanding of some of the basic issues confronting installations with hardware and systems software from many vendors and the problems to which open systems is said to be the solution. We will then go on to describe the world of open systems which aims to resolve these issues.

---

[1] Karl Popper, *The Open Society and Its Enemies*.

3.1 In the Beginning...

The Second World War gave a tremendous push to technology as governments started to spend money on new ways to fight and win the war. The classic example of this was the Manhattan Project when, in 1941, US and British scientists gathered in New Mexico to produce the atomic bomb - at a cost of over $2 billion. Similarly, scientists were gathered from all over the UK at Bletchley House to work on scientific approaches to such wartime problems as breaking the German Enigma code.[2] The result of this massive State sponsorship of science was a substantial leap forward in progress in a number of areas. One of these was in the development of the computer.

Several projects were important in the development of the computer. On the theoretical side, many see Alan Turing's work as fundamental[3] and most agree the first modern computer was ENIAC, the Electronic Numerical Integrator and Calculator. It was developed by two electronic engineers at the University of Pennsylvania, Presper Eckert and John Mauchly, to calculate artillery range tables. ENIAC was a massive machine with over 19,000 electronic valves. In 1947 Eckert and Mauchly set up their own company, Universal Automation Computers, or UNIVAC. However, within two years they had sold the company to Remington Rand.

Surprisingly IBM, which was later to gain such a hold on the computer market, was not very active at this time. Though during the war it had been involved in the Harvard University's Mark I computer it was really interested only in producing faster punch card readers and tabulators. In his autobiography, Thomas Watson Jr, son of the IBM founder, tells how the move into computing was not easy for the company. It had been very successful in the past but many staff felt this new technology could seriously affect their livelihoods. Watson explains that eventually the decision was taken to develop what was described as an electronic calculator and then, with the outbreak of the Korean War, to use that as the spur to move the company.

The first real IBM computer was the 701 - patriotically called the defense calculator. This was followed up by other models - the 702 and the very successful 705. IBM was finally committed to computing.[4]

Once IBM was committed to electronic computers it was in a very strong position to be successful in IT. In the early days businesses used computers just as

---

[2] This was done on Colossus, the first programmable electronic computer.

[3] For a detailed description of the work of Turing see Andrew Harvey, *Alan Turing: The Enigma of Intelligence* (London 1983).

[4] Thomas J. Watson Jr, *Father Son & Co.: My Life at IBM and Beyond* (London 1990).

faster tabulators. IBM salesmen then sold their new computers to exactly the same people who had previously bought their tabulating equipment. As Watson wrote in an article in the magazine *Nation's Business*: 'the invention of the computer was important. But the knowledge of how to put a great big system on line, how to make it run, and solve problems was probably four times as important.' The last sentence anticipates, albeit unwittingly, some of the problems of open systems.[5]

The company was remarkably successful. Indeed, within a very short time the computer industry was divided up into IBM and the rest - known collectively as the BUNCH (Burroughs, Univac, NCR, Control Data and Honeywell). The launch of the System 360 in 1964 confirmed IBM's hold. The S/360 and its successors, the S/370 and ES/9000, have dominated business computing for the last 25 years.

They are, of course, mainframe computers - large, essentially monolithic, devices which hold and manipulate their data centrally. They work well in those environments that have large amounts of data that logically sit together. Financial applications are well suited to the mainframe - the interworking of the general ledger with the accounts payable and receivable suggests that having them on a single machine is ideal. This is why most businesses did their computing on a single large machine.

3.2 Departmental and Personal Computing

Once computerization of the accounts was seen as successful, other parts of the business felt they too could benefit from computers.

The engineering and scientific side was an obvious candidate for computerization. However, as a general rule, the mainframe did not cope well with this and IBM was not familiar with this area. In 1957, two engineers, Ken Olsen and Harlon Anderson, set up a company (Digital Equipment Corporation or DEC) to offer computers specifically for this market. DEC marketed computers directly to engineers and scientists, and expanded from this base to sell elsewhere in the organization. It concentrated especially on departments not directly served by the mainframe.

Other companies became established in various niche markets and expanded from there. Two examples will illustrate the point. Hewlett-Packard, which had made its name in laboratory and scientific instrumentation, began to attach computers to its instruments and moved into more general computing as a result. Wang Corporation was very successful in arguing that computers were fine for numeric tasks but text-based tasks, such as word processing, required a new sort

5 Lessons in 'Leadership part XCIII', *Nation's Business*, February 1973, quoted in R.T. DeLamarter, *Big Blue - IBM's Use and Abuse of Power* (London 1986).

of computer. Wang successfully marketed a range of computers specifically for word processing.

The 1970s saw a lot of new thinking about how large companies were best structured and what emerged were flatter, more devolved business structures. Increasingly departments acquired their own machines but this did not mean that the mainframe was dead, quite the reverse. The corporate mainframe became more established, began to do even more tasks and grew at a remarkable rate. However, out in the departments new machines were being bought and different tasks computerized.

The invention of the micro-processor in the 1970s saw another computer revolution - the micro-computer. Companies like Apple, Commodore and Sinclair became household names and as they grew they started to sell into the business environment. In 1980 IBM set up a task force under Philip (Don) Estridge with the mission to develop an IBM micro-computer as quickly as possible, which it did. It was launched in August 1981 and became an instant success - selling over 30,000 on the day of its announcement. However, the desire for speedy development had a major consequence. The developers were quick because they bought off-the-shelf parts wherever possible. It took no time at all for others to come along and use these parts to build their own machines, often better than the ones they were copying. Companies like Compaq, Dell and Amstrad all made their name marketing IBM-compatible machines. Today there are approximately 36 million PCs in the world. It would be hard to imagine any but the smallest company without many PCs, either stand-alone or networked.

While this was happening, a separate strand of personal computing was developing based on the 32-bit micro-processor, originally developed by Motorola. The technical workstation, from companies such as SUN Microsystems and Apollo, offered relatively high-powered desktop computing to the engineering and technical community. Generally these machines ran Unix operating systems and by the end of the 1980s it was one of the fastest growing areas in computing. Just as DEC and H-P moved out of their original niche so the workstation vendors moved into general-purpose commercial computing offering departmental and, more recently, company-wide services via LANs and WANs.

3.3 The Problem of Multiple Systems

By 1990, a typical business of reasonable size would almost certainly have technical computers, specialist word processors, departmental mini computers, hundreds of personal computers and a mainframe. The mix of computers in such a company was becoming very complicated and the biggest problem was communication between these systems. The IBM machine could not communicate with the DEC, neither could communicate with the Wang, and the departmental computer simply made things worse. Many professionals worked on a PC. They analyzed data from around the company, often downloaded with difficulty from the mainframe, and they rarely sent that analysis back to the centre. Increasingly the information vital to business decisions was not available. Some writers have called the systems islands of information. There was the IBM island (or sometimes the IBM islands!), the DEC island, the Wang island and so on. The business needed to bridge these islands, getting computers working together to provide different perspectives of the company's business information.

3.4 The Way Forward

While it is always dangerous to force any series of events into a strict pattern, it does seem that the computer was invented in the 1940s, developed in the 1950s and established in the 1960s. The 1970s saw the growth of departmental computing and the 1980s the emergence of personal computing. In the 1990s users are attempting to bring together mainframes, minis and personal computers. The two key drivers of the 1990s are separate and yet connected.

The first is the move to distributed computing - spreading computer resources throughout the business and then sharing data, applications and computing power. Rather than buying even more machines or an even bigger mainframe, companies want to combine, in an efficient manner, all the systems they already have.

The second driver is open systems - the need to create environments where many heterogeneous machines can work together. These environments are often distributed environments, hence the two ideas are very close. However, an open system need not be distributed and a distributed system need not, in theory, be open. In practice, to create a truly company-wide distributed computing environment you will need to combine machines from different manufacturers and with different architectures - that suggests open systems. While this book is about open systems, we also cover distributed computing.

Chapter 4 Proprietary Systems and Networks

Give me a place to stand, and I will move the earth.[1]

This chapter outlines the development of proprietary operating systems and networks. We are using IBM as the prime example, simply because our knowledge of this is sounder, although we also cite DEC. No superiority of IBM or DEC operating systems or architectures is intended or implied - they are simply vehicles for discussing the development of operating systems since many other operating systems and architectures have a similar development profile.

4.1 Computer Systems

In 1964, IBM introduced a radical new architecture in the System/360 series of computers. The '360' was significant in that it meant that 360 degrees of the computing compass were addressed by the new architecture. Prior to System/360, IBM had delivered a variety of machines and architectures which were designed to do a specific job of work, scientific or commercial. These machines were coded by experts at a very low level, often writing instructions at bit level (0s or 1s). Because of the different machine architectures, code written for one machine would not run on another since the instruction bit pattern of one machine meant nothing to a different machine.

    With the S/360, IBM developed a machine code, or assembler, language which enabled programmers to produce code which would run on any model in the 360 series, giving some measure of portability. As the 360 architecture evolved into new machines, these programs could still be run on later models and even on the

---

[1] Archimedes, on the lever.

S/370 series when that was announced in 1970. However, these programs could not run on other manufacturers' machines because they had a different hardware architecture. Why should this be a problem?

4.1.1 Source and Binary Code

Source programming languages like assembler, Cobol and Fortran, are designed to ease the task of the coder in telling the hardware which instructions to execute in which order. They are not understood by the hardware since it deals only with bits which are either on (1) or off (0). This is where a 'compiler' comes to the fore. The compiler takes the code as written by the programmer and translates it into an executable module which, when loaded into the memory of the computer, is in *binary* form like '0011010001110...'. These 'bit patterns' can represent instructions and data. The same instruction will have a different bit pattern on machines of different architectures, for example a DEC VAX and an IBM AS/400. Similarly, data representations vary across machine architectures. This is known as *binary incompatibility*.

If the full bit pattern from a compilation by an IBM machine were loaded onto a DEC machine with its different architecture, it would almost certainly not execute. The reverse situation would also be true.

This explanation of binary incompatibility should also serve as an explanation of *binary compatibility*.

4.1.2 Application Binary Interfaces (ABIs)

In the previous section, binary compatibility was discussed at the level 'does the bit pattern mean something to the machine?'. If two machines share the same machine architecture but are driven by different operating systems, then simple binary compatibility will not give portability in general. One reason for this is that programs often make calls to the core of the operating system - these are called *supervisor calls* in IBM terminology. How these calls are treated depends on which operating system they are addressing.

This necessitates some agreed way of handling such calls and has led to the idea of application binary interfaces or ABIs. These are similar in concept to binary compatibility but go further. An ABI is a portability specification which outlines the following programming environment:

- instruction set (this is all binary compatibility cares about)
- method of making system calls
- table of system call entry points
- executable program format

- shared library mechanisms
- other interfaces.

This means that it is possible to take a program compiled on one system that complies with the ABI and ship it, via file transfer or media, to an ABI compliant system from another manufacturer, using a different operating system, and run it. The executable format applies only to similar architectures, for example, the Intel 80X86 range or the IBM Power architecture.

4.1.3 Operating Systems Concepts and Development

The concept of an operating system did not exist in the early days of computing and programming. All operations - I/O,[2] I/O verification, error checking etc. - were the domain of the programmer and, later, the programmer aided by the compiler. In fact, the programmer and compiler could 'see' the machine hardware and I/O devices. Consequently, much of the effort of programming went into handling hardware operations, checking for errors and retrieving and storing data rather than concentrating on the job the program was dealing with.

The development of operating systems took away a lot of the repetitive work which hampered early code developers and compilers and, in time, isolated them from the system hardware. Operating systems became much more than coding and effort 'savers', allowing multiple users to access the same database, single transaction programs to serve many users as well as scheduling batch work and offering timesharing facilities to end users.

A key concept in operating (and other) systems is that of the ***application programming interface*** or ***API***. An API is essentially a set of rules for a programmer or user to access system functions, with a 'guarantee' that the rules will be honoured across changes to the way those functions are implemented. As an example, imagine an operating system which can be freely accessed by a programmer. To get the time of day, the programmer might look at a particular data block maintained by the operating system. Let us say it is in the fourth field from the left of the data block and the programmer instructs the program accordingly. In subsequent rewrites, the operating system moves the time of day from field 4 to field 8. The original program will get some data back from field 4 but it will not be the time of day and the ensuing results will be unpredictable.

To get round this problem, most operating systems offer an API - in this case it could be a 'GETIME' instruction - which will relieve the program of knowledge of the internals of the system. The operating system would ensure the GETIME

---

[2] Input/output to devices such as magnetic disks or tapes.

instruction always got the time of day wherever it was stored and in whatever format, and delivered it to the requesting program.

Examples of systems which offer APIs are:

- operating systems
- communications
- database
- graphics.

An analogy, rather than a detailed exposition, should help the reader understand the concepts of hardware, operating systems, and API relationships.[3]

4.1.4 An API Analogy

Imagine a design engineering business which is growing rapidly. While the business is small, letters might be delivered personally or addressed to 'Jim D.'. This works fine in a small way but if the company grows rapidly, there would need to be a method established for inter- and intra-company communications. A simple scheme might be that all mail goes into box A, work to be done by secretaries in box B, and everyone uses the same name and address list for addressing mail. If the way the mail is shipped changes, or the typing pool acquires a word processor, this in theory is transparent to the designers since they continue to use boxes A and B.

The use of these boxes is in essence a type of API. In addition, if the 'addressing API' used forms like 'Chief Engineer, Mason & Dixon Co.', a change of chief engineer and even the location of Mason & Dixon would be hidden from the engineers and handled by the mail department.

A summary of our analogy is shown below:

Analogy	*IT Equivalent*
Engineer	Application
Administration	Operating System
Mail Department	Communications
Building/Office Hardware	Hardware

The analogy is not perfect and should not be extrapolated too far. It should give the reader a feel for the benefits of an 'isolation' layer with a defined interface(s) to it, in IT and, indeed, other organizational structures.

---

[3] Readers familiar with the idea of APIs should move on to Section 4.2.

The development of this 'isolation' of programmer or application from changing elements in an IT system is illustrated in Figure 6. This shows three sets of APIs from different periods of IT development. The two left hand boxes show the types of API available to early applications although a single application would not use them all as shown, except perhaps the 1970s case where the application-to-compiler API arrow represents the use of assembler subroutines. The right hand figure, however, does represent a single application using three different APIs, for example, accessing graphics, database and network services.

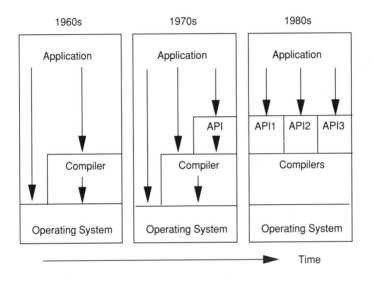

Figure 6. *Development of APIs. This is a conceptual diagram illustrating the methods by which applications in three 'eras' accessed system services.*

Suitable APIs allow users to be insulated from any particular operating system, although some remain operating system specific. Open systems are essentially concerned with 'open' APIs, and their design and implementation, within and across heterogeneous systems. Open systems are also concerned with relationships and interfaces between other types of non-application software found in IT systems. These we will deal with in Chapter 16.

4.2 Computer Networks

Using the IBM world as the vehicle again, we can examine the rise of networking from the humble origins of batch processing in the 1960s through to the complex network architectures, and ensuing problems, of today.

4.2.1 Networking Concepts and Development

In our discussion of the evolution of the operating system, we touched on the problems of programming in the early days. Once operating systems took much of the tedious and repetitive work off the programmer's hands, he/she was free to deliver function to the users. This took the form of **batch programs**, programs which ran under the control of the operating system and usually accessed files, reading and updating, and produced printed reports for end users. A typical program might have been a customer order program, maintaining the file of customer orders and producing reports for the accounts, shipping and other departments. The accounts department printout could be used for day-to-day invoicing and also for satisfying *ad hoc* queries which might arise. Queries like 'Who owes us more than a certain amount of money?' could be satisfied only by a tedious sequential scan through the printout by accounts personnel. One solution to this problem was to write another batch program to produce a list of all customers owing more than a certain amount.

This was often done and kept the relevant department quiet until another query was needed - and so it went on. In the end, the braver installations decided to write programs which 'talked' to the user and answered questions about the files by interacting with a user at a terminal of some sort. This was often a Teletype, where the user typed in his query in a form specified and understood by the program. The program would act on the query and deliver an answer to the Teletype print roll as a series of printed lines. With a bit more effort, the function was extended to use a visual display terminal instead of a Teletype. This is why simple visual display terminals are often called 'glass Teletypes'.

It is easy to see here the embryo of today's online transaction processing (OLTP) since what the querying users were doing was a specific unit of work, known as a transaction. Consider an example from the banking world. A bank has a transaction (not necessarily computerized) to enter money into a savings account. It is a fixed operation to do a very specific job. If this was coded as a program, it would be called a 'transaction program', accessed by a user at a terminal.

This sounds ideal but there were some major drawbacks in developing such applications in the early days:

- The terminal and network handling logic resided in the program, which made changes of terminal difficult and tied the terminal to that program while it was running.

- The programming was usually in assembler code, difficult to write and maintain and without the benefit of high-level calls to aid programming.

- It was very difficult for the programmer to cater for more than one terminal at a time, especially when there were multiple types of transaction. If these transactions were trying to update files as well as read from them, the task was more often than not beyond most programmers.

This phase of teleprocessing (TP) development is shown in Figure 7.

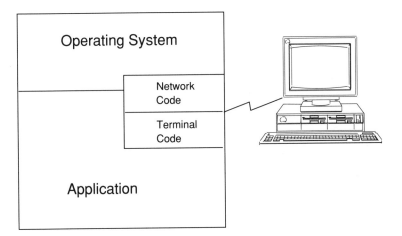

Figure 7. *Early Teleprocessing Programs. The incursion of the network code box into the operating system area indicates that the latter did offer some assistance to the programmer.*

By 1969, IBM had developed several systems to help people to write trans-action programs - names like BREAD, FASTER and CICS will be known to older IBM users! They offered programmers APIs to ease the programming task and transaction monitors to handle multiple terminals and transactions. CICS (Cus-tomer Information Control System) was the survivor when IBM rationalized its software offerings in the early 1970s. CICS was later given an interface to the Data Language/1 (DL/1) to assist in the management and integrity of data. A par-allel system was Information Management System (IMS), which also used DL/1. Both CICS and IMS survive today.

However, the problem of embedded terminal and network handling logic did not go away - it merely moved it to the transaction system which then inherited the problems the programmer had faced previously.

A schematic view of this phase of teleprocessing program development is shown in Figure 8.

Although this was less of a problem than before, it still 'locked' a terminal into the CICS system. The ideal situation would be to transfer the physical network and terminal handling code to a higher-level and free CICS to handle them at a logical level. An added benefit to such an architecture is that this 'higher level' function might be able to route the terminal into applications other than CICS upon request.

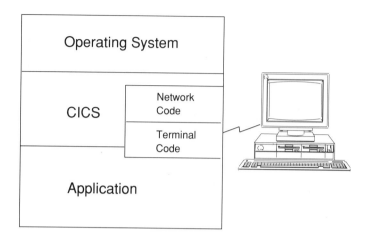

Figure 8. *Early CICS Environment*

The SNA architecture was designed to give a more rigorous structure for networking on IBM systems, and early implementations included the Virtual Tele-communications Access Method (VTAM) and the Network Control Program (NCP). VTAM is the 'higher level' we outlined above and NCP was the network function outboard of the main processor. You will see later that this is easily achievable using a layered architecture. Figure 9 illustrates the new regime in an architected environment.

It demonstrates the use of layering software to achieve, in this case, terminal independence of both CICS and the application. CICS was then developed as an OLTP system, free of the need to be concerned with the vagaries of ever changing networks of terminals.

VTAM is an implementation of part of the SNA architecture. Time Sharing Option (TSO) is a feature of the MVS operating system. What Figure 9 shows is a user terminal with the ability to access both TSO and CICS through the addition of the VTAM layer of software. Changes to terminal types are the concern only of VTAM and not TSO, CICS or the applications running under them.

IBM continued to develop SNA and its implementations through versions known as SNA-0, SNA-1 and so on.

Other major vendors had exactly the same problems we have described and they too tackled the issues with an architecture suited to their operating system environment. However, the introduction of new architectures by IBM, DEC, ICL and others compounded the problems of interoperability.

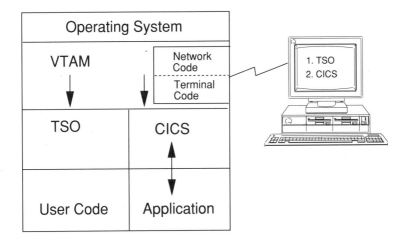

Figure 9. *CICS in the SNA Environment. Both CICS and TSO (Time Sharing Option) applications can be accessed via a simple menu presented by VTAM.*

Open Systems Interconnection (OSI) was one effort to devise a common, acceptable interoperability model for networks.

4.2.2 Network Architecture Development

Over a period of years, several vendor-specific network architectures evolved and, more importantly, implementations were produced on various platforms. The following list shows the major networking developments and indicates why, several years after those architectures were implemented, achieving complete portability and interoperability is not trivial. The architectures were initially designed to give interoperability between the vendors' own systems to attain marketing advantage. Interoperability between unlike systems was unknown except for such rudimentary vehicles as IBM 2780 file transfer, often implemented when users demanded some kind of link between unlike systems.

Proprietary Network Architectures: The network architectures from the major vendors were delivered over a period of some 15 years:

- 1960s 'OSA' - 'Onion Skin' Architecture from ICL[4]

---

[4] Jack Houldsworth's term from his book *Open Systems LANs*, Oxford (1991) ISBN 0 7506 1045 X.

- 1974 SNA - Systems Network Architecture from IBM
- 1975 DNA - Distributed Network Architecture from DEC
- 1976 DCA - Distributed Communications Architecture from Univac
- 1978 DSA - Distributed Systems Architecture from CII-H-B[5]
- 1978 TRANSDATA - from Siemens
- 1979 BNA - Burroughs Network Architecture
- 1980 IPA - Information Processing Architecture from ICL.

Other Proprietary Architectures: Two major architectures, built on network architectures, are worthy of note since they address the open systems goals of 'portability' and 'interoperability':

- 1987 SAA - Systems Application Architecture from IBM
- 1990 NAS - Network Application Support from DEC.

4.2.3 Isolation by Layered Architectures

All the vendor network architectures described above have one thing in common - they are layered architectures. Each layer has a role to play in the network but it only interfaces with, or 'speaks to', the layer above and below it. The same applied to our API company (Section 4.1.4), although it implemented a layered architecture possibly without realizing it.

This 'one-up, one-down' interaction is known as an $(n, n-1)$ layered architecture which effectively isolates each layer of function from those more than one layer away from it. Changes to the functions in one layer may not affect any other layers except, perhaps, the adjacent ones. If a layer-to-layer interface is changed, then only the two participating layers are affected. If the function of a layer changes without affecting the interface then the change is transparent.

Another layering implementation is known as $(n, n-k)$ layering, where k can be 1, 2, 3, 4 etc. Such an architecture does not have the change isolation that the $(n, n-1)$ architecture has, as we saw above. The two types of architecture are best shown diagrammatically, as in Figure 10.

Layering of functions in computer architectures not only affords isolation, but also gives the opportunity to offload and distribute such functions to the most appropriate place or layer, as IBM and other vendors did in their implementations of the various computer and network architectures. This is roughly the system

---

[5] CII-Honeywell-Bull. DSA was part of a grander concept called Distributed Systems Environment (DSE) which was meant to become an architecture for the design and implementation of distributed IT systems.

equivalent of application 'downsizing/rightsizing' discussed later in this book. In this context, it simply means putting (application) function where it is best placed to perform its job. For example, IBM 'downsized' SNA network function by putting elements in 'outboard' intelligent boxes such as the 3745 Communications Controller and the 3174 Control Unit as well as, in some cases, modems via Link Problem Determination Aid (LPDA).

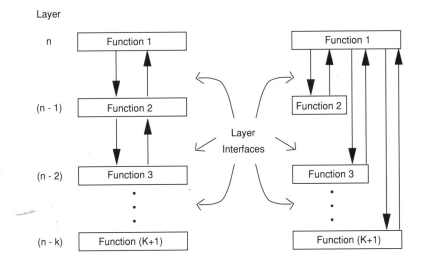

Figure 10. *Layered Architectures*

4.3 IBM's Systems Application Architecture (SAA)

Systems Application Architecture (SAA) is essentially an architecture built on other IBM architectures and implementations. It is a special case of 'open systems' since it was designed to operate across the major IBM platforms giving interoperability, maximum portability, and a common look and feel for the end user. The platforms in point, System/370, PS/2 and AS/400, came from very different sources and were apparently totally and irreconcilably incompatible. This would have posed a major problem for IBM and its customers since the latter could justifiably expect the systems bought from IBM to work together, even if they could not work with systems from another vendor.

Many vendors have accepted the fact that it is difficult to have a single hardware and software architecture that covers the requirements of users from inexpensive desktop PC to supercomputer or a machine supporting 10,000 terminals. In about 1970, IBM introduced the System/3, a mid-range computer aimed at organizations which wanted a computer but found mainframes expensive. System/3 was not a System/370 architecture machine because that would have rendered the cost of the machine prohibitive at that time. The problem of scaling down mainframe architectures to the desktop or small mid-range systems is common to all vendors. The reverse is also true.[6]

After System/3 came other systems such as System/36 and System/38 and, of course, the IBM Personal Computer or PC. In the early micro-processor days, IBM had assessed the feasibility of using System/36 architecture as the basis of a PC but decided that it would make it too expensive. A new, more appropriate architecture, the Intel chip, was used as the core of IBM's PC, eventually running Microsoft's DOS as the operating system.

The situation in the mid-1980s was that there were, for very good reasons, three basic machine ranges offered by IBM in the commercial area:[7]

- System/370

- System/3X (System/36 and System/38)

- IBM Personal Computer and, after 1987, the PS/2.

Although compatibility within these ranges was acceptable, compatibility and interoperability across them was difficult.

SAA was developed to provide consistency and interoperability across these platforms, and to protect the investment people had in the three architectures. It was announced in March 1987 and comprised a set of specifications and interfaces in three parts:

- Common User Access (CUA), an interface dictating how the system and applications interact with the user across each platform.

- Common Communication Support (CCS), which covers how systems work together to accomplish work across a network via consistent connection implementations.

- Common Programming Interface (CPI), which specifies a consistent way for programmers to interact with, and use, languages and other services (such as database). The CPI for Communications (CPI-C) provides a consistent programming interface for program-to-program communication across a network. It also facilitates cooperative processing, or the splitting of an application across a Personal Computer and another IBM computer, such as a System/3X or mainframe.

It is interesting to note that several key elements of the IBM SAA environment are reflected in the X/Open Portability Guides and CAE specifications - SQL and CPI-C are two major examples. X/Open licensed the APPC specification from

---

[6] See G.G. Henry, 'IBM small systems architecture and design - past, present, and future' *IBM Systems Journal*, Vol. 25, Nos. 3/4, 1986.

[7] Other vendors found themselves in a similar position.

IBM in 1989 for inclusion in its portability guides.[8] Both XPG and SAA specify ANSI standard languages as the basis for their respective programming APIs.

The growth of Unix has made major manufacturers like DEC and IBM market a Unix offering alongside their proprietary offerings. It does not mean, however, that these and other manufacturers are about to abandon their proprietary base - it means they must devise ways and means for the old legacy systems to live alongside the new. DEC is developing NAS and IBM is evolving an open architecture to include SAA and AIX (IBM's implementation of Unix), as well as non-IBM systems. IBM's Systemview and Information Warehouse are two examples of this open strategy.

4.4 DEC's Network Application Support (NAS)

In 1991 DEC published *The NAS Handbook*[9] outlining **Network Application Support**. NAS evolved from the earlier Application Integration Architecture (AIA) and, simply expressed, is a set of software APIs based on existing or emerging standards.

The NAS environment addresses what DEC sees as the main requirements for open applications:

- portability
- interoperability
- distributed processing.

Although initially implemented on DEC platforms, for example to give portability and interoperability between VMS and Ultrix, NAS has been ported to the Sun SPARC platform in the form of the NAS 250 package. The interoperability and portability offered by NAS will allow the porting to DEC platforms of applications developed using NAS on other platforms when available. In this respect it is very similar to SAA in offering APIs and specifications which can be implemented on other platforms should it be required.

NAS as an implementation acts as an interface between applications on a DEC system and the operating/networking parts of another vendor's platform. There are four sets of NAS application services:

- *Application access services*, providing options in the selection of user dialogue types and languages. For example, OSF/Motif, DECforms, 3270 emulation and PHIGS.

---

[8] A major subset can be found in X/Open's XPG4.

[9] Second Edition EC-H1190-58/91.

- *Information and resource sharing services*, offering a variety of ways to access application data, including remote access. It also addresses document handling and printing via such products as CDA Services and an ODA/CDA gateway.

- *Communications and control services*, aiding program communications via messaging protocols and cooperative services such as DECmessageQ and MAILbus.

- *System access services*, such as POSIX and DECrpc.

A Digital manual[10] lists the DEC products which make up the four categories outlined above and shows the standards on which the products are based.

4.5 Conclusions

Proprietary systems generally offer sophisticated facilities that in IT terms are mature. In particular, they have strengths in systems and network management and in their suitability for mission-critical applications. The fact that until recently proprietary systems have been all that was available has also meant that there is a massive installed base of such systems.

However, as we saw in Section 2.3, users need more than just systems maturity. They want a wider choice and a degree of interoperability between heterogeneous systems that proprietary networks do not offer. Much of this book is about resolving the conflict created by a major investment in proprietary systems and a demand for greater openness.

For some users the demands far outweigh the advantages of proprietary systems and the proprietary systems are being phased out completely. For others the proprietary system still provides all that they require and they continue to deal with their chosen supplier.

Most users fall between these two extremes. They are trying to create open environments based on their existing proprietary equipment with the intention of integrating new systems more easily. For those who are unerringly proprietary this book will be of no interest - they probably will not even have got this far. For those moving to open systems, either radically or pragmatically, this book should answer many questions and assist in identifying many of the major issues they will face.

---

[10] EC-H1558-48/92 - Guide to Software.

Chapter 5 Unix Systems and Networks

Curiouser and curiouser![1]

While this hectic activity was occupying the proprietary world, something was stirring in the AT&T Bell Laboratories where a 'pretender' to the throne of operating systems was about to make itself known. The pretender became known as UNIX. UNIX is seen by many people as the ultimate open system. The story of how it came to such prominence is a remarkable one.

5.1.1 UNIX versus Unix

The word 'unix' is used basically in two contexts in this book:

1. As an operating system architecture or specification which is independent of the hardware on which it is implemented or how it is implemented. Such a specification is the System V Interface Definition (SVID). Implementations of this we will call 'Unix' to denote a 'UNIX-like' operating system.

2. As a coded implementation from UNIX Systems Laboratories (USL), now part of Novell. This we will call UNIX.

5.2 The Origins of UNIX

In the mid-1960s a team from the Computer Research Group at Bell Laboratories in New Jersey developed, in conjunction with MIT, a computer environment called MULTICS. The environment was quite sophisticated but required substantial com-

---

[1] Alice, from her *Adventures in Wonderland.*

puting power, so much so that in 1969 one of the Group's senior staff, Ken Thompson, requested a new, larger, machine. When the request was turned down the team produced a scaled-down version of MULTICS, in machine code, on a borrowed DEC PDP-7. One of the team joked that 'if the original was MULTICS this must be UNICS', and the name stuck.

This UNICS, or more succinctly UNIX, had many advanced features and Ken Thompson and his team had been able to use their considerable ability to produce an excellent, state-of-the-art, operating system. It had an assembler, command interpreter and a hierarchical file store. However, it was designed by, and for, technically advanced users. It was not user-friendly in the way modern environments are. Indeed, the need to produce a scaled-down operating system ensured that many 'unnecessary' features were stripped out. Although never a single user system, UNIX was typically used in an environment where the user was also the systems administrator. As a result even the most routine administration tasks required the system to be taken off line. These are not criticisms of the original UNIX but are observations that became important as UNIX grew in popularity.

Once Thompson was sure the team had created a usable environment he again requested a new machine and proposed using it to create a text-processing system. His request was approved and UNIX was ported to a DEC PDP 11/20 in 1970. Success came very quickly when the Bell patent office selected for its text processing the UNIX system over a commercial one.

By 1972 the system documentation noted: 'The number of UNIX installations has grown to 10, with more expected.'[2] We suspect that in their wildest imaginations, the originators of UNIX would not have expected that it would be the fastest growing operating system in the world 20 years later.

5.3 The Portability of UNIX

Ken Thompson and a colleague on the original UNIX development team, Dennis Ritchie, were also responsible for another important product - the C programming language. They developed C in the 1960s and in 1973 they rewrote UNIX in C rendering UNIX portable. C compilers were soon to become available for a range of machines which then could become hosts for the UNIX operating system.

Traditional operating systems had been written for particular hardware implementations (and vice versa). The two would have a symbiotic relationship and combine to deliver the optimum speed and efficiency. Thompson and Ritchie realized that, providing performance was acceptable, there were benefits in allowing the same operating system to run on a wide range of hardware. This did not mean

---

[2] Quoted in D. Libes and S. Ressler, *Life with UNIX* (Englewood Cliffs, New Jersey 1989).

there was no requirement for hardware-specific features since code was often added[3] to exploit specific hardware features.

The financial benefits of the portability of UNIX are well expressed by Dennis Ritchie: 'It is easier to port UNIX to a new machine than an application to a new operating system'.[4] In other words, if you want an application on your machine that someone else has running under UNIX, do not port the application - simply port UNIX.

5.4 The Popularity of UNIX

UNIX is growing in popularity as you can see from Figure 11. There is no doubt that it has features and facilities that make it a good operating system for certain workloads. However, having strong facilities was not unique to UNIX. What was special about UNIX was that it came from AT&T. Not that AT&T had a strong track record in computer systems - quite the reverse. Due to a court ruling under America's anti-trust legislation, AT&T was not allowed to market actively computers or computer-related equipment. As a result there were no users outside AT&T until a handful of universities were given tapes of Version Four. Version Five was sold to universities for a nominal fee - but without support, warranty or bug fixes, and payment was in advance.

The features of UNIX, the fact it could run on a multiplicity of hardware platforms and its very low cost, made it extremely popular in universities. Furthermore it was available in source form which made modifications and extensions easier. Often these modifications would find their way into the next official release of UNIX. UNIX conferences and UNIX user groups like USENIX and later /usr/group, which became UniForum, were excellent sources of such new features. Furthermore, as AT&T had no commercial interest in the development of UNIX it was far easier for users to influence the product's direction. When Version Six was released in 1975, AT&T began licensing it to government and commerce.[5] It became popular in the US Department of Defense and in particular the Defense Advanced Research Project Agency (DARPA).

One institution using UNIX was the University of California at Berkeley, and when DARPA began looking for a site to develop UNIX further they chose Berkeley. They worked with staff, including Bill Joy, to develop a UNIX system

---

[3] Usually in assembler code.

[4] Libes and Ressler, op. cit.

[5] This time at a significantly higher price - arguing that it was still not making a profit and therefore not breaking the law.

that could take advantage of the virtual memory concept in the new DEC VAX. Bell agreed that providing the customer already had a Bell licence, then Berkeley could distribute its version of Unix directly to the marketplace. Versions distributed from Berkeley were labelled BSD - Berkeley Software Distribution.

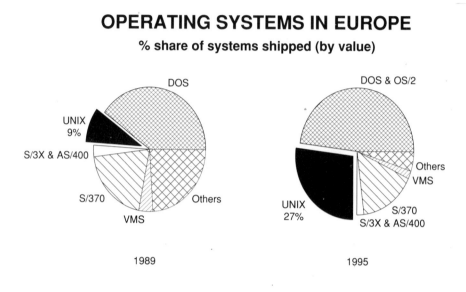

OPERATING SYSTEMS IN EUROPE
% share of systems shipped (by value)

1989   1995

Source: IDC (quoted in *Financial Times*, 22 October 1991)

Figure 11. *The Growth in UNIX Systems*

5.5 The Proliferation of UNIX

The late 1970s saw the development of micro-computers and associated technology which culminated in the highly successful IBM PC. Before developing DOS for the PC, Microsoft was developing a UNIX-like operating system for Radio Shack and Altos micro-computers. This was called XENIX - since UNIX was a trademark of AT&T. When Intel produced a 32-bit version of its PC chip it offered XENIX on the PC as well. By the mid-1980s XENIX was the most popular implementation of UNIX in the world. However, Microsoft was expanding rapidly and becoming massively profitable with MS-DOS. So it sold the distribution rights of XENIX to its largest distributor - the Santa Cruz Operation. SCO distributed XENIX but also developed their own version of UNIX for the PC and negotiated a deal with AT&T that enabled it to be called SCO UNIX. These two versions of Unix for the PC are together the most popular implementations of Unix in the world.

A more advanced chip was the Motorola 68000 CPU. A group of students at Stanford University used it in designing a relatively low-cost machine specifically to run UNIX. They licensed this hardware to a number of companies, the most famous of which was set up by a group which included Bill Joy, the Berkeley developer, and was called Stanford University Network - now abbreviated to Sun. XENIX was available for the 68000 but Joy's knowledge of the Berkeley implementation led him to produce a BSD-based version of UNIX for the Sun range. Again he could not call it UNIX so it was called SunOS. The relatively low cost of the Sun hardware and its popular SunOS operating system made it a pioneer and leader in the emerging workstation market.

Each different implementation of Unix has a different name - Digital Equipment Corporation's is called Ultrix; Hewlett-Packard's is called HP-UX; IBM's is called AIX, Sequent's is called Dynix; and so on. Only the AT&T code, and more recently that from SCO, may be called UNIX.

In 1984 AT&T was subject to a new anti-trust ruling that broke it up into a number of smaller companies but it was now allowed to participate competitively in the computer market. Clearly an important part of this participation would be the promotion of UNIX.

UNIX did not immediately make a profit for AT&T - quite the reverse. In 1986 the AT&T computer business lost an estimated $1 billion. Much of this was swallowed up in the attempt to develop its own hardware range and end its reliance on selling UNIX only as an add-on to another vendor's hardware.

The largest UNIX· vendor at that time was Sun, and in October 1987 AT&T bought a substantial, but not controlling, interest in Sun. In doing so the fortunes of AT&T UNIX became inextricably linked to one particular hardware vendor. AT&T announced that it would develop a new release of UNIX, to be called System V Release 4 (SVR4), in conjunction with Sun. It would be designed to exploit particular features of Sun's hardware and include features previously only found in SunOS - a BSD based version of UNIX. This caused many of Sun's competitors to feel that UNIX was being turned into a proprietary system.

As a result of this concern, May 1988 saw the launch of the Open Software Foundation (OSF) by seven sponsors - Apollo, Digital, Groupe Bull, Hewlett-Packard, IBM, Nixdorf and Siemens. Their initial objective was to develop an open operating system not dependent on AT&T and Sun. The OSF called its open operating system OSF/1, and the member companies agreed that in the future their own implementations of Unix would incorporate OSF/1. See Chapter 10 for details of the OSF.

The AT&T vision of a single unified UNIX was ruined but its response was rapid. It announced that the vendors committing to SVR4 were eligible to join UNIX International. UI would be able to influence the direction both of SVR4 and follow-on versions. Furthermore, the ownership of the rights to UNIX was passed to UNIX Systems Laboratory (USL). Within a year AT&T decided to keep only

85% of USL's shares - the remainder being offered on the open market. In December 1992 it was announced that, following discussions with AT&T, Novell Inc. would acquire USL as soon as agreement could be reached with the minority shareholders. That agreement was reached, in principle, in early 1993. Novell now own the rights to UNIX.

At first sight it would appear that there are two diverging UNIX implementations. We analyze the differences between OSF/1 and SVR4 in Chapter 17. However, generally the two are not that different - they both match all the commonly agreed standards in this area. Furthermore, it would appear that if anything the two are coming closer together. The original vision of Thompson and Ritchie, that of a single portable operating system that would run on a range of hardware implementations, seems to be almost fulfilled. What is now clear is that after their work things will never be quite the same again for customers or vendors.

5.6 UNIX Communications History

When initially conceived, UNIX had no communications facilities. The first communications programs to be added to UNIX were utilities called UNIX to UNIX Copy Program, or UUCP, which allowed the transfer of files across a network and the execution of commands by a user on a system remote from his own. According to Stuart Feldman, a UNIX historian, this was written by 'Mike Lesk of Bell sometime before January 1977'.[6] The main purpose of UUCP was the distribution and receipt of software by linked UNIX systems.

In 1969, the U.S. Department of Defense Advanced Research Project Agency (DARPA) began sponsoring the development of distributed computing over what was then considered a high-speed network called ARPANET. The development team was drawn from government, academic and industrial research sites which needed to transmit and receive files and mail from each other and also remotely log in to other machines on the network. This idea of networking a variety of networks they called internetworking, and the overall networker of networks they called Internet. Because of the diversity of the sites involved there were several physical connections used in the early packet-switching ARPANET network. The group developed a layered protocol to make transmissions independent of the carrier technology on the internet and called it Transmission Control Protocol/Internet Protocol - TCP/IP for short.

The Network Working Group (as they were called) documented their work through notes called Request For Comment or RFC. The original mission of the

---

[6] S.I. Feldman, 'An Architecture History of the UNIX System', *USENIX Summer 1984 Conference Proceedings*.

group was laid out in RFC 3, dated April 1969. It stated that 'the Network Working Group is concerned with the HOST software, the strategies for using the network, and initial experiments with the network'.

Despite its later development TCP/IP was *not* developed for UNIX, nor was it developed for mini-computers or workstations. However, it was developed to link heterogeneous machines and networks together.

In an effort to persuade sites to adopt their new protocol suite DARPA decided to make a low cost version available. As many universities were using BSD UNIX, DARPA funded Bolt Beranek and Newman, Inc. to develop a TCP/IP version for UNIX and subsequently funded Berkeley to integrate it into BSD UNIX. This gave Unix its much needed network protocol and as a result, it became even more popular. TCP/IP soon became the *de facto* networking standard for UNIX, and latterly Unix.

5.7 Conclusions

The use of UNIX is growing rapidly. It has moved from being used solely in technical environments by specialists to being used by many commercial organizations for their everyday business. As can be seen from Figure 12, 70% of respondents in a recent survey agreed to some degree that Unix was their operating system of choice.

Proponents of Unix talk of the massive savings in IT bills possible when companies move to Unix and this has created a lot of interest. Undoubtedly Unix hardware is cheaper than proprietary hardware.

However, IT expenditure does not consist solely of hardware costs. Hardware is a small and shrinking part of the total picture. Unix tends to require more management and more 'hands-on' support than proprietary systems do. Unix networking, which is usually TCP/IP, is not as functional or as automated as many proprietary systems. An assessment of the savings from pursuing a Unix strategy needs to look at the total cost of ownership and not just a part.

If Unix bigots tell you that Unix systems are far cheaper than proprietary systems then at the same time proprietary system zealots exaggerate the failings within Unix. We would simply point out that Unix systems are improving all the time - so any supposed gap in functionality is closing. At the same time prices of proprietary systems are falling so any perceived hardware savings will be shrinking.

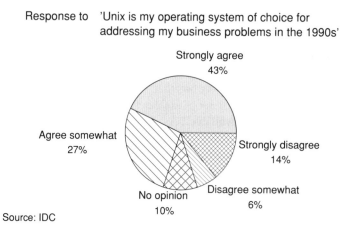

Response to 'Unix is my operating system of choice for
addressing my business problems in the 1990s'

Figure 12. *The Growing Popularity of UNIX for Business Computing*

Taking account of the full picture is 'business as usual' for most IT people and we hope this book will provide you with a similar broad perspective.

Chapter 6 Today's Network Environment

For mine own part, it was Greek to me.[1]

In the preceding chapters we have looked at several strands of IT development:

- proprietary systems and proprietary networking protocols
- UNIX and UNIX-like operating systems and TCP/IP - the networking protocol widely used in UNIX environments
- how different systems and different networking protocols have created a computer environment made up of discrete domains - islands of information.

The first networking architectures to emerge were proprietary. IBM's System Network Architecture (SNA) was developed so that IBM machines could communicate with each other in a layered manner. The initial announcement was of an architecture or model, a framework within which specific networking solutions could be developed. Other vendors also developed their own network architectures (see Figure 15).

This was fine until you tried to get dissimilar machines to communicate. It was like a meeting of the United Nations, where each delegate spoke in his own language. When the French ambassador speaks the others have to listen to what is being said via a translator. Leaving the analogy now, if you wanted to make a DEC machine talk to an IBM machine, you got it to talk SNA or the IBM machine to talk DECnet.

Nobody suggests that making one system 'speak the language' of another is the ideal solution but for many it is the pragmatic solution. Chapter 15 looks at the various options in a little more detail.

---

[1] William Shakespeare, *Julius Caesar*.

Many years ago someone had the bright idea of creating a new language, one that could be spoken by everybody in the world. It was called Esperanto. The main advantage claimed for Esperanto was that nobody would have an unfair advantage when it was spoken because it was not anybody's native language.

There is a computer equivalent of Esperanto called Open Systems Interconnection or OSI. OSI is a networking protocol specially written so that dissimilar systems can communicate in a language other than their own. It was developed soon after SNA was announced, and we will now examine the origins and development of OSI.

6.1 OSI 'Networks'

While UNIX and proprietary systems were treading their diverging paths, it was becoming apparent that, short of everyone adopting a single existing network architecture, there was a need for a standard, agreed way of communicating between unlike network architectures. The dilemma is illustrated in Figure 13.

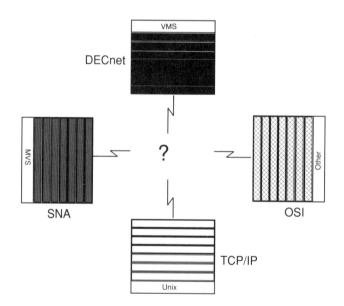

Figure 13. *The Multi-architecture Dilemma*

The solution to this problem was seen as key to high function interoperability.

6.1.1 The OSI Standards

Jack Houldsworth, now an ICL Fellow in Open Systems, did some fundamental work on network systems design in the late 1960s and early 1970s. Much of his work was adopted by the International Standards Organization (ISO) which, in 1977, began the task of defining a framework and set of rules (protocols) which would enable systems, supplied by different vendors, to connect and communicate. The standards evolved by the ISO organization are know known as the ***Open Systems Interconnection*** standards, and in 1983 the OSI Basic Reference Model became an international standard.

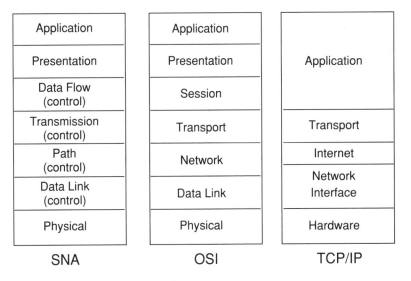

Figure 14. *SNA, OSI and TCP/IP Layers*

The longer-term goal of OSI is the interaction of applications, using a common set of well-defined communications architecture, protocols and services, in a multi-vendor network. These standards are still evolving, generally working up from the physical layer to the application layer, and adding network management function over time.

OSI defines two environments, the ***open system environment***, which is made up of OSI protocols, and the ***local system environment***, which is everything internal to a particular system. OSI is not concerned with the implementation of the local systems, only the standardization of the formats and protocols between end users attached to local systems. Open systems may be implemented on any hardware/software platform provided they conform to the OSI standards - see the OSI definition of 'open systems' in Chapter 2.

If OSI had pre-dated the other network architectures and been adopted by the major vendors, the interoperability issues faced today would not have arisen. For better or worse, the vendors went their own way.

Figure 14 shows three major layered architectures - OSI, TCP/IP and SNA. In Chapter 11, we will show practical examples of these architectures (Figure 87).

6.2 Network Choices

The networking choices for most sites today fall into three categories - proprietary, OSI and TCP/IP. Figure 15 shows how these have emerged over the last 25 years.

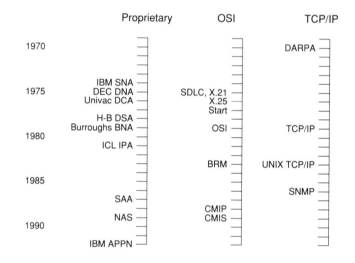

Figure 15. *Development of Major Network Architectures.   Legend: H-B is Honeywell-Bull, BRM is the Basic Reference Model.*

Within each of the different proprietary architectures there has been development similar to that happening with TCP/IP and OSI.

The unusual thing is how network systems have altered in recent years. A few years ago most companies, when asked about their network directions, would have said 'we use SNA but plan to move to OSI'. Now those same companies use a variety of networking protocols, joined by bridges and routers, but plan to move to more open systems. Figure 16 plots the current and planned use of various protocols by some of the USA's largest companies.

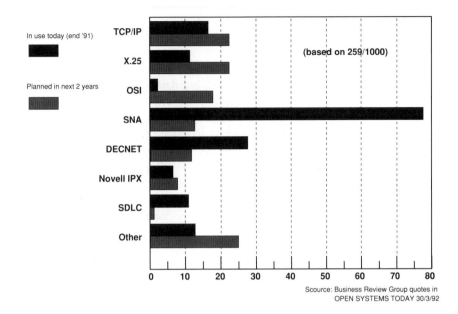

Figure 16. *Fortune 1000 Protocol Use: Now and in the Future*

6.3 Conclusions

There is no doubt that TCP/IP and OSI offer far greater interoperability between heterogeneous systems than proprietary systems. So, when organizations open up their networks, they must opt for TCP/IP and/or OSI, rather than a proprietary solution.

For UNIX systems, the fastest growing area of computing, TCP/IP has long been the network architecture of choice - in preference either to proprietary systems or to OSI. This has led most open systems environments to be TCP/IP based. Indeed many organizations have been tempted to disregard OSI altogether.

This has created a dilemma because the functionality of TCP/IP is generally inferior to both that of proprietary networks and of OSI, with the result that the decision to move to open systems has been based on two conflicting demands. On the one hand, the clear advantages of opening up the network. On the other, the added difficulties of managing and operating that open network.

The need to combine the popularity and openness of TCP/IP with the manageability and openness of OSI has been seen for some time. As a result the ISO Internetworking Joint Technical Committee JTC/SC6 (responsible for OSI interoperability) announced in July 1992 its intention 'to make overtures to the

Internet Activities Board[2] aimed at encouraging future convergence between OSI and TCP/IP communications and protocols'. At the same time user organizations are actively encouraging such a convergence. For example the UK CCTA, who as we saw in Chapter 2 define open systems as matching OSI, is widening its view of the OSE beyond a strict OSI-only policy. Similarly the X/Open CoMIX initiative (see Chapter 13) has also addressed the 'convergence' idea with a document on coexistence and migration.

In April 1993, the IAB and ISO agreed to cooperate on future standards to allow TCP/IP and OSI to coexist and provide a feasible migration to OSI. This agreement was given the unlikely name TUBA (TCP/UDP with bigger addresses). The cooperation is, however, evolutionary and open to changes in direction when practical options are considered in detail.

We stated in our introduction our belief that any decision to move towards open systems should only be made on its business benefits. The benefits, of course, need to be weighed against the problems before any firm decisions are made. Our hope is that in the future those problems are far less than they are today and it does appear as if this change is increasingly taking place.

---

[2] The body responsible for TCP/IP development.

Chapter 7 Distributed Computing Concepts

Not bound to swear allegiance to any master, wherever the wind takes me I travel as a visitor.[1]

The distribution of computing systems today outside the confines of the mainframe 'glass house' is a result of several strands of IT development. These include the the rise of the proprietary minis, PCs and latterly Unix systems, from desktop to large multi-user machines. Since computers themselves are already distributed, even in a single enterprise, one might think that distributed computing is already with us. This is not true since what we have are distributed computers, often totally autonomous. Distributed computing really means a coordinated sharing of data and programs across a network. Although the Unix world grew up to represent a high degree of distributed computing, the rest of the world did not. The development of distributed computing is more of a necessity than a wonderful invention.

The computing tasks undertaken to run a business are often the same in both single central sites and in true distributed systems. Distributed computing tasks need not take place on systems separated by great distances, as the name might imply - they may well be side by side in the same room. What *is* distributed is the computing work.

People are often confused by terminology such as distributed computing, client/server, cooperative processing and distributed database. We will now present some scenarios, in increasing order of complexity, to clarify some of these terms.[2]

The IT department of a company might employ one or more of the following techniques:

---

[1] Horace.

[2] In so far as they have been defined - they do not appear in accredited dictionaries like the *OED* or *Webster's*.

- A single computer with local and remote terminals attached. This is the traditional mainframe or mini-computer environment. All jobs, transactions and database accesses take place on that single system as seen in Figure 17.

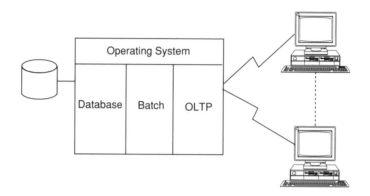

Figure 17. *Single Image Computing*

- Several autonomous computer systems, each having its own work to do, perhaps exchanging data occasionally with the other systems. The characteristics of this environment are the placement of work in an organization on the most appropriate system. An example of this is a large organization with an IBM mainframe for the financial and other commercial work, one or more VAXes in engineering and technical departments and some HP machines for various other purposes. Although the work on these systems may have initially have been unrelated, it is often found that as the systems develop, some kind of interaction is needed. Normally, this took the form of file transfer. We will call this a *distributed computer* environment. This mode is shown in Figure 18.

- A scenario similar to that above, with the addition of a network joining the systems together to enable file transfer, remote login and so on. The remote login facility means that a user on one machine can use one of the remote machines as if he were actually attached to it. He can also issue commands from his system but have them executed on a remote system. File transfer over a network is a common feature of such environments. This we will call a system of *networked computers* as shown in Figure 19.

- An enhancement of the previous scenario is one where computing functions, such as payroll or scientific work, are performed across more than one system. In addition, database access may span more than one system across a single logical, but physically distributed, database. This situation, with lesser and greater variants of it, we will call a *distributed computing* system, essentially a set of discrete computers. It is often called a ***networked computing*** system and is shown in Figure 20.

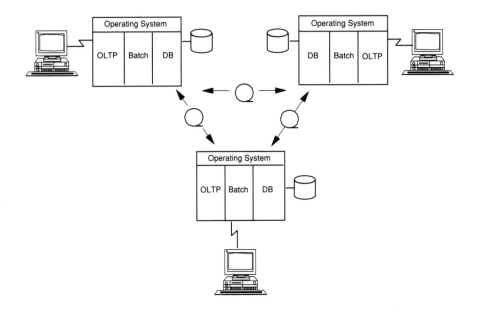

Figure 18. *Distributed Computers*

Such distributed computing scenes can arise in a number of ways:

● as a deliberate policy where systems are added to a network from scratch to meet the developing needs of an organization,

● as a strategy to devolve computing from a traditional mainframe environment to a distributed one, which may or may not include the original mainframe,[3]

● in order to integrate existing and future heterogeneous systems within an organization.

This is why distributed computing is often the key to moving to an open systems environment (OSE). The first two scenarios above (Figures 18 and 19) are less difficult to implement, operate and manage if the environment is homogeneous, for example all VMS VAXes or in an IBM SAA setting. No standards outside those of the chosen vendor need worry the implementing organization. It is the third case, the OSE, (Figure 20) where standards hold the key to successful integration and that is why they are so important.

---

[3] See Chapter 12.

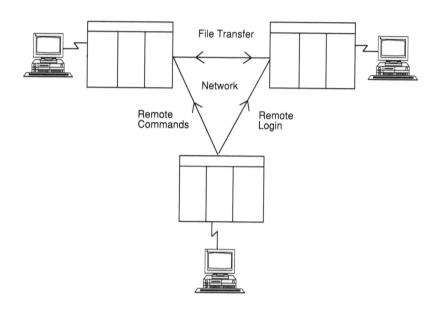

Figure 19. *Networked Computers*

In traditional data processing, computer access was via an unintelligent (or dumb) terminal and all computing activity took place on a single system run by the IT department. These terminals were later endowed with intelligence, such as the ability to draw simple graphical shapes, or perform vector to raster conversion operations, but were still totally dependent on the main system.

When the micro-processor arrived the face of computing began to change. The IBM Personal Computer made its debut in 1981[4] and began to find its way into many large organizations on the desktop. Applications such as spreadsheets, accounting and so on became popular, especially among finance personnel. The arrival of more powerful PCs and bigger disks rendered the early small PCs almost obsolete. It did not make financial sense to discard them and buy the latest model every time one was announced. In addition, some PCs were being configured to perform specialized work such as database access, calculations and archiving. It was not a large step to realize that it was not feasible for everyone to have such power and function on his or her own PC, and the ideas of sharing power came into being.

---

[4] 1983 in the UK.

The idea of doing one's personal job on the PC and using shared systems for things common to several people gave rise to the ***client/server*** concept, which is also very popular in Unix environments.

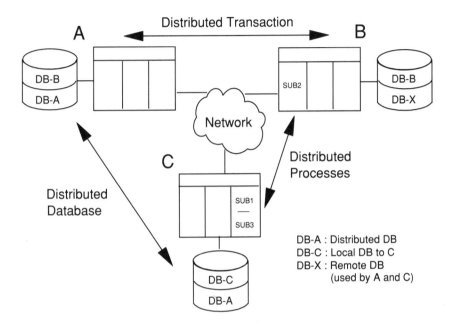

Figure 20. *Distributed Computing*

This scenario was one step removed from the terminal-mainframe in that:

- the PC could perform useful work alone, unlike a simple terminal
- the PC could use one or more server machines for work more suited to them when necessary.

A similar sort of development occurred in the Unix world, although it did not have the same original affinity with the mainframe that many PCs had.

7.1.1 Client/Server Concepts

A simple example of client/server computing is an intelligent machine (client) requesting a service from another machine (server) across the network to which they are both attached.

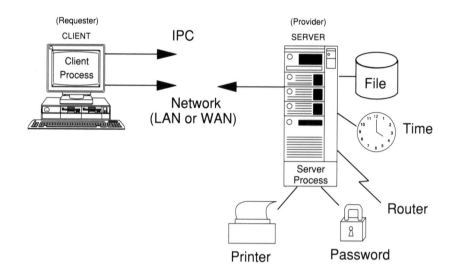

Figure 21. *Server Types*

Many people's idea of a server is a 'file' server on a local area network (LAN). While this is very often the case there are a variety of server types, as shown in Figure 21. Here the server has a number of functions or services to offer prospective clients:

- data
- process or program execution
- time
- printing
- routing.

Of course, all the server functions need not reside on a single machine.

In essence, the way transparent client/server systems work is for the user or program on the client system to request access to some resource (such as a file record or the time) assuming it is local. Local in this context means 'on the same machine'. There is some intercepting function on the client that detects that the requested resource does not reside on the client, but elsewhere in the network. The interceptor then:

- locates the system which has the resource requested

- issues instructions to kindred software on that system to access that resource and pass it back to the caller via the interceptor.

The requestor (or client) is then handed the desired resource. The way this 'action at a distance' is achieved is via calls across the network between processes outside the requesting program. This is often called 'interprocess communication' or IPC.

7.1.2 Interprocess Communication

Normally programs, processes or subroutines perform a task and then pass control to another set of related code. Although the programs may exchange data and parameters, they do not communicate with each other. IPC is a technique whereby programs invoke functions in other programs to complement their own functions. This program-to-program communication forms the basis of much client/server work. A schematic view of IPCs is shown in Figure 21.

IPC is often used in OLTP systems and takes one of three basic forms:

- conversational communications
- remote procedure call (RPC)
- message enqueue/dequeue.

The three communications vehicles are actually network APIs for interaction between processes or programs on different systems. We will deal with each of them in turn, starting with conversational communications, shown in Figure 22.

Conversational communications: There are different implementations of conversational communications, for example:

- OSI conversational model
- IBM SNA conversational model (Advanced Program-to-Program Communication or APPC).

In the conversational model, three basic things happen:

1. determination of the location of the application to communicate with
2. establishment of a connection[5] between the participating applications
3. an interactive exchange of data, possibly half-duplex or full duplex, which can be asynchronous.

---

[5] A conversation in SNA, a dialog in OSI.

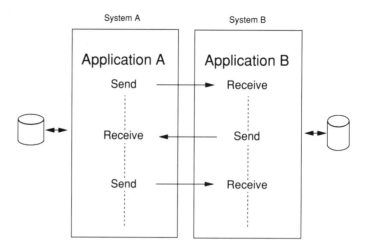

Figure 22. *Conversational Communication*

Remote Procedure Call: The RPC mechanism is shown in Figure 23.

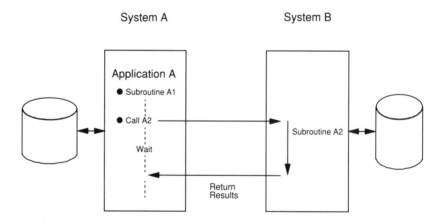

Figure 23. *Communication via RPC*

Message enqueue/dequeue: The message queueing method is gaining in importance because of the potential independence of the underlying transport protocols. A well-defined Message Queueing Interface[6] (MQI) permits transparent exchanges between applications on dissimilar systems across a variety of network types.

---

[6] A form of API.

There is an ISO initiative in the area of message queueing known as OSI/MQ, with a remit 'to define a protocol for remote queue access'. The work began in late 1989 and is expected to be adopted as an international standard towards the end of 1994.

The message enqueue/dequeue mechanism is shown in Figure 24. It is not strictly an API but specifies an abstract service definition as an application layer standard. The project uses OSI TP[7] facilities as a basis and, not surprisingly, has been assigned to the OSI TP group as 'a data transfer' mechanism for use with OSI TP. The design, however, does not exclude other transport protocols such as LU6.2 and TCP/IP.

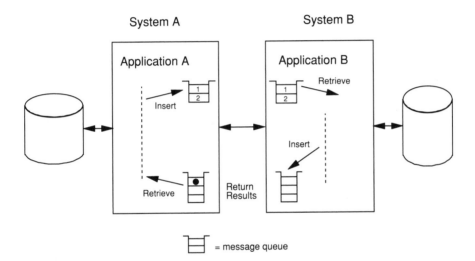

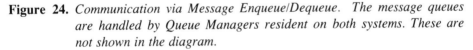

Figure 24. *Communication via Message Enqueue/Dequeue. The message queues are handled by Queue Managers resident on both systems. These are not shown in the diagram.*

It is anticipated that the specified OSI/MQ facilities will be used by queue manager products. A queue manager is a messaging system service which offers message queueing facilities to applications and communicates with other queue managers on remote systems.

Let us examine a few of the characteristics of the three methods of systems communication.

Conversational Processing: In this form of IPC, a conversation (or session) is established between two programs on a peer-to-peer basis. Once the session has

---

[7] See Chapter 16 for a discussion of OSI TP.

been established, the rules or protocols for further exchanges are agreed and a two way conversation can begin.

Conversational or cooperative processing is a special case of the client/server mechanism where participating nodes might flip-flop between client and server modes.

Remote Procedure Call: The RPC method involves the calling up of a program on a remote system and handing it a task to do.   This is not peer-to-peer and represents more of a master-servant relationship. The process is usually synchronous, that is, the sender of the RPC waits until a reply is received before proceeding with other work. RPCs are often used in client/server processing where the server function is predetermined[8] and usually passive when implemented by server software. An application can, however, make the process a little more dynamic.

Message Enqueue/Dequeue: In this method, the exchanges between programs are made via queues, both input and output.   The program uses a message queueing API to pass a request to a service or resource. If that service resides on another system, the queue manager on the requesting system will communicate with its peer on the system containing the service or resource.

One benefit of queues is that they can be implemented on many different systems, allowing an ordered 'store and forward' mechanism for shipping data and transactions across heterogeneous networks. This IPC method is gaining acceptance in the distributed computing environment.

7.2 Remote Data Access

We have implied already that data can be accessed by a program on a system that does not have that data resident on it, and have seen in brief how the data is located and retrieved, essentially transparently to the program. How does the programmer view this data in the context of the program? The world according to the programmer is shown in Figure 25 whereby files he wishes to access are made to appear local, that is, reside on the machine that the application runs on.

What we have just discussed is the concept of remote data or file access. One implementation of this is the Sun Network File System *(NFS)*, another is the Distributed File System *(DFS)* from OSF. Both of these are discussed in Chapter 16.

---

[8] For example, a file server.

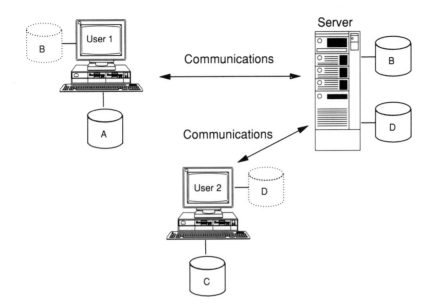

Figure 25. *Remote Data Access (Conceptual). User 1 treats files A and B as if both were both local, even though B is on the Server. User 2 treats B and D as local in a similar way.*

7.3 Remote Process Access

As a logical extension of the remote data access mechanism, it would be useful to be able to access programs, other than server programs, to perform certain computing tasks on a remote computer. One reason for this is that the remote machine may specialize in a particular process, for example a Cray machine doing matrix manipulation or other numeric-intensive tasks.

Conceptual remote process access is shown in Figure 26. User 1 is running a program on his system but calls the other system, the process server, to carry out part of his computation. A real life example of this is the case of molecular modelling. In such studies, the user works in three phases - creation of a model, a computation and finally a display of the results.[9] The computation part of such modelling can take from minutes to many hours on an ordinary workstation, tying up that resource for the duration. A simple use of remote process access is to perform the create and display phases on the workstation and the computation phase on a server Cray machine. We shall see later how this server function might

---

[9] For example, electron density plots represented in various colours.

be spread across many machines using the 'threads' facility of the OSF Distributed Computing Environment (DCE).

Again we have outlined here the concept of remote process access. One implementation of this is the Apollo (now H-P/Apollo) Network Computing System *(NCS)*. NCS is covered later in the book.

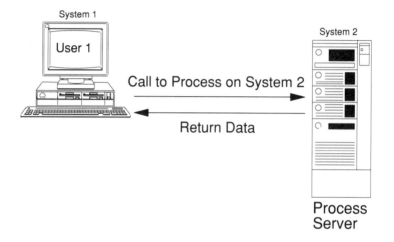

Figure 26. *Remote Process Access*

Structure of Distributed Computing

The access to distributed data and programs can take several forms, as outlined earlier in this chapter, from simple remote data access to data and process sharing. Figure 27 summarizes the kinds of processing we have considered and will consider further in Chapters 16 and 18.

Although the figure shows the different modes of computing with clean boundaries, it is possible to mix and match the modes. This is especially true when using conversational programming techniques. For example, it is possible to envisage a scenario where both the database and the application are split across the workstation and the mainframe. Using X Windows, the presentation logic and window manipulation can also span both systems.

The decision as to which mode should be used will probably be decided on business, technical, financial and other grounds, such as geography and networking technology. Hopefully it will not be chosen on a whim or the desire to be 'leading edge' in the IT world.

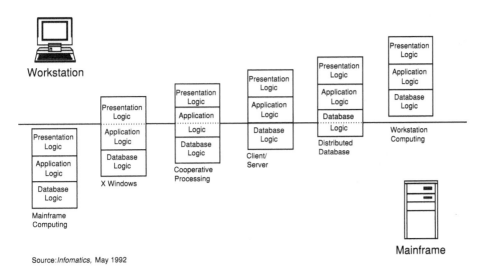

Source:*Infomatics*, May 1992

Figure 27. *Distributed Processing Summary.   Although functional splits are shown at a single boundary in each part of the figure, there may be more than one.*

7.4 The ISO Open Distributed Processing Model

The ISO ODP model[10] is a high-level model for distributed processing in heterogeneous environments. It is the work of a joint ISO/IEC SC21 committee. Because of its abstract nature and level of maturity[11] we will discuss it only briefly here, in spite of the word 'reality' in the title of this book.

The ODP project was initiated in 1987 as a working group and incorporated the work of a CCITT group specifying the Framework for Distributed Applications (DAF). DAF was OSI-based, but in 1988 another work group was initiated to work on the more generic ODP. The European Advanced Network Systems Architecture (ANSA) consortium is the main 'driver' of ODP and includes as sponsors:

- British Telecom
- DEC

---

[10] Called in full the Basic Reference Model of Open Distributed Processing (RM-ODP).

[11] It reached the CD (Committee Draft) stage in November 1992.

- GEC/Plessey Telecom
- Hewlett-Packard
- ICL
- Olivetti.

In conjunction with ANSA, ODP is also driven by a few vendors, including IBM and Unisys, as well as academics, consultants and researchers from various PTTs.

The goal is the production of a Reference Model for distributed computing which caters for the by now familiar requirements of portability, interoperability and, in this case, scalability and manageability. Although couched in rather formal terms, the model can sometimes be related to things well understood in IT, for example a nucleus can be seen as a processor.[12] In general, though, the subject is for experts only.

The model talks about the different aspects of ODP in terms of *viewpoints*, essentially treating the problem in a modular fashion, and discusses the interfaces between them. The viewpoints dealt with by the ODP model are:

- *Enterprise Viewpoint*. The Enterprise Viewpoint is designed for the management view of the ODP system and describes this system in terms of what it is supposed to achieve for the organization. The term 'management' has a similar meaning to that used in the OSF's Distributed Management Environment in that it relates to people, actions and policies.

- *Information Viewpoint*. This viewpoint follows on from the Enterprise Viewpoint in looking at the information processing requirements identified in it. ODP aims to produce an Information Model specifying information structures, their relationships and the flow of information between them.

- *Computation Viewpoint*. The Computational Viewpoint concentrates on the structure of applications in a distributed environment and its goal is network and system transparency. The resulting Computational Model complements the Information Model by specifying a suitable structure for programs in a distributed environment, their processing requirements and the communications between them. The attributes of modularity and parallelism are prescribed to enable the combination, linking and general use of programs in distributed systems.

- *Engineering Viewpoint*. The Engineering Viewpoint is less concerned with hardware maintenance, as one might guess, than with general manageability and support of the whole ODP system. Characteristics of interest here are security, performance, and reliability in the design of a distributed system.

---

[12] For an account of ODP more readable than the official ISO documents, see the report by Ernst and Young, *Open Distributed Processing (ODP) - Concepts and Standards*.

- *Technology Viewpoint*. This viewpoint focuses on the hardware and software components which comprise the distributed environment. It seeks to model the hardware, software, I/O devices, storage and communications interfaces for use in the creation and maintenance of such distributed systems.

It should be noted that the five viewpoints are not of equal maturity with the Enterprise and Information viewpoints lagging their Engineering and Computational counterparts. The RM-ODP work and documentation is structured as follows:

- Part 1 - Overview and User Model[13]
- Part 2 - Descriptive Model
- Part 3 - Prescriptive Model
- Part 4 - Architectural Semantics.

Each of the viewpoints has a corresponding language to describe ODP functions and their relationships.

Like most modern specifications and architectures, the ODP Reference Model has an ODP Object Model relating required activities with objects which comprise the whole system.

ODP, in common with many reference models, is evolving slowly, whereas the drive towards distributed processing is rapid and accelerating. The success or otherwise of the ODP model will depend on how well it complements and assists the pragmatic and standards-based approaches to distributed processing today and in the future. It would seem common sense for ODP to ensure that it is consistent with other related technologies such as OSF DCE, the Object Management Group's CORBA[14], and the work of X/Open in the field of distributed computing.

It is unlikely that the ODP model will gain *de jure* status before 1995 or 1996.

7.5 Conclusions

Today, most businesses have a significant investment in IT. The migration to open systems is therefore not going to be straightforward - it will have to take account of the existing situation. As a result, it will require a considerable amount of planning and thought. This thoughtful consideration requires knowledge of the whole area of open systems and standards. We hope that the succeeding chapters will provide a grounding in these areas.

---

[13] The User Model was previously called Part 4.

[14] Common Object Request Broker Architecture.

Some would let you believe that success in open systems is a matter of luck. We have found that the more you know, the luckier you become at solving problems!

Part 3
The World of Standards

Chapter 8 Open Systems - Where and Why Standards?

Standard ... *An authoritative or recognized exemplar of correctness ... some definite degree of any quality.*[1]

We have seen in the preceding chapters that relevant and agreed standards are central to the implementation of open systems. The need is not limited to the areas of simple portability and interoperability. To structure our discussion, we will expand the areas affecting open systems which need standardization under three headings:

1. portability
2. interoperability
3. user interfaces.

Using these classifications, we will discuss each area briefly and show why standards are needed to achieve openness in that particular area. The actual standards evolving to meet these needs are covered in Chapters 13, 14 and 16.

Portability Requirements

Some key areas affecting the portability of applications across platforms are listed below:

- programming languages and APIs (e.g. OLTP)
- database
- graphics
- object oriented technologies
- program development and CASE.

---

[1] *Shorter Oxford English Dictionary.*

Portability requirements for applications are shown as application programming interfaces (APIs) in Figure 28. What the figure shows is an application shielded from its hardware and operating system environment by a set of APIs. The major APIs are database, network, system and graphical. There are other supporting services shown, such as OLTP and security. The isolation of the program in this way makes it easily portable to other environments which support those same APIs.

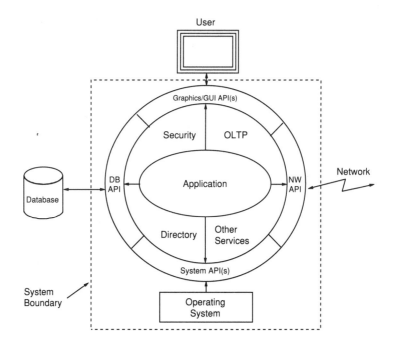

Figure 28. *Portability Requirements in Applications*

Interoperability Requirements

The major types of processing on today's IT systems which aspire to seamless interworking of heterogeneous systems are:

- transaction processing (OLTP)
- distributed computing
- management
- security
- database
- printing.

Figure 29 shows the interoperability requirements as a set of schematic relationships between entities called *resource managers* (RM). We will discuss these here since they appear again in Chapter 16.

Resource managers are sets of software which look after and control certain resources on a system which are accessed and used by applications. Some resources may be invisible to the application and some accessible via APIs. An example of this is an application accessing a database using an SQL API (visible) where access to that database in controlled by the security RM (invisible). Other examples of RMs are shown in Figure 29.

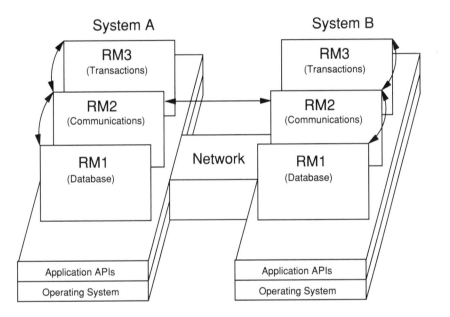

Figure 29. *Interoperability Requirements. The arrows in the diagram represent interfaces between the various Resource Managers (RMs). Similar RMs on different systems interact via the network arrows between the Communications RMs. It is of course possible for RM3 to interact directly with RM1 on the same system but this is not shown in the diagram.*

User Interface Requirements

These are discussed in Chapter 14 and are of two types:

- GUIs
- shells.

Using this structure, we will outline each topic and any issues affecting portability and interoperability. In Part 4, 'The Paths to Openness', we will examine both pragmatic and standards-led solutions to many of the problems identified in this chapter.

This list represents, in one form or another, the requirements put forward in the Xtra, Forrester, GUIDE 82 and other findings discussed in Chapter 2.

Portability, interoperability and user interfaces are key concerns for many IT organizations, which are expected to support a business organization now, and in the future. The questions IT managers and others might be asking are: 'How do we ensure that our system remains open as we progress?', 'Would you recommend waiting until all the necessary standards have been defined?', 'Do we have to sacrifice any existing IT functions or facilities that we rely on when we move to the open environment?'. These are the $64,000 questions in open systems and the answers surely lie with the individual companies, their IT strategies and the people employed to implement them.

8.1 Standards in Context

Someone has said: 'The nice thing about standards is there are so many to choose from'. This can be a major source of confusion to many people, so we will try to put the wide world of IT standards in perspective.

Firstly, a set of software, however popular, is rarely a 'standard' in its own right. OSF/1 is not a standard and neither is System V.4 - they are simply implementations of one or more standards specifications. System V.4 and OSF/1 are POSIX, XPG3 and SVID3 compliant and, as far as standards compliance is concerned, they are identical. Similarly, the OSI and POSIX standards are paper specifications and not software implementations.

Another key concept to be grasped in understanding open systems (and indeed, proprietary ones) are application programming interfaces, layered architectures and the relevant inter-layer interfaces. Consider the following example to illustrate the point.

There are standard specifications for TCP/IP communications. If an IT organization did not want to be tied to TCP/IP but wanted the option to use it and, for example, OSI when necessary, it would need to seek a standard at a higher level than these two protocols. This higher-level standard might permit a choice of lower-level communications or, in an ideal case, transparently use whatever communication stack happened to be there at the time - TCP/IP or OSI.

This point is illustrated in Figure 30, where two levels of API in a simple layered architecture are shown.

The programmer using API 1 needs to know whether he is addressing SNA, TCP/IP or OSI, whereas the programmer using API 2 does not.

Although 'API 2' has more flexibility than 'API 1', it does not dispense with the need for standards at the lower levels for the Transport Independent Layer to interface with. A corollary is that if you mandate a standard at a lower level, you may be restricting your options in the OSE.

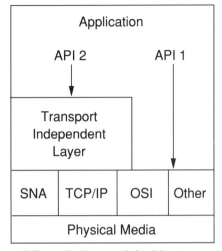

A Pseudo Layered Architecture

Figure 30. *Levels of Standard APIs*

Certainly, if you insist on a particular hardware or operating system platform, your are severely limiting your options for interoperability.

8.2 Portability

Portable programs, utilities or other software are those which are able to run on more than one platform without change.

'Portability', like interoperability, has many degrees. To one IT organization, portability of applications across PCs might be everything it needs for its business. For another, complete portability of complex programs involving database, graphics and so on across many platforms may be mandatory.

There are several levels of acceptable portability:

- Binary compatibility, where the compiled machine code will execute on another machine as it stands.

- Compatibility via an application binary interface (ABI).

- Source compatibility where an application will run unaltered on another machine but needs to be compiled into machine code for that platform.

- Fourth generation language (4GL) compatibility. An application written in a 4GL can be moved to another platform if that platform supports the same 4GL. There can be some issues where block mode and character or line mode applications are concerned, though some 4GLs can cope with this.
- Mixtures of the above.

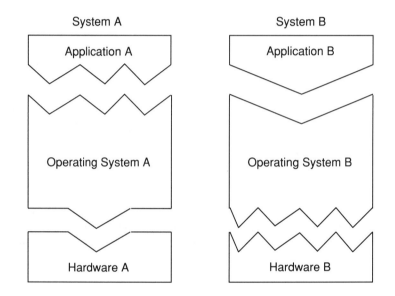

Figure 31. *The Issue of Portability*

The portability issue is shown schematically in Figure 31. When the unique application-operating system interfaces are shown diagrammatically as meshing outlines, it is obvious that application A will not run on system B because of its unique interface with operating system A (and vice versa).

8.2.1 Programming Languages

The languages in which a program is written, or the way code is generated by a 4GL, is of paramount importance to OSE portability. Putting machine-dependent assembler code aside, the major languages in use today are Cobol, Fortran, C and PL/I with growing use of Ada and Pascal. There is obviously a need for standards in the languages themselves as well the API calls issued from them to invoke various functions.

8.2.2 Database

There are three main types of database model in use today:

1. hierarchical
2. network
3. relational.

There are other types of database model in use, for example, the emerging object oriented databases, but these three are dominant. In the UNIX world, the relational model is by far the most popular DBMS.

The first two types of database are traversed by the programmer's knowledge of the connections between the various records in the database. In other words, as a programmer, you need 'navigational' knowledge to find your way around the database. The third type, the relational database, is composed of flat (or sequential) files. Relationships between records are established by the presence of a field common to two or more files. These files are referred to as 'tables' in relational terminology. In the first two database types, relationships are established by physical pointers in the database and as a result they are often inflexible. They are therefore used in areas where specific function is acceptable and they can be tuned for performance. They do not lend themselves to *ad hoc* queries as the relational model does.

An example of a hierarchical database application is a bill of materials system using IBM's DL/1 database, where an assembly is broken down into its constituent parts. Figure 32 compares the three database types.

An example of a relational database application is one which calculates the average salary bill of a department from two tables. One contains salary-personnel details (X-Y), the other personnel-department (Y-Z) details. The two are logically *joined* to give the effect of a salary-department (X-Z) table which the application uses. In Figure 32, the link between the two tables is 'Y'.

The question of portability of database programs is a thorny one. Most proprietary databases are confined to the suppliers' platforms for example, DB2 and IMS are for IBM platforms only.

The most flexible database type is the relational model, accessed via the Structured Query Language or *SQL*, pioneered and developed by Dr Ted Codd when he was employed by IBM. One reason for the growth of SQL is this flexibility and the fact that almost every system can support flat files or tables. SQL as a language is now in the public domain and a developing ISO standard.

The implementations of relational (SQL-based) databases usually differ from supplier to supplier. Simple, non-procedural SQL code is almost certainly portable across implementations.

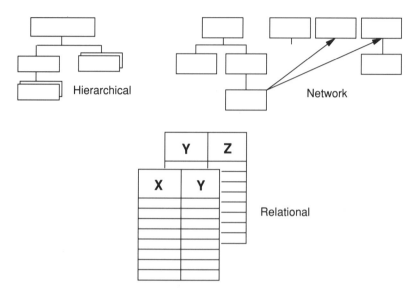

Figure 32. *Data Base Types*

However, since most applications are developed using vendor-specific tools and 4GLs, applications are usually non-portable, as are the actual databases.[2] Although we said that relational databases use flat files, presented as tables, that is only the programmer's view. The way they are physically stored and indexed is specific to the vendor implementation.

Datamation[3] lists nearly 150 DBMS varieties from over 100 vendors. The platforms involved range from PCs through to mainframes, with the majority of the DBMSs supporting SQL either directly or as an option. This list has implications for the open tenet of 'vendor independence'!

The work of the ISO/ANSI committee and the SQL Access Group in standardizing the SQL relational language is dealt with in Chapter 13 under 'Portability'. In Chapter 16, under 'Interoperability', we look at the standards for distributed database from these same bodies.

---

[2] It is possible to unload a database as a flat file and reload it into another type but this doesn't help the application.

[3] 'A DBMS for every user', August 1992.

8.2.3 Graphics

The use of graphics is growing in importance for many applications. We are not talking here about simple business graphics and pie-charts, but sophisticated, colour, three-dimensional graphics shown on screens capable of displaying pictures made of colours selected from 16 million available colours and shades ('true colour') for advanced design work. Advanced graphics are increasingly being used in pharmaceutical, television, science and many other areas, in addition to traditional areas like CAD/CAM and mechanical design.

Early graphics programming had similar drawbacks to early application coding - it was usually platform-specific and non-portable. A certain low-level set of code (primitives) would mean something to one type of screen but nothing at all to another.

It was also very difficult to do anything at all clever, like shading a shape, without considerable effort and use of CPU cycles. When you consider that a 3D diagram is made up of 20,000 or more shaded polygons, creating such a figure in pure software was not feasible. There was a need for a higher level of programming language specification or API to make life easier for the graphics developer, especially if it could be made public and standard.

A graphics API is a set of graphics subroutines and utilities that help the programmer to define, display and modify graphical data at a level higher than simple device-level coding. It is aimed at creating platform-independent graphics programs, which, for the sake of understanding, can be compared with Cobol programs in terms of intended system independence. Like Cobol, these APIs need to be agreed and standardized before they confer attributes of portability across heterogeneous platforms.

Following its formation in 1977, SIGGRAPH (Special Interest Group on Graphics) developed the earliest recognized standard graphics API called 'Core' (short for *Core Graphics System*) - a 3D graphics system - but it was not approved by ANSI or ISO as a standard. A subsequent API, Graphical Kernel System (GKS), was modelled on Core but only handled 2D geometry. It was, however, endorsed by ANSI and ISO and led to the development of further APIs for 3D graphics.

Graphics functions are made available to the user by a combination of features supplied by:

- application code
- graphics API code
- graphics adapter hardware.

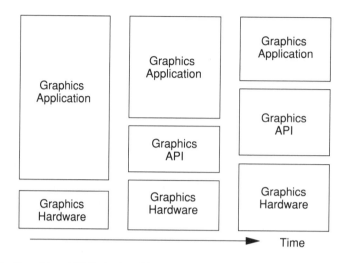

Figure 33. *Graphics API Relationships*

Normally, the aim in graphics development is to shift the burden of graphics code from the application programmer to the API, which in turn will try to use hardware to perform function for it and ultimately for the programmer. An example of this is the shading of a polygon or triangle using hardware and then using combinations of them to display a 3D picture. The generation of the whole picture using software alone, with or without an API, would often put an intolerable load on the system.

The development of APIs and hardware adapters is shown in Figure 33.

Developing standards for graphics has the advantages of minimizing programmer learning time and making programs written to appropriate standards portable. The three main areas where graphics standards are seen as key are:

- user interface to graphics programs
- graphics program to device interfaces
- graphics program to graphics program interfaces.

These standards efforts are discussed in Chapter 13.

8.2.4 Object Oriented Technologies

Object oriented technology is one area of computing that is generating increasing interest. As shown in Figure 34, it is estimated that the revenue generated by object products will increase tenfold between 1990 and 1996.

TOTAL REVENUE FROM OBJECT PRODUCTS

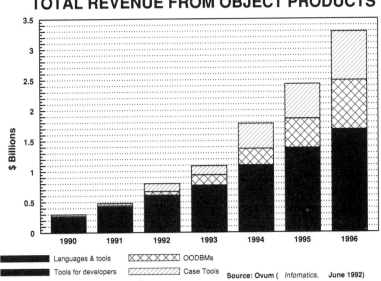

Figure 34. *The Growth of Object Oriented Technology 1990-1996*

At its most simple, object orientation is a technique for creating software modules that can easily be reused, either replicated or modified, many times over. This ability to be reused cuts down the costs and time normally associated with program development. Its relevance to open systems is that if the programs written using object oriented technology are written to agreed standards then they will be portable from one machine to another. In addition, if the message passing between them follows an agreed standard, they will also be able to interoperate efficiently in an object-based client/server environment.

Objects, Messages and Classes

To understand object oriented technology it is important to understand a few basic concepts. The first is the idea of an 'object'. The Object Management Group's 'Object Management Architecture Guide' defines an object as: 'A combination of a state and a set of methods that explicitly embodies an abstraction characterized by the behaviour of relevant requests.' Perhaps a little explanation is required!

Dr. David Taylor explains[4] the idea of objects by using the concept of an automatic guided vehicle in a warehouse. The vehicle can exhibit a range of behav-

---

[4] In his excellent book *Object Oriented Technology: a manager's guide*, (Reading, Mass. 1990).

iours, or methods: moving up and down, forward or back, loading and unloading as it goes. At the same time it maintains information about its characteristics. Some characteristics are inherent - pallet size and lifting capacity; other characteristics relate to its current state - contents, location and speed. These characteristics are variables. To equate this to an object you would then say that it carries out its behaviour or methods (that is, what it can do) by changing its variables (that is, its characteristics).

Like the warehouse vehicle the object is complete in itself. It is entirely self-contained because everything it 'knows' is expressed in its variables, everything it does is expressed in its methods. An object is a software module - a full program consisting of a number of individual modules working together.

These modules, or objects, work together through messages passing between them. The messages are very simple - they contain merely the name of the object the message is for and the name of the method to be carried out. If the method requires specific information to know precisely what to do, this is included as a collection of data elements called parameters.

Of course many objects will be identical. In the example of the warehouse there could well be more than one automated vehicle. It would be a ridiculous waste of time to redefine everything about the object again. Instead the groups of identical objects are referred to as a class and the multiple occurrences of an object within that class are referred to as instances. In other words an object is an instance of a particular class.

Though many objects will be identical there will also be many objects that differ from each other only slightly. In the example of the warehouse one automated vehicle might be designed to pick up palettes and another designed to pick up rolls. They are both adaptations of a basic automated vehicle - they inherit basic characteristics of the vehicle and then add some of their own. If the automated vehicle is a class then adaptations of that class are sub-classes. We can extend the analogy because trucks designed to pick up palettes may be split between those that pick up large palettes and those that pick up small - a sub-sub-class.

In traditional programming developers were limited to specific data types and had to define such data types - e.g. text, number, maximum and minimum ranges of the number and so on. With object orientation they can define new data types by combining traditional data types and packaging them together taking key features from the traditional data types. This is known as abstracting. The packaging together of data types into abstracts is how the object is created.

Of course it is very difficult to define some very complicated things as a series of data types packaged together. It is not how we think of complicated things. An aeroplane, to use another example from Taylor, is itself a single object, but nobody designing an aeroplane would think of it only as a whole. They would have to break it down into a number of parts - the wing, the fuselage, the engine, and so on. In other words, the aeroplane, though an object, is made up of a number of other objects - it is a composite object. The designer is aware both of the whole and the individual parts that make it up.

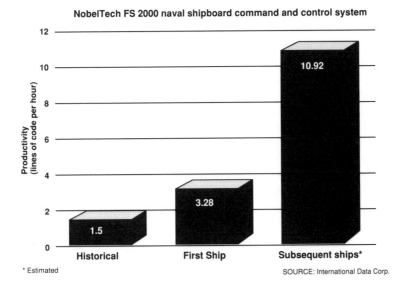

Figure 35. *Object Oriented Programmer Productivity Increases*

In summary, the power of object oriented technology can be understood as follows:

- An object can be defined as having methods and variables.
- It is programmed easily using data abstraction. As the use of object orientation grows, so developers discover the object they require, or something very similar, has been defined before. Their object is one of a class. All they need to do is take the class and amend it so their object becomes a sub-class.
- As the program grows and more complex ideas are brought on board so objects can be collected together to form a composite object which makes the whole program easier to understand.
- These individual objects, composite or single, communicate with each other through a simple messaging system and together create a complex program.

The key benefit of object orientation is productivity increases. NobelTech, which produces command and control systems for the Swedish armed forces, estimates productivity will increase 600% using object oriented techniques. The graph in Figure 35 shows the increases documented. Benefits like this may not be open to every organization but they are the source of much of the interest in the technology.

Where are Standards Needed?

The potential advantages of objected oriented technology are such that many organizations, both user and supplier, are moving towards using it. If open systems are to be achieved, then it is vital that this important part of the computing environment has some agreed standards. The Object Management Group (OMG), a non-profit association of information system companies, has set out to establish some.

The OMG deals with an Object Management Architecture with certain key standard components. The first component is called an ***object request broker*** - the mechanism for messaging between objects. We have already described how objects interwork with each other through the passing of simple messages. If objects are to be portable to different environments, and perhaps more importantly if they are to interwork with other environments, then the messaging methodology needs to be standard. There is no point having one object send a message in a form the other objects do not understand.

The object request broker will need to address such issues as a name service - each object needs to have a name and a location known to the other objects; request dispatch - there needs to be a way of expressing the method to be invoked; parameter encoding - an agreed way of representing the parameters of the method to be invoked and many others.

The second component of the architecture which needs a standard approach is that of the object oriented database - or, more correctly, the interfaces to it. The need to allow multiple access to objects means that some sort of database management system is required to 'keep order'. However, as we have already explained, objects do not use traditional data types, rather new data types are created through the process of data abstraction. Therefore a traditional database management system is not usable and an object oriented database management system is required. The database itself can order things however it chooses, but the interface to it must be standard to allow programs to access objects no matter which object oriented database they are held on.

These examples, the object request broker and the database API, are two obvious areas within the technology that need standardization. The Object Management Group is working on these today. In the future it plans to work on the creation of an object oriented language and a range of data architectures as well.

8.2.5 Program Development and CASE

Early standards for program development meant agreed ANSI languages such as Cobol and Fortran, the so called third generation languages or 3GLs. More sophisticated methods of developing programs, without necessarily having to code every function, were introduced later and became known as fourth generation languages or 4GLs. These tools were developed and became programming projects where documentation, charts and so on were kept on a computer along with the code. These environments were named computer aided software engineering environments or *CASE*.

The need for standards in CASE is very like the need in network architectures. Vendors each developed their own CASE tools and architectures without any attempt to resolve how they would interoperate with other vendors' solutions. The areas that require standardization are

- data exchange between different CASE tools
- the structure and format of a CASE repository
- the method for accessing a CASE repository.

There have been attempts at standardization in all three areas and these are discussed in Chapter 13.

8.3 Interoperability

The interoperability problem can be envisaged in a diagram similar to Figure 31 on page 86 where the communications subsystems of two systems do not mesh.

Interoperability means different things to different people. It can range from simple IBM 2780 file transfer to total data and program transparency where a user or programmer neither knows nor cares where files and processes reside but accesses them in a simple fashion as if they were resident on his or her own machine.

We would see that system A is unable to communicate properly with system B because of the uniqueness of the communications interfaces. Standards, we can now see, mean agreeing what the interfaces should be between applications and operating system and between communications subsystems or layers. This is shown schematically in Figure 36.

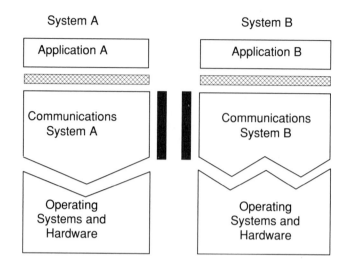

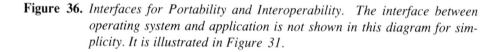

Figure 36. *Interfaces for Portability and Interoperability. The interface between operating system and application is not shown in this diagram for simplicity. It is illustrated in Figure 31.*

The solution to the portability and interoperability issues is a set of agreed interfaces between:

- the operating system and the application
- the communications software and the application
- the communications software on one system and that on the other.

The hatched areas represent agreed interfaces for application portability and for communications interoperability. You will note that the operating system to hardware interface can still be unique but this does not affect the portability and interoperability.

8.3.1 Security

Security often appears at the bottom of open systems IT checklists, and if it does appear it is usually because someone thinks it should be there but does not know what to do about it. It is probably the most important issue in open and distributed computing systems. The evolution of open networks, the advent of computer viruses and the interoperability needs in modern IT make security a key issue for any organization.

The word 'open' implies a *laissez-faire* attitude to controlling access to key IT system resources. Most stand-alone systems have some form of security, usually involving passwords. If such systems are linked in an OSE, then problems can arise in controlling access to resources across systems. In any distributed system, open or otherwise, security warrants careful consideration. To bring out the issues, we will examine some of the security concepts of relevance.

Security Concepts

Authentication: This means proving to the system that 'you are who you say you are'. To explain what this means in a distributed environment, let us use another analogy.

If you visit an IBM location, you will need to register with security at reception your identity and reason for entering the building. Once the staff are convinced you are a legitimate visitor you will be issued with an access badge, valid for that day. This badge must be worn during your movement around the building since it proclaims that you have been ***authenticated***. You are then free to roam around the building as long as you carry the badge.

In heterogeneous networks, unless there is a global authentication mechanism supporting individual authorization mechanisms on the nodes, then each access to a resource on any node may require separate authentication. If the environment supports transparent access to remote data and processes, distributed transaction processing and databases, the overhead of this would be intolerable.

Platforms which have such problems cannot really be said to be open since they do not exhibit the key characteristics of portability and interoperability.

Authorization: There may, however, be some areas in the building which are closed to everyone except certain IBM staff.[5] To enter such an area you will need access ***authorization***. Someone will need to refer to a list to see if you are authorized to enter that area. In IT security terms, this is known as an access control list (ACL) as it defines who can access which resources - the resource in this case being a specific part of the building.

To bring the analogy closer to a distributed systems environment, authentication means you are accepted by the security system as a valid user of the network of systems. At a lower level, there will be authorization systems on the various nodes to check which resources on that node you are allowed to access. Just because you as a user are authenticated and authorized to use a VAX at some location on the network, that does not mean you can run every transaction and access every database. The ACLs will dictate what you can and cannot do on that VAX, even when you are authorized to access it.

---

[5] For example, a development laboratory.

Data Encryption: If you are excluded from accessing resources on certain nodes, there are ways you might eavesdrop on data being transferred between nodes. Data in this sense can include passwords as they are being entered, perhaps on a remote system. To reduce the security exposure to this, data and passwords are often scrambled or, more technically, *encrypted*. Data is encrypted at one end of its journey and *decrypted* or unscrambled at the other. This is achieved by the use of encryption/decryption *keys* which 'lock' the data at its source and 'unlock' it at its destination.

Other terms you may come across in security discussions are:

Confidentiality: The need to safeguard critical data, files or objects from unauthorized disclosure.

Data integrity: The need to safeguard critical data, programs or objects from unauthorized modification.

Non-repudiation: A function to allow the proof of origin or delivery of a message or data.

The three basic threats to an IT system are:

1. loss of confidentiality of data

2. loss of data integrity

3. loss of data availability.

It is these exposures that need standards to be defined for both single systems and, more importantly, for networks of heterogeneous systems. Some of the elements of security are physical, such as locked rooms and keylocks on terminals. However, much of the security needs to reside in the system software and network elements of IT systems.

8.3.2 Database Interoperability

We dealt with the portability aspects of relational databases in section 8.2.2. In a distributed computing environment, two major database scenarios can be envisaged:

- databases on different systems, for example RDB1 on system A and RDB2 on system B.

- a database split across two or more systems, for example RDB3 spread across systems A and B.

There are obviously issues that demand attention in such environments, such as control of simultaneous updates, integrity and recovery of data and databases.

Examples of such distributed databases are illustrated in Figure 37.

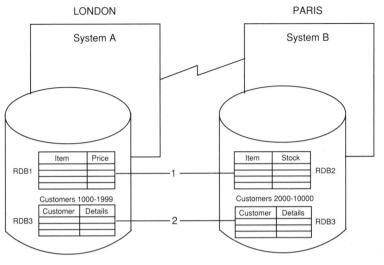

1. Distributed database - combined they are an Item-Price-Stock database
2. Distributed tables - combined they are a complete Customer-Details database

Figure 37. *Examples of Distributed Databases*

It is a major task to implement such scenarios even with a single relational database implementation involved. The problems are compounded when the databases are different, especially in the OLTP environment. Yet distributed database standards and distributed OLTP standards are required if any large commercial organization is to adopt seriously open systems across all areas of its computing. That is why we have made these subjects a key topic in this book.

8.3.3 Online Transaction Processing (OLTP)

There are several definitions of online transaction processing we might quote, but the best way to get a feel for OLTP is to look at the words that make up the acronym.

A *transaction* is a 'discrete unit of work', updating a personnel record when the person marries, for example. The word *online* means the action is carried out there and then (that is, synchronously) and not, for example, queued for batch processing overnight. The word also carries the idea that the initiator of the transaction is acting via a terminal or workstation, although this is not always the case. Transactions can be initiated by programs, stored procedures or other transactions (from the same or other systems).

This type of processing is sometimes called ***real time*** because the processing of the unit of work (usually involving the access and update of one or more databases) is done immediately, thus representing the 'real time' state of the art of the business related to that database.

About 25 years ago, most commercial data processing was done in what is called ***batch*** mode since large batches of data were processed by a single program. A typical batch program could be the updating of a public utility customer file to reflect the day's payments made by consumers (in batches). Such files were often sequential so a query on a particular account would need a program to search through the whole file. As new consumers were taken on, forms would be filled in and sent to the IT centre for keying onto punched cards and then put in batches ready for processing against the file. The new customers would then be added to the customer file by a batch program, copying the old file, adding the updates and creating a new file. With tape-based files, this was the only way to update a file.[6]

As database access methods improved, it became possible to make single specific queries or updates on a file using a suitable program. Special programs were written to do specific tasks and these were latterly invoked from a display terminal. If the task was an update or delete function, the action would not be performed directly on the database but spooled to a temporary file. Later, the actions would be vetted by another program and the file update or delete performed or not according to the success of the vetting process.

In time, monitors were developed to maintain the integrity of databases when running user programs against them. The benefit of such systems was that updates could be done there and then, that is, in ***real time***. Queries too could be classed as real time since the data is always current. This was not the case in the old batch days since the update runs were usually performed in the evening or overnight so the resulting data was always a day out of date. A generic name for these systems is ***transaction processing systems*** and the characteristics of leading edge ones are that they:

- have high availability
- are capable of high transaction rates
- support many users simultaneously
- cater for online (terminal) input and output
- can control multiple transaction types and databases
- can assign and change priorities of transactions or users
- give good response time from the user entering the query to receiving the answer or acknowledgement.

---

[6] Called grandfather, father, son versions of the files.

- have recovery facilities for failed transactions
- implement recovery facilities for databases as a result of failed or rogue transactions (these facilities might be integral to the transaction processing system or use an existing database system)
- can be split across more than one system in either client/server mode or transaction shipping mode
- free programmers from details of the OLTP implementation and allow them to concentrate on processing data as requested by the user.

In general, transaction programs perform a set of functions, and a transaction processing system might have many such programs. One reason for this is that the programs can be kept relatively small, reducing loading overhead and main storage requirements. For example, an online personnel system might be documented as follows:

Figure 38. *Sample Personnel System*		
Transaction Code	*Program Invoked*	*Function Performed*
PERSU	PER001	Update record
PERSD	PER002	Delete record
PERSS	PER003	Display record
PERSC	PER004	Update salary field
....	....	....

The way such a system would operate is thus:

1. The user enters data on a screen, usually preformatted. For example, imagine the user enters:

    PERSD 21567

    where PERSD is the transaction code and 21567 is someone's personnel number.

2. The transaction processing system reads this input and, using a table similar to the one above, finds the program associated with PERSD, in this case program PER002. The program is loaded into main storage by the OLTP system and executed using the data supplied - in this instance 21567. In our simple case, the program PER002 would delete the record of 21567 and inform the user that this had been done.

3. If program PER002 is requested again whilst still in storage it may be reused without going through the lookup and load sequence.

4. The system will then invite the user to enter his next transaction code and associated data.

This is a very simple outline of transaction processing systems most of which work in similar fashion, as outlined in Figure 39.

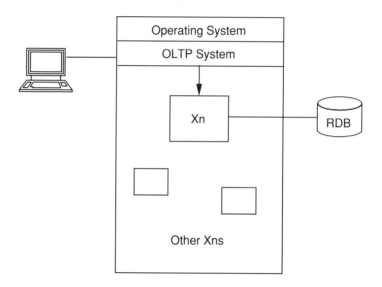

Figure 39. *Non-Distributed OLTP Systems. 'Xn' is popular shorthand for 'transaction'.*

Most transaction programs are quite small and perform only one or two application functions. There are a number of reasons for this:

● A transaction program which does, for example, all the payroll functions outlined above would be large, difficult to maintain and would not lend itself to distributing function across systems.

● A single large program could handle only one type of transaction at a time unless very cleverly coded to be multi-threading.

● Such programs are quickly loaded and given control.

● It is possible to prioritize transactions.

It is important to note the difference between a ***business transaction*** and a ***system*** transaction.

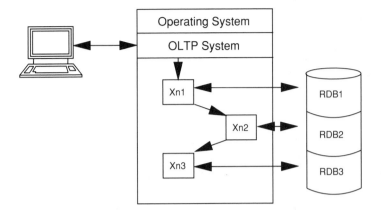

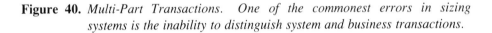

Xn1, Xn2, Xn3 are related system transactions
performing partly one business transaction

Figure 40. *Multi-Part Transactions. One of the commonest errors in sizing systems is the inability to distinguish system and business transactions.*

Take the example of a transaction to take an item of stock from a warehouse. To the user this is a single transaction - to the system, it may be several. There may a transaction to verify that the user is authorized and that the part number keyed in is valid. Control may then be passed to another, related transaction to remove the item of stock from the stock file. This transaction in turn could pass control to another transaction which updates a ledger and perhaps other files. Information which needs to be passed on to succeeding transactions is often called a *scratch pad* or save area. An example of the use of this would be passing the part number from transaction to transaction in our example. Such a transaction flow is shown in Figure 40.

The structure of the business transaction as represented by discrete system transactions lends itself to distribution of function across more than one system. The only issue with this is how we pass the common information (save area) required by each step on to the next step. We will see a little later how the Encina OLTP product handles this.

The name *transaction monitor* is often used to describe an OLTP environment rather than a specific set of code, for example ACMS or CICS. Such an environment might comprise:

- a set of APIs for use by the programmer to perform various tasks within a transaction program

- language support for the programmer, typically Cobol and C
- file control for non-relational files such as DEC's RMS or IBM's VSAM
- relational database support, either integral or external with a defined interface to the monitor
- database integrity, especially across systems
- system-to-system communications over different network protocols, for example TCP/IP and DECnet
- distributed OLTP communications
- support for terminals, screen mapping and GUIs
- systems management tools for performance measurement, software distribution, network management and so on
- a program development environment
- internationalization, sometimes called National Language Support
- manuals, sample code, tutorials and other enabling materials.

An important part of an OLTP system is the ***transaction manager*** (TM). The main jobs done by the transaction manager are:

- handling communication between the user terminal and the transaction program API
- cooperating with the database manager (often called the resource manager in the OLTP context) in maintaining transaction and data integrity and synchronization
- interfacing with the communications manager for things like peer-to-peer communications.[7] If you remember, the general name for this kind of interaction is interprocess communication (IPC) with the three major types - remote procedure call (RPC), conversational and message queueing interface (MQI).

Many OLTP programs do not use a TM but have embedded similar function in the application. Unless the program is capable of handling the many transaction-terminal relationships, then a copy of the program is needed for each requester. This mode of operation is totally unsuited to large OLTP volumes of many transactions per second. It is sensible to centralize these functions in a TM instead of each program reproducing them. The task of the programmer is then to ask the TM for the input received from a requester via an API and to perform database accesses through another API. There will also be some data processing between the API invocations, representing the business logic of the transaction.

---

[7] Sometimes called program-to-program communications.

There are some important tasks to be performed by an OLTP system, the main one being the integrity of data on the system. In OLTP systems handling many transactions and more than one database or file, certain disciplines are essential and these are outlined briefly here.

Data Integrity: There are four key characteristics vital to data integrity in any database system, commonly known as the 'ACID' tests. The acronym expands as follows:

- *Atomicity* - the changes made to the system by a transaction must be accomplished entirely or not at all. If a transaction cannot complete, any changes made must be rolled back or undone.

- *Consistency* - the transaction must change the state of the system from one valid state to another valid state. The results of a transaction must be reproducible and predictable.

- *Isolation* - means that changes made to shared resources by a transaction do not become visible outside the transaction until the changes are committed. This means, for example, that if a transaction has updated 2 out of 4 related records it intends to change, another transaction cannot access any of them until they have been committed.

- *Durability* - the changes made and committed by a transaction will survive subsequent system or media failure. This is normally achieved by logging changes to indexes and data and registering commit points within or at the termination of a transaction program.[8]

Concurrency Control: This is a mechanism for controlling concurrent transactions attempting to access a single database. This is necessary to avoid situations like two transactions reading a copy of a record, updating it and replacing it. The last transaction to replace the record will know what the record contains but the earlier update by the first transaction will be destroyed.

One mechanism used to prevent this, and other integrity exposures, is called *locking*, sometimes known as serialization of update access. When a resource is accessed with update intent by a transaction, that resource is locked to other transactions until freed by the original transaction. Such locking can be at disk volume level, file or database level, physical block level or record level. Obviously, the more discrete the locking, the easier it is to have concurrent access - volume-level locking is unacceptable, while record-level locking is the ideal.

---

[8] These ACID properties are built into the TPC benchmarks specifications from the TPPC (Transaction Processing Performance Council) to eliminate some of the loopholes in the Debit/Credit and TP1 benchmarks which often yielded widely different results for machines of comparable power.

Commitment Control: This function of an OLTP system is the one that provides the ACID property of durability. When a transaction makes a series of logically related updates to databases, the commitment control ensures that all updates are committed together and are permanent. An example of lack of such control is a fictitious personnel system. There are two databases involved, the personnel database and the payroll database. An employee is promoted and this is reflected in the personnel database. Obviously he is due a pay rise and this is about to be reflected in the payroll database when the system fails. The employee is not pleased when he receives the next salary advice in his new position.

The topic of Two Phase Commit (2PC), which avoids such problems, is covered in Section 8.3.4.

Having explained OLTP, can we define it? There are two definitions of OLTP which we feel are appropriate:

- 'An OLTP system is a system which manages a complete unit of work with online access to, and update of shared data, with integrity, at a reasonable cost.'[9]

- 'A transaction is a set of database updates whose effects are to be considered indivisible.'[10]

They seem as good as any if a definition helps you to understand what OLTP is.

The question may have arisen in your mind: 'What have standards got to do with this?'. The answer is that OLTP systems and their transaction programs are not portable, do not interoperate and do not have a common user interface. They cannot, therefore, be open. The APIs through which the programmer invokes teleprocessing and database functions are different across systems. In some cases, the APIs on two transaction processing systems on the same machine might be different. Standards related to OLTP and some current OLTP systems are discussed in Chapter 16.

8.3.4 Distributed OLTP

Distributed transaction processing is really a generic term used in different ways. The common theme in most interpretations is the splitting of work across more than one system. One way of looking at it is to imagine that the processes and databases which resided on a single mainframe are now spread across several systems. We will illustrate this mode of OLTP with two systems, although there could be more.

---

[9] Used in an IBM presentation.

[10] From a UI document, *Tuxedo Transaction Processing System.*

There are a number of ways these two systems can interact in a distributed OLTP environment. Our two-system OLTP environment is shown in Figure 41 to aid the discussion. Imagine that OLTP-A on system A receives a transaction code which causes it to invoke transaction Xn1, and pass it some data. Imagine that Xn1 needs access to databases DB-A and DB-B.

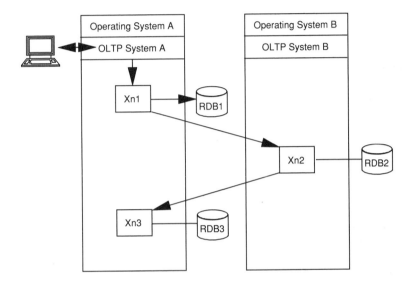

Figure 41. *Distributed OLTP*

Some of the ways the systems can interact are as follows:

1. Xn1 obtains data from database RDB1 in the normal way and uses a gateway to request data from database RDB2. Such gateways are common in Unix RDBs, as are other ways for a transaction on one system to access data on another system. This is known as *function shipping.*

2. System A receives a user request to execute Xn1. System A however, determines that Xn1 resides on system B and passes the request on to system B for processing. On completion, the results of Xn1 are passed back by system B to system A and thence to the user. The user may not be aware that the transaction did not execute on system A. This form of OLTP is called *transaction routing.*

3. Xn1, after performing some processing of its own, can invoke another transaction (Xn2) on system B, which gets the data from database RDB2 and passes it back to Xn1. Xn1 may even have an interactive conversation with the user and one or more transactions on system B. In addition, Xn2 may

need to invoke a third transaction, Xn3, on system A.[11] This form of inter-action is called ***distributed transaction processing.***

The interaction between distributed OLTP systems brings its own problems, but also raises the issue of database update synchronization where the databases reside on different systems. The problem of multiple database update is addressed by the notion of ***two phase commit*** (2PC).

Two Phase Commit

Two phase commit is a form of architecture or specification which, like many architectures in open systems, has different implementations. It seeks to maintain the ACID property of ***atomicity*** where transactions either commit changes completely or abort. 2PC is of great importance where transactions span multiple systems and databases.

In 2PC, all updating resource managers, for example database, agree to make the changes permanent. There are, not surprisingly, two steps in this procedure:

- prepare (to commit)
- commit or abort together.

Two phase commit is normally a function of the transaction manager which, like the starter of a race, asks if everyone is prepared then sounds the gun. If he is happy with the start, the race continues, if not he sounds the gun again and aborts the race.

Interoperability Summary

We have outlined the various ways that heterogeneous system can interact and interoperate. Simple file transfer interoperability is rarely a problem. Interactions involving OLTP and databases are much more of an issue, particularly if the systems in question have their own proprietary database and OLTP systems.

As a general principle, if any subsystems on unlike systems need to interact with each other, there need to be agreed rules for that interaction. They may be the rules of one of the participating systems or rules set by an independent body. These, as we are now aware, are called standards.

8.3.5 Management of Heterogeneous Networks

Much has been written and said about open systems functionality, the benefits of distributed computing and so on. An area which is often bypassed is the manage-

---

[11] It could easily be on a totally different system.

ment of multiple systems with some degree of interoperability. Because most sites cannot start from zero IT investment, the challenge can be envisaged as shown in Figure 42.

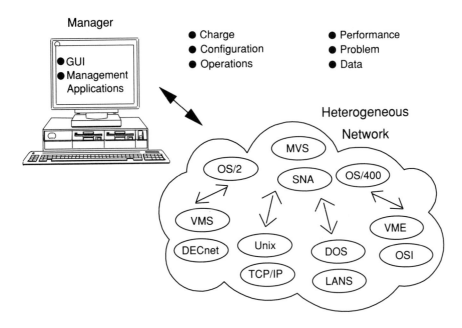

Figure 42. *The Scope of Heterogeneous Network Management*

Again, the problem of disparate systems working together without an agreed set of rules applies to the management of a heterogeneous network. It applies even if standards have been agreed and adopted for all the other problem areas, such as OLTP, database and security. Most vendors have developed management tools for their own systems but are now extending them to cater for other systems. To avoid major changes to such tools each time a new system joins the network, some standards or standard tools are necessary.

8.3.6 Printing

The major user requirements for printing, particularly in downsized or distributed computing environments, might be summarized as follows:

- to print documents in an office location, data centre or location with the same results

- to put printing as close to the end user as possible
- to print output from host and workstation applications
- to view output from host and workstation applications
- to move print files easily among environments.

Printing is probably the open systems subject where the pragmatic approach wins out since people want printout today and not after the leisurely standards bodies have done their work. However, in the long term there must be standardization. Mainframe-based systems can manage printing easily, on distributed heterogeneous systems the simple act of printing your document can be a nightmare. If it is a compound document comprising image, text, colour, perhaps data automatically included from elsewhere, the problem can seem insurmountable. So despite short-term pragmatism this is still a key area for standardization.

8.4 User Interfaces

A key element of the IEEE definition of open systems is 'portability of people'. What does this actually mean? It can be viewed in two senses. Firstly, from the systems programming and systems management point of view, it can be viewed as truly open systems needing the same skills whatever the platform. In reality, this is not true for proprietary systems and sometimes difficult even across Unix implementations. The second interpretation is that of the end user view of applications being used. If the look and feel of applications were the same across different platforms, then the user need not be aware of the platform. If a common look and feel is implemented, then the payroll systems on the VAX will look exactly like the ledger system on the H-P, even though they are doing totally different things.

Most proprietary systems have developed some form of menu interface to ease the task of the end user in entering data or interacting with the system in some way. However, these menus or *front ends*, as they are often known, can be different across different applications on the same machine. Often they were left to the whim of the program designers, and the result was a plethora of different screen layouts and, worse still, many ways of using the keyboard to interact with the system. The use of 'gold keys', 'PFkeys', 'Alt C', and 'Ctl D'[12] can confuse even the most enlightened user, especially if an attempt is made to map keyboards. The need for a common 'look and feel' for applications and a consistent method of interacting with them becomes evident.

In Chapter 14 we will examine some of the user interfaces developed as a result of these needs (and to gain marketing advantage!).

---

[12] Well-known jargon to devotees of non-intuitive systems interaction.

8.5 Conclusions

The requirements for portability, interoperability and manageability in heterogeneous distributed environments demand standards. These standards need to be owned, specified developed and delivered to the OSE community as quickly as possible. In subsequent chapters, we will look at the bodies charged with, or assuming responsibility for these standards. In Chapters 9 and 10 we describe the bodies and consortia which specify and develop standards and deliver working implementations of many of them.

Chapter 9 Standards - Setters and Specifiers

Candidates should not attempt more than six of these.[1]

We concluded from our discussion of open systems in Chapter 2 that openness came from standards adherence. It would be fair to say that the move to open systems is essentially one of standardization. In this chapter and the next we shall look at those organizations and industry bodies that are involved in the creation and implementation of standards.

In Chapter 2, where we sought to define the scope of open systems, we came across the expressions *de jure* and *de facto* standards. These are both Latin phrases much used by those discussing or writing about standards. The first, *de jure*, means literally 'by right' or perhaps better in this context 'rightfully'. To illustrate: PHIGS (the Programmer's Hierarchical Interactive Graphics System) is rightfully a standard because the official standards body, the International Standards Organization (ISO) has specified it as an ISO standard - ISO 9592 - 1. Hence PHIGS is a *de jure* standard. By contrast *de facto* means 'in fact'. *De facto* standards are simply products that because of their wide use and acceptance become standards 'in fact', that is, in reality.

Whether a standard is *de jure* or *de facto* is usually irrelevant and the boundary between the two can often be blurred anyway. We use the term *de jure* to describe only those standards approved by ISO - other writers use it to describe standards agreed by any public standards body. There is no correct answer and, beyond understanding the basic thinking behind the terms, unless you wish to engage in a debate on semantics, just be aware of the two phrases.

Beware of treating *de jure* standards as more important than *de facto* - this is not always the case. There is no guarantee that a *de jure* standard will actually be

---

[1] Hilaire Belloc, on the Ten Commandments.

used widely enough to achieve the goal of openness. For example the *de jure* standard in communication, OSI, is not widely accepted.

The majority of open system environments run TCP/IP: OSI is not a requirement. Similarly, in the graphics arena the *de jure* standard is PHIGS but the majority of advanced graphical applications use the Silicon Graphics proprietary GL (Graphics Library) product. Perhaps the point to make is that, *de facto* or *de jure*, they are still standards.

In this chapter, we will discuss the work of the major standards bodies and consortia which influence open systems. Other groups involved in standardization, such as ISO PHIGS, are covered in Part 4 of this book, 'The Paths to Openness'.

9.1 ISO

The International Standards Organization (ISO), formed in 1947, is a voluntary international federation of standards bodies. ISO is a United Nations agency with no government allegiance. Its mission is to promote standardization across many areas of human activity including, obviously, IT. The ISO membership is limited to country standards organizations[2] and the standards they promote are

- voluntary
- public.

In the IT arena, there is a cooperating ISO/IEC[3] committee called the ***Joint Technical Committee 1*** or JTC1. The associated subcommittees of JTC1 prepare standards in many IT subjects, for example:

- OSI (FTAM, VT, management)
- Graphics (GKS-3D, PHIGS)
- Database (Remote Database Access or RDA)
- Distributed transaction processing (DTP)
- Office (ODA, ODIF).

ISO's mission is carried forward by over 20,000 people in nearly 3000 subcommittees and working groups. To date, ISO has published nearly 8000 standards, not all relevant to IT. The unwary IT organization which commits to complete standardization might take note here.

Generally ISO only adopts standards that have come to it via the national standards bodies that make up its membership. There is a tendency to accept only those

---

[2] For example, ANSI is the US member of ISO.

[3] See Appendix D for explanations of this and other terms in the list below.

standards that have acceptance in the market, and standards status through some other organization. There have been some exceptions to this rule of which the most noteworthy is OSI. OSI was developed by ISO with the intention of creating standards in the area of communication because while standardization in this area was seen as a definite requirement, it was not forthcoming. The problem with developing such speculative standards has been well demonstrated by OSI because it has not become widely established - though this may change over time.

9.2 Other Standards Bodies

9.2.1 International Standards Bodies

There are a number of international standards-making bodies which are important. The CCITT (Comité Consultatif International pour la Télégraphie et la Téléphonie) makes standards in the area of telecommunications. Like ISO it is a part of the United Nations but is secondary to ISO. Many CCITT standards go on to become ISO standards, for example, the X.400 (88) standard is the same as ISO 10021. There is also CEN (Comité Européen de Normalisation) and its subsidiary organization with a special remit in the area of computing and electronics CENELEC (Comité Européen de Normalisation Electronique).   These are the standards-making bodies of the European Community.

9.2.2 National Standards Organizations

Most industrialized nations have their own national standards body which is a member of ISO and makes its own, national, standards. In Britain the body is the BSI - the British Standards Institution. The predominance of the United States in computer manufacture and usage means that ANSI (the American National Standards Institute) is of particular importance in the IT area. Increasingly JIS, the Japanese Industrial Standards Committee, is gaining in stature too.

9.2.3 Government Standards Bodies

In most industrialized nations the government is one of the biggest IT users. The need for different projects within a department, and even different departments, to share information has meant that a number of governments and government departments have introduced their own standards. In the United States there is FIPS, the Federal Information Processing Standard. An example of a FIPS standard is FIPS-151-1 which endorses POSIX 1003.1 (1988). Just to confuse us even further with acronyms FIPS is defined by NIST - the National Institute of Standards and Technology, a US government agency which specifies procurement rules. FIPS is a cross-department standard in the USA. The US Department of Defense specifies its own standards too; for example, TCP/IP can match certain military standards (Mil-Std-1778 and 1777 for TCP and IP respectively).

At this point we should perhaps mention GOSIP. GOSIP is the Government OSI Protocol and both the UK and the US governments use it - though UK and US GOSIP differ in several important respects. As we will see in Chapter 16, the OSI model allows you to select which specific standards within the model you will use - your standards profile. GOSIP is simply the government's profile of OSI standards.

9.3 IEEE

IEEE is the Institute of Electrical and Electronic Engineers, the world's largest technical professional organization and a leader in standards development.

UniForum is a Unix user group which was a prime mover in promoting standards for the Unix environment. UniForum, previously known as */usr/group*, handed over the development of many standards to the IEEE POSIX committees in 1984. Some form of standardization was obviously necessary to avoid proliferation of Unix varieties. POSIX is a generic name now given to the set of standards in the process of definition by the IEEE. The name stands for ***Portable Operating System Interface for Computing Environments***, the 'X' being poetic licence to denote association with 'UNIX'. Note the fourth word in the expansion of the POSIX acronym. It describes a portable *interface* not a portable *operating system*.

POSIX standards are classed as either 'approved', 'balloting', or 'working' in increasing order of the maturity of the specification.

The POSIX subcommittees contain personnel from the major hardware and software vendors on a part-time basis, as well as other technical people from interested organizations. They meet on a regular basis to develop their particular standard or profile from initiation, through the working and balloting phases to acceptance as a 'standard'.

These interface definitions gives guidelines to the application on how to address the operating system, and to the operating system on how to respond. In this way, any operating system implementing this interface can support any POSIX-compliant application. The POSIX interface obviously has its origins in the Unix arena but is today applicable to other operating systems, as we shall see later.

UniForum still maintains technical committees looking at a variety of requirements among Unix users and developers. They continue to provide input to the POSIX sub-committees outlined in Chapter 13.

The length and complexity of the groups' work will indicate to even the non-technical reader that there is more to 'portability and interoperability' than meets the eye. For the avid technical reader, Appendix A expands on the work of the 1003.xx groups at some length, giving even more detail than Chapter 13.

9.4 X/Open

X/Open was founded in 1984 to 'create a market for open systems'. Today, it is a not-for-profit firm owned by computer vendors, who are known as X/Open Corporate Members - Amdahl, DEC, HP, IBM, NCR (AT&T), Sun, and Unisys (USA), Fujitsu, Hitachi, NEC and Groupe Bull, ICL, Olivetti and Siemens in Europe. OKI Electric (Japan) were involved but withdrew early in 1993. The consortium's members include 90 user corporations, and its mission in essence is to expand the market for open systems computing. The original categories of X/Open membership as they stood in September 1992 were:

- X/Open User Council
- X/Open Independent Software Vendor (ISV) Council
- X/Open System Vendor Council.

Between the XPG4 launch in October 1992 and December 1992, X/Open has restructured its membership categories in order to open up the X/Open process to everyone with a commitment to developing, promoting or using open systems.

New Categories of X/Open Membership

The members of the associate member councils (User, ISV, or System Vendor) can take one of the following options:

- Requirements membership - influences the X/Open strategic directions, establishes the agenda of the annual Xtra World Congress, shapes the detailed discussion topics, and creates the Open Systems Directive. This membership is free to existing User Council members.

- Specification membership - gives the same rights as a shareholder (for example DEC, IBM, HP and so on) during the detailed development of Technical Specification Guides. The fees for joining individual work groups vary depending on the activity level of that group. Any member who joins all the work groups gets a seat on the Technical Strategy Committee.

- Verification membership - offers immediate access to X/Open's existing and emerging test software for members who produce enough open systems products to require in-house testing facilities.

Membership rights include sending a voting representative to all the group meetings, receiving all paper and electronic mail produced within the group, including early access to draft documents, and receiving a copy of all publications produced by the group.

It is interesting to note that UNIX Systems Laboratories (USL) became a full technical member of X/Open at the end of 1992 and left early in 1993.

Aims of X/Open Company

According to John Totman, former director of User Relations at X/Open, 'X/Open is:[4]

- supplier-independent and international
- a forum for both suppliers and customers
- an integrator of component "standards"
- an accelerator of standards maturity
- a certifier for compliant products
- *not* a standards body
- *not* a technology consortium.

Its aim is to combine existing and emerging standards to define a comprehensive, yet practical, Common Applications Environment (CAE). It is X/Open policy to use approved *de jure* standards where they exist, and adopt widely supported *de facto* standards in other cases.

X/Open has a technical strategy:

- To provide a framework in which X/Open member companies can develop and approve open systems specifications which are aligned with formal standards, building where appropriate on the work of focused consortia.
- To manage a process by which X/Open member companies can validate their conformance to these specifications.'

X/Open technical programmes to support these aims are listed in figure 43.

---

[4] Presentation given to an IBM (UK) audience, 21 July 1992.

Figure 43. *X/Open Technical Programmes*		
Interoperability	*Application Portability*	*User Interface*
Data Interchange	Application Development	Human/Computer Interface
Distributed Applications	C Language	
Systems Management	Cobol	
Interworking	Data Management	
PC Interworking	Internationalization	
Transaction Processing	Object Oriented Technology	
	Operating System Commands	
	Operating System Interfaces	

9.5 Internet Activities Board (IAB)

We covered the basic development of TCP/IP when we looked at the history of UNIX in Chapter 5. The question may arise as to who drives and controls the development of these protocols. By 1979, there were so many people involved in the development of TCP/IP that DARPA convened an informal committee to coordinate and guide the design of the TCP/IP protocols and the underlying architecture. This group was called the Internet Control and Configuration Board (ICCB), and met regularly until 1983.

In 1983, the committee was reorganized and the Internet Activities Board (IAB) was formed to direct the research and development of the protocols in a more structured manner. The work was then progressed via Internet task forces, each chaired by a member of the IAB. Each task force worked on a given problem, or perhaps a series of issues, as its project.

A sample of the hundreds of RFC subjects is given here to show the diversity of the IAB's activity in the TCP/IP area:

RFC to discuss host extensions for support of IP Multicast
Official ARPA-INTERNET protocols

RFC specification for PC-based mail systems
Communications support for fault-tolerant systems
Privacy enhancement for Internet electronic mail
End-system to intermediate-system Routing Exchange Protocol
Protocol specification for NETBIOS service on TCP/UDP
Concepts/methods for Netbios services over TCP/IP or UDP transport
A distributed protocol authentication scheme
ISO transport services on top of TCP
External Data Representation (XDR)
X Windows protocol specification
Network requirements for scientific computing
Report of the Workshop on Environments for Computational Mathematics

The Internet community had been growing rapidly since Unix adopted TCP/IP and in the late 1980s it was growing at 20% per month. To cater for such explosive growth, the IAB was reorganized to take in members from communities outside the TCP/IP research groups, who were moved into a subsidiary group. The IAB and related groups are summarized below.

- Internet Activities Board (IAB) - guiding body
- Internet Research Task Force (IRTF) - coordinates research and architecture activities
- Internet Engineering Task Force (IETF) - working groups dealing with shorter-term issues and problems than the IRTF
- Network Information Center (NIC) - deals with Internet documentation and administration
- Network Operations Center (NOC) - responsible for the management of key Internet networks and gateways.[5]

Detailed information on RFCs can be obtained from the NIC whose address can be found in Appendix B.[6]

9.6 Conclusions

There are so many standards and standards setters that your organization needs to decide which ones are relevant to its needs. Where standards clash or overlap,

---

[5] Operated by BBN.

[6] For more information on these and other standards bodies, see the comprehensive books by 88Open and Peter Judge referenced in Appendix C.

you should establish your order of precedence for standards based on business need and benefit. For example, IBM's order[7] is shown in Figure 44.

Precedence	Category	US Example
1	International Standard	ISO/IEC 9945-1:1990
2	Accredited National Standard	ANS X3.159-1989
3	Accredited Voluntary Standard	IEEE 1003.1-1990
4	Government Procurement Specification	FIPS Pub 151-1
5	Industry Specification	XPG3
6	Vendor Specification	SVID Issue 2
7	Implementation	4.3 BSD

Figure 44. *IBM Standards Precedence*

The significance of the order means that function in one layer can be implemented provided it does not compromise a standard in a higher layer. DEC have a similar standards-based compliance hierarchy:[8]

- *de jure* standards such as ISO and ANSI
- consortia standards like OSF and X/Open
- *de facto* standards, for example, TCP/IP and Postscript
- DEC corporate standards, which are formulated when no suitable standards exist in the categories above.

As you can see, there are many different standards organizations, often working in similar areas. While they do, usually, work together and try not to produce different standards in the same area there are times when some standardization of the standards bodies is required.

Any organization interested in open systems could spend a lot of time monitoring the output of different standards bodies - it could even join in their activities. That would not necessarily make it any easier for it to move to open systems. Indeed, the sheer volume of material produced by the bodies and written

---

[7] Not necessarily the same as yours since IBM is a vendor.

[8] Source - IDC, *DEC NAS Strategy.*

by industry pundits could exclude all other work in an IT department. There is no easy answer and most people learn by reading the computer press, attending the occasional industry conference and listening to representatives of various vendors.

We would recommend relying less on the press and vendors' representatives than on conferences. Not because what the press and the representatives say is wrong but because unless you are very informed you cannot contradict or evaluate their theses. In a conference, however, there is usually a large audience who between them constitute a group far more knowledgeable than any individual, and you have the chance to evaluate several points of view.

The buck will stop there, we feel - the issues in proprietary and open systems environments are essentially the same, even if the platforms involved are different. The differentiator between vendors is not whether they are 'proprietary' or 'Unix' but the quality of their whole range of offerings in the OSE and their ability to deliver the 'goods' safely and on time.

Whatever route you use for gathering and evaluating the information, it is a fascinating area. If nothing else providing us, the authors, with the chance to earn an honest crust!

Chapter 10 Standards - The Implementers

There's a long, long trail a-winding,
Into the land of my dreams ...[1]

Producing dense volumes of standards and specifications is a difficult task in itself but producing implementations of them is also a major hurdle. In this chapter we will deal with OSF and UNIX International, implementers of Unix, and cover two major bodies, SPAG and POSC, which are attempting to implement usable environments based on standards and pragmatic 'supplements'. We will also look at one standards-based environment that is currently gaining significant support - COSE.

10.1 Open Software Foundation (OSF)

Chapter 5 outlined some of the reasons for the emergence of the Open Software Foundation. It was founded on 17 May 1988 with seven major manufacturers as sponsors - Apollo, Digital, Groupe Bull, Hewlett-Packard, IBM, Nixdorf and Siemens. Shortly afterwards, Philips joined as a sponsor, followed by Hitachi. It was formed as a non-profit organization with a mission of 'the development and delivery of an open and portable software environment to which vendors and users have equal input and access'.

Today, the OSF has more than 350 members and is staffed by over 260 people. Members include computer manufacturers, software development companies, commercial end users, research organizations, universities and government bodies.

The guiding principles of the foundation are given as:

---

[1] World War I song, words by Stoddard King, music by Zo Elliott.

- technology offerings based on relevant industry standards
- an open process actively to solicit inputs and technology
- a timely, vendor-neutral decision process
- equal and early access to specifications and software
- hardware-independent implementations
- technical innovation through universities and research
- reasonable, stable terms for licensing.

OSF aims to provide software which has the three major characteristic of portability, scalability and interoperability. Scalability means software designed and implemented with no inherent limitations of functionality because of the size of the platform on which it is implemented.

10.1.1 Technology and Innovation

The open technologies sought and delivered by the OSF are not the result of work by gurus locked away in a secret room at the OSF HQ in Cambridge, Massachusetts. The technology is solicited from organizations inside and outside the OSF membership via an open process called a 'Request for Technology' or RFT. In selecting technologies for inclusion in the OSF Open Computing Environment, consideration is given to the views and recommendations of:

- OSF membership
- non-member technology submitters
- industry consultants
- standards groups.

The RFT process is shown in Figure 45.

During the development of a selected technology, OSF will provide members with early access to versions of the code under development. These are called 'snapshots', and they enable recipients to evaluate and port the technology to their particular environment. It also allows them to assess and comment on its functionality.

The OSF open process goes beyond just the evaluation and delivery of technologies. Its activities include research, education, technical support, assessment of market needs for technologies and the development of ideas by special interest groups.

- The OSF Research Institute works with universities, industry laboratories and government research bodies to assess future directions and possible RFTs from the OSF.

- The OSF Educational Services create, deliver and license course material on OSF technology offerings.

- The OSF Software Services offer various levels of tailorable technical support to licensees of OSF technology.

- The OSF Portability Laboratory provides on-site support to members' personnel in the use of OSF technology. The laboratory also exchanges ideas and technology with participating OSF members.

- There are OSF Special Interest Groups (SIGs) and membership meetings which help to create ideas on open systems technology for future consideration.

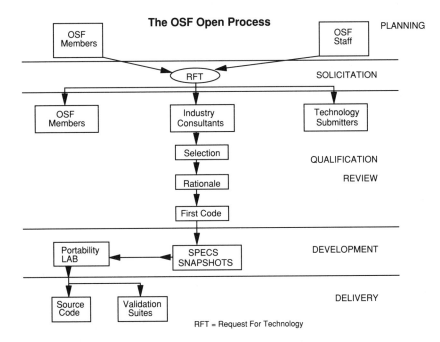

Figure 45. *OSF Request for Technology (RFT) Process*

To date the OSF has announced five specific products, and we have explained these more fully elsewhere.

- OSF/1 (Chapter 17)
- OSF/Motif (Chapter 14)
- The Distributed Computing Environment (DCE) (Chapter 18)
- The Distributed Management Environment (DME) (Chapter 18)
- The Architecture Neutral Distribution Format (ANDF) (Chapter 18).

The availability of these products is shown in Figure 46.

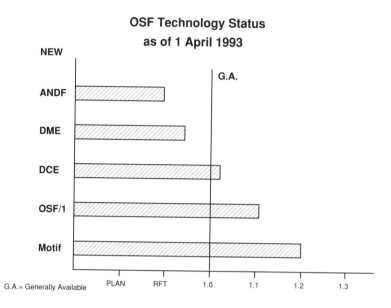

Figure 46. *OSF Products - Availability and Release Dates*

10.2 UNIX International (UI)

10.2.1 Origins and Mission

Unix International was formed shortly after the Open Software Foundation in 1988. Since December 1988, UI has been working with its members to solicit requirements for the evolution of UNIX System V and related technologies. UI is a working requirements body and the actual System V UNIX code is developed and enhanced by a sister body, UNIX System Laboratories (USL).

Each year, UI publishes its *Roadmap* which defines high-level requirements which UI members have indicated they would like USL to deliver reference implementations. The Roadmap is covered after the description of the UI technology open requirements process.

The UI Open Process

Like OSF, UI has an Open Decision Process to decide the best way to evolve

System V and related products. The Process works as follows:[2]

- The UNIX International Steering Committee (UISC) examines market needs by reviewing documents like the X/Open Open Systems Directive (OSD) and other industry requirements.

- The UISC charters investigative teams, made up of representatives from interested UNIX International member companies, to do detailed market studies in specific technology areas (e.g. kernel enhancements) and end user market niches (e.g. desktop computing). These studies examine the business case for features, including market analysis, priority, and required timeframe for the features.

- The UISC evaluates information from these investigative team reports and develops a list of features that should be introduced into the UNIX International Roadmap.

- Once per year the UNIX International Executive Committee (UIEC) approves a revised Roadmap.

- The UISC charters work groups of representatives from interested UNIX International members and other companies to develop feature requirements for specific elements of the UNIX International Roadmap.

- If the requirements are for enhancements to existing reference technology, then the completed requirements are delivered to the related reference technology provider for development.

- If the requirements are for new technology, then the UIEC selects a reference technology provider to develop the technology and integrate it with the UNIX International member defined base. This selection process is described in detail in the UNIX International document 'Guidelines for Selecting Reference Technology Providers'.

- The identified reference technology provider develops a product overview and detailed specifications (including API definitions) against the requirements.

- The product specifications are reviewed by the associated UNIX International work group to ensure the specifications accurately implement its original product requirements.

- The identified reference technology provider places the completed product specification under change control, and UNIX International makes an associated draft API definition available to the industry for use in application

---

[2] Reproduced with permission from *1993 Roadmap for UNIX Systems & Related Technologies*, Revision 4.31, 93/02/02.

development, independent implementations, and for use by industry standards bodies as a base for *de jure* and *de facto* standards.

- The reference technology provider gives UNIX International members Early Access to the reference implementation at appropriate intervals in the development process.

- The reference technology provider releases a reference implementation of the technology.

- The reference technology provider publishes final APIs.

- The final APIs are referenced in the UNIX International Anatomy of Interfaces document.

- System vendors make functionality conforming to the published API available to end users.

The role of UNIX International is essentially that of a market research group and requirements analyzer. It presents requirements to the chosen reference technology providers.

The UI/USL interaction is outlined in Figure 47.

10.2.2 Request for Proposal

In April 1993, UNIX International issued a Request for Proposal (RFP) pack soliciting technology for Application-to-Application Linking Reference Technology. The RFP is similar in concept to the OSF Request for Technology (RFT).

The RFP was addressed to reference technology suppliers and has the following steps in the process:

- Suppliers must register intent to submit proposals with UI

- Development proposal to be submitted to UI

- UNIX International issues clarification requests

- Final proposals submitted to UI

- Evaluation of proposals to be completed

- Final selection made by UNIX International Executive Committee.

The RFP 'specifies the functional requirements for a reference technology to enable UNIX GUI applications to provide object linking and embedding functionality in compound documents.' Object Linking and Embedding (OLE) was introduced in 1992 by Microsoft for linking and embedding objects between documents from different desktop applications. The RFP seeks to provide such functionality for the UNIX environment, pending the outcome of the OMG's efforts in this area.

The timescale for this particular RFP is about 5 months. It can probably be assumed that there will be further RFPs issued by UNIX International.

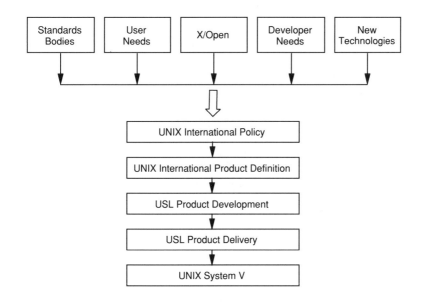

Figure 47. *The UI/USL System V Development Process*

10.2.3 The UI Roadmap

The Roadmap is a list of desired features and functions requested by UI members for inclusion in UNIX and the UI-ATLAS distributed computing framework. We will illustrate the Roadmap principle by reference to the 1993 version and cover the technical content in Chapter 18.

The structure of the Roadmap is a detailed requirements matrix, a reference technology availability guide and descriptive information about the contents. It covers the UNIX operating system itself and the UI-ATLAS framework, which is described in Chapter 18 of this book.

Milestones for UI Requirements These are the steps in the development of UNIX and UI-ATLAS requirements:[3]

- work group creation, where a team develops the detail of a stated requirement
- building block requirements, the formal output of a work group
- technology provider identification

---

[3] The terms used here are from the UI documentation.

- target deployment timeframe, concerned with when the technology will be generally available to end users.

The requirements matrix is too large to reproduce here but can be found in the UI 1993 Roadmap.

Reference Technology Milestones During the development process, the technology providers identified in the requirements process work to the following milestones:

- technology specification containing draft APIs, data format and protocol definitions to satisfy UI member building block requirements

- early access to the technology by UI members

- reference technology availability, the time when the reference technology is complete and available to system vendors from the technology provider.

10.3 Petrotechnical Open Software Corporation (POSC)

Petrotechnical Open Software Corporation was set up in 1990 by a group of major oil companies as a non-profit-making, vendor-neutral organization. 'POSC's primary mission is to define, develop and deliver, through an open process, an industry standard, open systems *software integration platform* for petroleum upstream (exploration and production) technical computing applications'.[4]

The major Founding Sponsors of POSC are:

- BP Exploration Inc.

- Chevron Corporation

- Elf Aquitaine

- Mobil Oil Corporation

- Texaco Inc.

In simple terms, POSC is a consortium of oil companies and it seeks to specify a set of standards which these companies will use in particular areas of computing. Software and hardware vendors may join the consortium but it is undoubtedly dominated by the user companies.

The core of POSC's work, the software integration platform, is not a new product. Rather it is a set of already existing standards which POSC has adopted to resolve specific issues. Together these standards will, in theory, create a complete, integrated, platform. POSC has said that as a last resort they may define new technology or standards specifications - but only if what is already available does not meet requirements.

---

[4] POSC, *Opening the way to the Future.*

POSC's Base Computer Standards Endorsements

Operating System Services	User Interface Services	Program Services	Data Mgmt Services	Data Inter-change Services	Graphic Services	Network Services
POSIX XPG3	X Window Motif	Fortran C	POSC Data Model POSC APIs PEF		GKS PHIGS X Window CGM	TCP/IP OSI
▶XPG4	▶IEEE 1201	▶ C++			▶PEX	

▶ DCE	Security Services/System Management Services	▶ DME
	Hardware/Software Platform	

Source: POSC Technical Program Overview

Figure 48. *POSC Base Computer Standards Endorsements*

As a starting point to its work POSC set out a suite of base computer standards which it plans to move towards. The standards endorsed and the long-term direction are shown in Figure 48.

In addition to this base specification POSC plans an exploration and production data model, for defining data elements specific to the industry; a data access specification containing an API and a user interface style guide to ensure a common look and feel for software applications.

Whether POSC will be successful is unclear, though the initial signs are very good. POSC is of interest to us because it is a new way of working, with users clearly driving the requirements and using their buying power to force software standards and integration on suppliers. Furthermore, they are bringing standards together and integrating them, often in new ways. Standards integration is an important part of real open computing and POSC may well be leading the way for others to follow in the future.

10.4 Standards Promotion and Application Group (SPAG)

If POSC is dominated and controlled by users then the antithesis of POSC is

SPAG. SPAG, the Standards Promotion and Application Group, is a company that represent the collective voice on open communications systems development in Europe of a number of the leading IT vendors:

- Alcatel
- BT
- Bull
- DEC
- HP
- IBM
- ICL
- Olivetti
- SNI

SPAG's long-term mission is 'to stimulate, support and promote the environment for credible multivendor interoperable products and services, supporting computer networks across multiple enterprise organizations based on open international standards (OSI and ISDN for example). SPAG's ultimate objective is the creation of a truly competitive, open market in which user and procurers can purchase Open Communications Systems products with confidence that they will interoperate'.[5]

SPAG became a registered company in 1986, though the Group had been around in embryo since 1984. It was set up in response to the need, identified by the Commission of the European Communities, to harmonize Europe's IT and telecommunications standardization effort in order to improve its overall competitive edge. The Commission originally established a programme for pre-competitive research and development which was to form the basis of the current ESPRIT (European Strategic Programme for Research in Information Technology) programme.

This early work identified the importance of interoperability of multivendor standards. It is in this area that SPAG now focuses its attention through its PSI programme.

PSI, the Process to Support Interoperability, is described by SPAG as 'a global framework for interoperability'. It is a legal 'branding' which is granted to products which conform to the PSI standards profile. Those products which are branded are guaranteed to interoperate and SPAG has a framework to resolve any issues of non-interoperability.

The idea behind PSI is to provide users with what is in effect an insurance policy against non-interoperability. SPAG market the PSI mark as being 'synony-

---

[5] SPAG 1992, *Process to Support Interoperability: Participants' Handbook.*

mous with "guaranteed interoperability" '. The advantage for vendors is that their products can be receive the PSI Mark which can be a very useful marketing tool and 'vendors' is not limited to SPAG members.

On 8 April 1993, SPAG announced the appointment of the first independent PSI Operator after a series of negotiations. The new PSI Operator is the US Department of Defense's Joint Interoperability Test Center (JITC), which can now test and register products seeking PSI conformance. These in turn can be referenced in procurements.

10.5 Common Open Software Environment (COSE)

The Common Open Software Environment was announced in March 1993. It is not like the other subjects of this chapter in that it is a product rather than a group of vendors or users; there are thus no members, no offices and no fees to join. Six companies committed to COSE at the initial announcement:

- Hewlett-Packard
- IBM
- Santa Cruz Operation
- Sun Microsystems
- Univel
- UNIX System Laboratories.

DEC announced its support for the COSE initiative in June 1993.

At its most simplistic COSE is a standard profile. So many areas of computing have multiple products and multiple standards addressing the same problem that COSE provides a common approach to some of those areas.

COSE provides benefits both for users and developers. For users, it will allow them to access data and applications transparently from anywhere in the network. For developers there will be a high degree of commonality among the development environments of those vendors supporting COSE - leading to a reduction in the time taken to get new applications to market on a range of platforms.

The environments which COSE plans to address are outlined below.

Common Desktop Environment

The common desktop environment essentially incorporates existing technology from the six vendors, aiming to be scalable across a range of client/server platforms. The desktop environment will support:[6]

---

6 These are taken from the COSE technology factsheets.

- electronic mail, group calendar, text editing, audio and other productivity tools
- task/window management and online help
- procedural and object oriented application integration with facilities for drag-and-drop, linking, embedding and data interchange
- dialog and forms building with icon editing
- graphical object and file management
- security features including start-up, login, locking and authentication.

The environment was demonstrable on the day of announcement but the group intends to publish a specification for the environment and submit it to X/Open for inclusion in the XPG specifications. In June 1993, X/Open announced the formation a new desktop work program to complement the COSE Common Desktop Environment specification. The group is called the X/Open Common Desktop Environment Group.

Networking

This part of the COSE mission is to provide the tools necessary for developers to build distributed applications. The major distributed computing technologies today are:

- OSF Distributed Computing Environment (DCE)
- SunSoft Open Network Computing Environment[7] (ONC+)
- Novell NetWare.

The six vendors will deliver and support these three environments to allow integration of UNIX desktops with NetWare services.

Graphics

In an attempt to isolate graphics applications from specific graphics hardware, the six companies will provide a consistent application environment via common APIs and interoperability protocols. They intend to support the X Consortium's imaging and graphics facilities, namely:

- Xlib/X for basic 2D graphics
- PEXlib/PEX for 2D/3D geometry graphics
- XIElib/XIE for advanced imaging.

In addition, there will be cooperation to standardize in the areas of programming documentation, validation testing and test suites.

---

[7] Part of the UI-ATLAS framework.

Multimedia

Multimedia covers the manipulation of audio, video, graphics, image, speech and telephony. COSE intends to develop a standards specification to provide users with consistent access to multimedia tools in a heterogeneous environment. It will achieve this by jointly defining:

- an infrastructure called Distributed Media Services (DMS)
- multimedia access and collaboration tools for their use and called the Desktop Integrated Media Environment (DIME).

The specification will be delivered as a single submission to the IMA's (Interactive Multimedia Association) Request for Technology.

Object Technology

Object technology will allow programmers to develop more complex applications faster by re-use of previously developed objects. The six COSE partners are working to accelerate the delivery of a suitable object-based technology. The work in this area will support and utilize the efforts of the Object Management Group (OMG), for example, the use of CORBA (Common Object Request Broker Architecture) in future products.

Systems Management

In a heterogeneous network of systems, there is still a need to manage those individual systems in areas such as performance monitoring, data backup/restore, configuration management, security, problem determination and recovery. It makes sense to have a consistent approach to systems management tools for heterogeneous environments. COSE's initial efforts will focus on:

- user and group management, including security
- software installation and distribution management
- software license management
- storage management (backup and restore)
- print spooling and management
- distributed file systems management.

Late 1993 should see a COSE 'roadmap' explaining its plans in more detail.

10.6 Conclusions

In this chapter we have looked at four organizations which are planning and implementing standards and we have looked at one standard environment. The fact that such groups exist, and are seen as being important, should tell us that standards on their own are not sufficient. Raw standards are like the raw ingredients for a meal - you need to do some work to make a satisfying meal.

The reality of open systems is that users can buy products that meet all the necessary standards and discover that they do not interwork.

In the area of the desktop, COSE may well be resolving this but the approach is unproven and the scope limited. If you operate in the petroleum industry then the POSC consortium is actively working on standards interoperability, and there are other industry-specific organizations. However, most companies do not have this advantage. The task of creating an interoperable environment then falls on company IT departments. They may be able to use SPAG and similar bodies as a guide, they may be able to take some components of their environment from COSE, but the key tasks still fall upon them. It is important that both users and vendors resolve this problem. POSC and SPAG have led the way as organizations. The COSE approach has led the way as an agreed solution. Let us hope others follow.

Part 4
The Paths to Openness

Chapter 11 Preamble

Who dares, wins.[1]

11.1 Overview

This section is aimed at installations migrating sizeable systems to the open environment - the replacement of a single system by a Unix or other system does not concern us here.

In the course of this book, we have alluded to various types of computer installation which aspire to 'openness', but have not really differentiated between them. It is perhaps opportune to do so now before moving on to migration or evolution issues and to place today's installations into one of three categories, ignoring the 'green field' sites which are installing their first computer system.

There is a huge variety of IT installations in existence, from the very small to the very large corporations, with many systems purchased from many vendors. Although each of the vendors involved would claim that the organization would have been far better off purchasing all its systems from 'them', the reality is different. Most systems were bought on a 'best for the job' basis and, since no vendor is perfect, this inevitably means heterogeneity in the network.

One of us[2] was fortunate or unfortunate to be at a gathering of a manufacturing special interest group where some speakers were relating their experiences in 'using open systems'. One speaker claimed he had moved to open systems and saved a lot of money. What he had in fact done was to use an abandoned Sun workstation with cheap, existing ASCII terminals to create a machine shop system

---

[1] Motto of the SAS.

[2] T.A.C.

for monitoring work flow. The fact that the workstation ran Unix completed the 'proof' that going to open systems was easy and saved money. The near certainty that the application was non-portable and the system did not try or even need to have heterogeneous interoperability did not seem to blunt his enthusiasm. Let us be clear here; this book does not address this kind of installation but those with much larger challenges. Such installations might have proprietary and Unix systems with a variety of network architectures, proprietary, TCP/IP and even OSI.

The following section draws on the work of X/Open in illustrating that all installations are not equal and that the issues they face in the open systems world vary enormously. A single solution will definitely not suit all requirements.

11.2 The IT Spectrum Today

Pragmatic open systems 'thinkers' will recognize that, except for 'green field' situations where no IT infrastructure exists, certain things are not going to go away because of the cost - in money and disruption terms - of throwing them out:

1. PCs and PC software. The US Business Research Group estimates that the number of networked PCs will increase from 17 million (out of 36 million in total) in 1991 to 47 million (of 69 million) in 1995. This must have a profound impact on planning an open systems strategy where an organization has a significant number of PCs.

2. Unix workstations, servers and multi-user systems.

3. Proprietary hardware and operating systems, such as mainframes and minis.

4. Apple Macintoshes.

5. Special systems, such as PICK and MUMPS, running on a variety of platforms.

Understanding open systems is not only a technical task, but also involves understanding the difference between installing a Unix application for 20 users and achieving true open systems integration across a large enterprise, such as company #603 discussed below. Both are often called open systems environments but the resemblance ends there.

The IT sites described below are extracted from the X/Open 1990 Open Systems Directive (OSD), where sites are identified by a representative who has an assigned attendee number (#). Each sees different problems and implementation challenges, some of which we have listed. The detailed analysis of issues as reported in the OSD and from other IT surveys is presented in Chapter 2 in 'Definitions - Do They Match User Requirements?'

Attendee #301 - Division of a Technical Association

- Systems environment - mainframes, minis, 350 workstations, 1600 terminals and PCs with MVS and Unix.
- Major concerns:[3]
    - Open systems have a tendency to cost more than many proprietary products.
    - C compilers and libraries are not all compatible.
    - Systems administration tools tend to be inadequate on open systems.
    - ISV[4] product releases often have major data incompatibilities on different architectures.

Attendee #603 - Manufacturer

- Systems environment - mainframe user (VMS and MVS), 30,000 terminals, 10,000 PCs, 5000 Apple Macs and 5000 workstations from a variety of sources.
- Major concerns:
    - low confidence that claimed benefits will materialize in the absence of substantiating data
    - incompatibility between competing 'open' systems products
    - multiple, immature, incomplete and evolving standards
    - multiple competing, non-integratable 'open systems'
    - justifying high initial cost of installing critical mass required to realize significant initial benefits.

Attendee #803 - Insurance corporation

- Systems environment - classic mainframe user, own network, 500,000 transactions per day, also has 18 Unix systems installed.
- Major concerns:
    - systems management and accounting
    - data and software distribution
    - integration in a homogeneous environment is much easier than in a heterogeneous one
    - transaction monitors.

---

[3] Quoted verbatim here from the OSD.

[4] Independent Software Vendors.

Attendee #806 - Application Development Company

- Systems environment - Single host Unix systems with ASCII terminals.
- Major concerns - None that are unexpected.

11.3 Conclusions

The first thing to note about this simple classification of today's IT installation is that the tactics which might lead the IT site represented by attendee #806 to openness, almost certainly will not help the others. They are very different in their IT platforms and their perceptions of the issues raised in moving to open systems. The admonition to 'go Unix on RISC hardware' without serious thought and planning is patently nonsense for the other installations. There are various reasons why this admonition can be risky but three stand out:

1. The business benefits are not spelled out - only possible savings in the IT area.
2. The installation has a massive investment already in hardware, software and training.
3. The disruption to the business of the company caused by such a simplistic move, if unplanned, could well be terminal.

The other panacea often proposed is downsizing or, more recently, rightsizing. We will examine these concepts, which are used interchangeably, and look at the some of their implications in Chapter 12.

Chapter 12 Downsizing and Rightsizing

There's no such thing as a free lunch.[1]

The IT industry is undoubtedly going through a revolution. That is nothing new - in Chapter 3 we talked about how computing produces a revolution every ten years: in the 1960s the mainframe, in the 1970s the departmental computer, in the 1980s the PC and now, in the 1990s, the attempt to integrate these disparate platforms.

One result of this revolution is the growth in the number of surveys trying to understand what is going on. We came across so many in researching this book that it is hard to imagine that IT managers ever do any real work since they must spend all their time answering questions. We did our own survey of IT surveys and can announce that the most asked survey question at the moment relates to 'downsizing'.

The questions relating to downsizing, and 'rightsizing', produced widely differing results. While the differences may be accounted for by examining the exact wording of the question and the make-up of the survey sample, it is clear that one can draw almost any conclusion one likes and produce surveys to prove it. On the one hand we could show that 80% of IT sites are considering downsizing, and on the other that only 17% are.[2]

Whether everybody or nobody is downsizing or rightsizing is unimportant. The question you, the reader, must ask is: 'Should my organization be considering it?' Our answer to that is that you should certainly be considering it. Whether you actually carry it through depends on the conclusions you come to.

---

[1] Robert Heinlein, *The Moon is a Harsh Mistress*.

[2] The first figure is from Forrester Research, quoted in *Integration*, June 1992; the second figure from a KPMG survey quoted in *Infomatics*, July 1992.

This chapter will raise some of the issues that you need to think about.

12.1 Downsizing and Rightsizing Defined

Downsizing is a term used to describe the movement of applications from a large system to several smaller systems. An example of this is the removal of a multi-site stock application from a mainframe to discrete PCs in each stock location.

Rightsizing is an exercise to decide the best place to implement new applications. It often applied to new applications whose nature possibly precludes a mainframe solution. An example of this is a new stock application which is eventually placed under autonomous control in the warehouses on discrete systems.

The first thing to note about downsizing and rightsizing is that they do not have 'open systems' (whatever that means in this context) as a prerequisite. It is perfectly feasible to downsize from a proprietary mainframe to proprietary minis, even from a different manufacturer. DEC did this quite successfully with PDP-11s and VAXes during the 1970s and 1980s, surrounding large IBM and other mainframes with departmental applications.

The second thing to note is that downsizing is not new. IBM introduced its own downsizing in 1975 with the 3790 distributed system and other industry-specific systems which delivered IT functions at the place where they were needed. One of the first tasks of SNA when it was announced was to support such distributed function. The IBM 8100 system followed in 1979 and the PC in 1981, taking quite sophisticated function to sites remote from the mainframe. Similarly, as we have already mentioned, DEC VAXes were purchased as departmental machines in organizations with large IBM mainframes.

Why is there a sudden interest in downsizing and rightsizing? There is no simple answer but a number of factors are evident:

- The organizational structure of many businesses is becoming less hierarchical and more distributed - so a distributed rather than a mainframe computing strategy often supports the business.

- The way the computer industry has evolved has resulted in a focus on distributed computing.

- The price of mainframes is perceived to be high in comparison to both mid-range and PC systems supporting the same number of users. As a result businesses are very interested in non-mainframe solutions.

- Multiple small machines rather than one large one are perceived by many businesses to offer greater flexibility and therefore ability to react quickly to changing requirements and market conditions.

- The growth of easy-to-use packages on the PC has meant that the PC has become firmly established as a business tool in a way that the mainframe terminal never was.

- The application development backlog of most mainframe sites makes a packaged solution, often on a new PC or departmental machine, a competitive option.

Whatever the reasons for the sudden keen interest it is true to say that though it may not be a new phenomenon it is certainly a new craze!

Treating downsizing and rightsizing as the same for the moment (they are both simply moves to distributed computing), let us try to classify the options available:

- complete host mainframe replacement with networks of PCs or workstations

- removal of some existing host applications to a distributed system or systems

- putting all new applications on distributed (non-host) systems

- putting appropriate new applications on distributed (non-host) systems

- splitting applications, new or old, between the host and the distributed systems - in other words, using cooperative processing or client/server techniques.

There can of course be an element of mixing and matching the options outlined. Whichever of these moves is made, the solution is likely to be (but not necessarily) the type in which the host can participate as a server, except in the first case of course.

12.2 Examples of Successful Downsizing and Rightsizing

One of the hardest things to discover is how successful particular companies have been in their IT projects. The computing press and the myriad consultancy reports have given numerous examples (though in fairness to some of the examples the accuracy of these is not always certain). We quote five different downsizing case studies:

United Airlines: According to *Computer World*, United Airlines will save between \$3.5 million and \$4.5 million by moving a crew scheduling application from an IBM 3090/600S to four Silicon Graphics IRIX-based multi-processors, seven IBM RISC System/6000s running AIX and 52 X terminals.

Royal International: According to *Computing*, Royal International, part of the Royal Insurance Group, cut £700,000 off its costs by moving an accounting application from an HP3000 to a network of 90 PCs.

Vernon's Pools: *Computer Weekly* reported that Vernon's Pools saved £3 million over five years by downsizing away from its IBM 4381 to a Pyramid server.[3] Not content with that, it is now looking at downsizing this to a network of PCs.

Burmah Castrol (UK): A report from Xephon Consultancy entitled 'Downsizing for IBM Users' has a chapter written by Steve Wright of Burmah on how it is downsizing its two IBM type mainframes to IBM AS/400s. After almost three years substantial savings had been made including being able to dispose of one mainframe.

Taylor Woodrow:[4] Taylor Woodrow is one of the UK's largest construction companies with a turnover in excess of £1.2 billion. In mid-1989 it decided to replace its IBM 3081KX mainframe, supporting around 450 users, with a distributed RISC System/6000 Unix solution. It now runs its business on five IBM RISC System/6000 and about 200 PCs. The project is seen as being very successful and, given the downturn in the construction industry, very timely.

The original drivers of the project were essentially technical. The users were demanding more sophisticated systems having seen what was available on their PCs. At the same time, the existing systems were starting to become outdated. It was perceived that before long IT could become an inhibitor to a dynamically changing business, and that maintenance was taking up more and more time and money.

The decision was taken to move the workload from the mainframe to a number of Unix-based machines. Unix was chosen not only because typically Unix-based machines were low cost but also because Unix provided a good base for the creation of an Open Systems Environment. Some key applications would be replaced with packages but others, written in Natural and Adabas, could be ported across from the mainframe.

The decision proved timely because just as the project got underway, the construction industry saw a massive downturn in business. As a result, the requirement to cut costs became paramount. Taylor Woodrow estimates that it has saved around £800,000 per annum on its IT budget. This has enabled it to deliver the service to user companies at significantly reduced costs.

Cost savings are only one benefit of the project. Users are now receiving a better service, more flexible and more able to meet their changing demands. Furthermore the company is well positioned to take advantage of the latest advances in technology, positioned as it is on a modern hardware platform.

Taylor Woodrow puts the success of the project down to the skilled staff it had. Many already had experience of UNIX, of managing large projects or of imple-

---

[3] It is possible that the Pyramid is more powerful than the 4381 it replaced, which seems a rather odd 'downsizing'.

[4] We are grateful to Ken Smith, the IS Director of Taywood Construction (Services) Limited, for agreeing to be interviewed for this section.

menting complex networks. As a result there was little need to hire expensive outside consultants who would, inevitably, increase the costs of the project. Furthermore the lessons learned by the in-house staff are now benefiting other projects within the organization.

The accounts above represent five studies of computing transition: four from IBM and one from HP. Of the five transitions, one is to proprietary mid-range, two are to distributed Unix, one is to centralized Unix and one is to PCs.

Life would be very easy if at this point we were able to draw out the factors, common to all these cases, that made them successful. If we were then able to examine some notable failures and show that this golden thread of success factor was missing we would have made considerable progress. But it is not as simple as that. There really does not appear to be a common factor that made these examples successful. (The Taylor Woodrow example suggests skilled staff are the key to success - we do not have enough information on the others to judge if this is indeed a common factor.)

The one common factor is that in each of the examples the result was a significant reduction in IT costs. This is an important factor because there is nothing like a newspaper article detailing how XYZ company managed to achieve 'a saving of £3 million' to produce a memo from the chief executive to the head of IT asking why they are not downsizing too.

12.3 Advantages of Downsizing and Rightsizing

There are a number of advantages claimed for downsizing and rightsizing. In this section we will look at the main ones and examine how realistic these claims are.

12.3.1 Cost Savings

A recent survey by Hoskyns showed that the prime motive for downsizing, in 59% of sites questioned, was cost saving.[5] There is no doubt that in simple 'MIPS for money' terms smaller systems do offer a far better deal than large systems. *Datamation* claimed: 'The cost of an instruction in a PC environment is about 3% that of a mainframe'.[6] As you can see from Figure 49, the cost differences are wide across the whole spectrum of systems.

---

[5] Hoskyns survey quoted in Rightsizing Supplement to *PC Week*, 15 September 1992.

[6] *Datamation*, 15 February 1990.

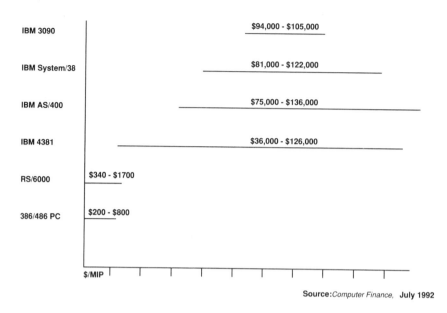

Figure 49. *Cost per MIP of Popular IBM Systems*

The figures are interesting and suggest that there are major savings to be made by moving to smaller systems. However, caution is required. To base a strategy on these figures alone would be erroneous. To use a rather extreme analogy, if we showed the cost of a journey in an articulated lorry from one end of Britain to the other and set it against the cost of doing the same journey in a small van it is certain that the articulated vehicle would be more expensive. However, two points need to be born in mind. The first is that the distance travelled and the raw cost of a lorry against even a fleet of vans is only part of the equation - we need to include other costs such as the full cost of a fleet of van drivers against the cost of an HGV driver. The second is that any business that handled modern freight palettes would be committing commercial suicide to sell off its articulated lorry and replace it with vans - they could not do the tasks relied on to run the business. The point is that the raw cost of the hardware is only one part of the equation.

The Gartner Group has done considerable work on the costs of end user computing, particularly PCs and PC LANs. It found that people costs account for a significant portion of the five-year cost of ownership figures. It estimated that end user operations and support accounted for 55% of the five-year people costs. More significantly, Gartner noted that the five-year cost of ownership for standalone PCs has nearly doubled since 1987 despite dramatic increases in PC price/performance.

In a different study the Meta Group calculated that an extra 0.5 persons per LAN should be budgeted into a downsizing proposal just to cover the annual on-going costs associated with network management.[7]

These figures suggest that the hidden costs may be quite large. Perhaps more worrying is the suggestion that identified costs are often far greater than calculated. An article in *PC Magazine* compared LAN costs as perceived by user departments with actual figures and these are shown in Figure 50.

Figure 50. *Perceived versus Actual Costs of PC LANs*		
Item	*Perceived Costs*	*Actual Costs*
Supplies	5%	5%
Maintenance	5%	5%
Outside Help	5%	15%
Internal Costs	5%	45%
Software	20%	10%
Hardware	60%	20%

In addition to these costs there are other factors. For example:

- the cost of program conversion and code migration
- the cost of retraining, rehiring and other employment changes
- the cost of parallel running during the change over
- the opportunity cost of any increased initial capital outlay.

The list is not exhaustive but does give an indication of other issues that need to be borne in mind.

In the preface we talked about the short-sightedness of making IT decisions based on solely on potential savings - when most organizations spend around 1.5% of turnover on IT it is not worth risking the business for uncertain savings. The size of the savings which some organizations and media articles claim from downsizing are impressive and should not be dismissed. However, if they are the sole driver to change then you may be taking a gamble. The stake might be the whole business, the prize a possible saving - not a particularly wise gamble.

---

[7] Quoted in *IBM System User*, August 1992.

12.3.2 Business Need

According to the Hoskyns survey already cited one quarter of all organizations downsizing give as their reason 'business restructuring'.

The current trend in business is to move away from monolithic, hierarchical structures, to flatter, more devolved ones. As part of this, business units are becoming profit centres with responsibility for their own revenue and expense. It is often the case that a flatter, more devolved, IT infrastructure seems to match business needs better.

Many organizations wish to reorganize in a more fundamental way - what might be referred to as *business process re-engineering*. In this, all the old processes and their supporting systems and structures are replaced. The drivers for this might be rapid change in the business environment, overly complex structures which tend to evolve in large organizations as they develop or problems caused by a lack of control due to poor process.

There is no doubt that IT systems should work for businesses and not the other way round. It must therefore follow that IT systems should help the business and not act as a brake on it. As the business changes so the IT structures must change too. The reasons for and against IT change in this way are very specific to each business. It would therefore be impossible for us to draw out any general lessons except one - take care.

12.3.3 Technical Unsuitability of Current Systems

As companies develop and change and as systems mature it often emerges that the IT is unable to support the business for technical reasons. There are many reasons why this can occur, and not all will suggest downsizing as a possible improvement. However, some will:

- Cost of maintenance - many installations, especially those which are mainframe based, develop their own applications. As the business alters so an increasing amount of time is spent maintaining and changing applications. The cost of this can become prohibitive and a new start, perhaps with a packaged solution, is required. A greater selection of packaged solutions is available for mid-range and PC systems than for mainframes.

- Application backlog - as increasing time is spent maintaining applications so less time can be spent developing new ones. The result is that many IT installations have long application backlogs. This can have a serious impact on the business. Development of new systems is often seen as being far cheaper and easier on smaller systems where there are many powerful tools far less expensive than those for the mainframe. Again, the answer may be packaged solutions for the reasons given above.

- Lack of 'usability' tools for users - the growth of PCs and workstations has produced a plethora of ease-of-use facilities: firstly, graphical user interfaces, and secondly, tools like spreadsheets. Neither of these are typically found on the dumb terminals of a mainframe and can put the brakes on acceptability and wide use of systems.

Downsizing and rightsizing can have real advantages in these cases. However, caution is required. If you downsize a bad system you will simply get a bad distributed system. What is more, the system will be new. It is likely people have found ways of coping with the old system and its problems have been ameliorated. Starting again and delivering a bad solution can be disastrous. If the reason for changing is the technical insufficiency of the current solution it is an obvious but nonetheless important point that the new solution should be architected to remove these deficiences.

Cost savings, changing business needs and technical insufficiency are together very good cases for changing systems and downsizing. Some companies, however, have learnt that there can be some very complicated problems. The difficulty is finding those who are prepared to talk openly about the problems they faced unless they have actually resolved them.

A Cautionary Tale

Perhaps the most quoted example of serious problems has been the Performing Rights Society.[8] The PRS decided to downsize from an ICL 2966 mainframe to a 10-way multi-processor Pyramid server. The cost was expected to be £10 million but the system was planned to save more than £3 million every year.

The Society's database was around 20Gb though the nature of tasks the system was expected to perform were quite complex. The result was the database required up to 30Mb of memory per user, night-time batch runs ran into daytime work and the system could not support 100 active and 200 *ad hoc* users.

It is clear that the machine was wrongly sized, though in fairness the PRS was breaking ground to such an extent in this area that any sizing was likely to be rather haphazard. In addition, it appears that in an attempt to improve the service the system design was overly complex.

The question for us is whether there are any lessons. Unfortunately, apart from the obvious 'don't buy a machine too small for the job' there do not appear to be any at this stage. To imply that the problem was a lack of planning, technical incompetence or anything else would be unfair as none of this is certain.

---

[8] In fairness to the Performing Rights Society it must be stressed that we were unable to verify these facts with them and have pieced them together from press reports, most particularly in *Computing*, 12 November 1992 and *Computer Weekly*, 19 November 1992.

What is important is that the PRS has involved itself in considerable expense as a result of its unfortunate venture into downsizing. It has also suffered considerable embarrassment. Its experience provides an ideal response to any chief executive who sends a copy of the 'we saved £3 million through downsizing' article to the IT department.

12.3.4 Disadvantages of Downsizing and Rightsizing

The case of the Performing Rights Society shows that the biggest disadvantage to downsizing is failure and the consequent expense and possible business catastrophe that can occur. However, there are other issues that need to be considered.

Security: A mainframe is far easier to make secure than a distributed system. On a mainframe security can be enforced by limiting access only to certain levels of information. In distributed systems it is common to limit access only by not putting certain information on a given server. When security controls are taken further than this, users may encounter difficulties as they move from one part of the network to another, and between networks - constantly encountering the security mechanisms set up to control unauthorized access.

According to Price Waterhouse, 65% of companies suffer a financial loss through lack of information security and 7% suffer loss which nearly cripples them.[9]

To suggest that these are problems that are insurmountable is not true. However, security is more of a problem in a distributed environment and when considering downsizing should be a major area of examination.

Systems and Network Management: the management of distributed systems and networks is not a trivial task. We have already talked of the need for 0.5 support staff for each LAN. The issue is more than that, though. The current state of technology is such that distributed network environments lack proper control in many cases. Issues like capacity management, software distribution, configuration and version control management, problem rectification and so on must be fully examined.

Mainframe systems and their networks are inherently easier to manage because of their centralized nature. Anyone considering downsizing such environments should pay serious attention to how they plan to manage their systems and networks after the move.

Support: A further potential problem is service and support from suppliers. A mainframe and its associated peripherals often come from one source and even though the source of the problem may be difficult to identify the source of the

---

[9] Quoted in Open Systems Project workshops brochure.

solution, that single supplier, is easy to see. When there is a heterogeneous networked environment that relationship is lost. This might seem like a minor point but the reality is that today the level of experience in most IT organizations in LAN technology and distributed computing is limited. That means reliance on the supplier is increased. The ability of suppliers to 'pass the buck' cannot be overlooked.

That is not to suggest for a moment that this is a reason to abandon a downsizing venture. Rather the point is made so that in planning you can ensure that you have the best staff on hand within your own organization and look seriously at bringing in new staff if necessary.

12.4 Summary

So far we have looked at the advantages and disadvantages of downsizing. We have also looked at some successes and a failure in this area. The question we have avoided is whether your organization should downsize or rightsize. That is because as far as we are concerned the difference is irrelevant - they are all moves to either a single smaller system or, more usually, distributed systems.

The other question we have not yet answered is where the mainframe fits in all this activity. A recent survey of Fortune 1000 companies' IT managers found that about one-third of the servers in use today in their organizations are mainframes. In addition, research by the Gartner Group indicated that the average workload (in CPU power terms) planned to be 'downsized' from mainframes was 22% in organizations which were considering it. The conclusion of these findings seems to be that the mainframe does indeed still have a major role to play.

12.5 Downsizing Considerations

We started off by saying that what was required before deciding whether or not to downsize was a consideration of the issues. Having looked at the advantages and disadvantages in an abstract way we felt it would be helpful to set out, in a series of checklists, each area and the issues involved. By its nature, and for completeness, this repeats a little of what has already been said. On the other hand it should serve as a helpful summary of the issues an organization will face.

Hardware: This is an obvious need but is probably not as important as the choice of enabling software - both system and application - that runs on it. This may even dictate the hardware platform. The popular options appear to be:

- PCs/PS2s and other Intel-based systems
- RISC machines (Sun, IBM, DEC, HP and so on)
- proprietary systems (OS/400, VMS, for example).

The third hardware choice may cause a few raised eyebrows but a look at the TPC-A price per TPS (transactions per second) will show that several proprietary systems are comparable to the best Unix/RISC systems.

Software: This is of major importance as to whether a downsizing exercise (of any class) will achieve its objectives and deliver the perceived benefits. The types of software to be considered are:

- migration tools, compilers and CASE for the new or downsized applications
- OLTP, database and networking software to support the application environment.
- operating system(s).

The operating system may be a foregone conclusion based on the choice of other software.

Skills: It may seem obvious to say that skills are needed to effect a transformation like downsizing, but it is often forgotten in the dash to gain the benefits. If an organization does not have the skills they will need to buy them in, either individually or as a systems integration (SI) package. The types of skill appropriate to the move are:

- end-to-end design skills for seeing the exercise as a whole and not as the installation of a series of boxes and software
- network skills
- database skills
- operating systems and related software skills
- performance skills
- project skills.

Project Plan: Again obvious, but it is on a proper project plan that the following are identified:

- The sponsor of the move. This is usually a senior manager who backs the exercise, removes any non-technical barriers to progress and is ultimately responsible for the success or failure of the project.
- The benefits of the move, both tangible and intangible.
- The deliverables of the project.
- The exclusions, personnel, timescales and all the other elements of a good project definition and project plan.

It should not be forgotten that after installation, someone will be charged with operating and maintaining the set-up. That person should be involved at the outset in assessing the feasibility of the task and can then flag service level expectations which cannot be met *before* the systems are implemented.

Benefit Analysis: This is simple but less obvious - it should answer the question 'Why are we doing this?'.

A final piece of advice - talk to someone who has downsized, successfully or otherwise.

The astute reader will have noticed that we have laid out the requirements in reverse chronological order and roughly reverse order of importance. 'Let's get some Unix RISC boxes and get on with it' is probably not the best approach to downsizing - or any other IT project.

12.5.1 Rules of Thumb for Distributed Processing

There are three basic approaches to distributed processing and, for that matter, downsizing of any reasonable scope:

- reactive
- proactive
- strategic with delivery of solutions after one or two years of planning and pilots.

Each has its benefits and shortcomings and these rules of thumb might help you assess the best approach for your organization.

1. Do not stretch the state of the art in technology.
2. Let the installation schedule drive the technology needs.
3. Capitalize on your existing investment, tools and experience.
4. Consider the differences between distributed data access and distributed data management.
5. Choose your inter-process communication (IPC) method carefully so that you do not limit your expansion capabilities.
6. Cater for network connections of different types since only new sites have the luxury of single supplier systems.
7. Prototype any network connections for function, performance and, above all, manageability.
8. Get the users and operations people involved - they are the people who have to manage the system after all. They should be in a position to point out impractical elements of the design at an early stage.
9. Remember that multiple platforms, heterogeneous or homogeneous, will require more detail in the planning, customization and implementation phases.
10. Make your own cost case - do not borrow someone else's.
11. Learn about the subject.

12.5.2 Implementation Checklist

1. Preliminary steps
   - application(s) identification
   - management approach and decision process
2. Preliminary platform selection
   - application availability on that platform
   - workload characteristics
   - control - centralized or delegated to remote sites
   - architecture
   - experience on that platform
3. Feasibility prototype
4. High-level design
5. Project plan with quantified deliverables
6. Identify sponsor(s)
7. Planning steps
   - application(s) definition and sizing
   - specify system(s) configuration(s)
   - installation approach
   - installation tools and facilities
   - automation levels, responsibilities
   - management process
8. Installation(s) plan
9. Operations items
   - central systems operator interfaces
   - system support services defined
   - back-up/archive functions defined
   - performance management
   - availability management
   - change management
   - problem management
   - application support
   - network support.

12.5.3 Downsizing Resource Requirements

When applications are migrated from a mainframe to another system, it should not be assumed that they will need the same resource. For example, if an application 1 used an x MIPS machine as measured by some benchmark, then two $0.5x$ MIPS UNIX systems as measured by the same benchmark will suffice. It is more than likely that the application will be either rewritten or bought in as a package. The installation is then faced with an *ab initio* calculation as to the resources needed to support the application.

The process of estimating resources for downsized applications is exactly the same as estimating resource requirements for any new application, including any client/server interactions.

In addition, there are other key considerations such as the acceptable availability. If, for example, the availability was 98.5% on the mainframe system, you may be faced with designing a more complex system to guarantee such high availability on the downsizing platform(s). This will add to the cost. If the extra cost is not acceptable, then you need to assess the cost to your company of a lower availability, say 95%, for the application. This is a real issue with some Unix platforms where the system needs to be taken out of service to make any changes which impact the kernel.

12.5.4 Application Dependency Matrix

Another issue which must be addressed in downsizing is the dependency of offloaded applications on other applications, either on the mainframe or elsewhere.

The matrix shown in Figure 51 is of the sort that needs to be drawn up for applications which are either taken from the mainframe and put elsewhere, typically on a 'workstation', or new ones which may or may not have links with existing applications wherever they may reside. The examples are not from real life but are meant to illustrate a principle.

In order to 'downsize' the payroll application and put it on a machine other than the one on which all the applications presently reside, it is necessary to provide some measure of 'interoperability' between the two platforms since the applications are linked. In this case, the link is with the ledger application which remains on the mainframe. There are then things to consider about the link, for example:

- What protocols will be used to link them (LU6.2, RPC etc.)?
- Will it now involve two different transaction and database systems and what are the consequences?
- What multi-system recovery and security techniques will be used ?
- What is the effect on performance of the 'split'?

- What data back-up method will be used - host or downsizing platform?

Figure 51. *Downsizing Dependency Matrix*				
LINKS	*Payroll*	*Accounts*	*CAD/CAM*	*Ledger*
Payroll	/////////////////	Y		
Accounts	Y	////////////////		
CAD/CAM			////////////////	
Ledger		Y		/////////////////
New Application 1				
New Application 2		Y		Y

On the other hand, it appears that CAD/CAM can be taken away quite easily as long as the application runs on, and is accessible via, the new 'downsizing' platform. The same applies to new application 1 but not to new application 2 which needs a link to the accounts and ledger systems. Note that although the new application 2 was never intended to run on the mainframe, it nevertheless still has a dependency on it.

Assuming interoperability is required, it will also be necessary to assess the level of complexity required, whether a static client/server relationship will suffice or whether more dynamic cooperative processing needs to be designed.

12.5.5 Manageability Issues

If a single mainframe application is moved to a single system with no mainframe links, there are probably no major issues. However, if the downsizing results in distributed systems, then there are some issues which need to be addressed:

- Do the systems and users have the same access to external systems and data that the original host offered?
- Is the data accessible to all who are authorized?
- How is the data to be managed (back-up, integrity, security)?
- What plans are in place for managing the network?
- Who will do systems and network performance monitoring and capacity (projection) planning?
- Are the hardware, software and other items auditable?
- Who looks after media (paper and printers for ribbons, tapes for back-up)?

- Do you have processes in place for problem, change and availability management?
- Is there a central help desk for reporting problems?

It is unlikely that the *end user* will be responsible for any of these items. In that case, who is?

12.6 Conclusions

Some companies have had considerable success from downsizing, both in terms of financial and business advantage. Others, though less well publicized, have suffered financially and doubtless their business has suffered too.

Whether the risks outweigh the advantages is particular to each business. The need to look at all the aspects has been emphasized throughout this book.

One final thought which will perhaps provide some encouragement. The number of companies downsizing and rightsizing is growing all the time. That growth is producing an increasing pool of IT personnel with the knowledge required to make such projects successful. The initial companies have been pioneers. The Performing Rights Society, the most publicized failure, would undoubtedly have been more successful if those involved in the project had had more experience.

Should an over enthusiastic sales person remark that 'it is all very easy and there are no problems', propose that he/she takes the risk and agrees to cover all costs, including liquidated damages, if the project fails!

Chapter 13 Standards for Portability

I have recently been all round the world and formed a very poor opinion of it.[1]

What is *portability*? Dennis Ritchie, of Unix and C fame, claims that an application is portable if it takes less effort to move it to another platform than to rewrite it. Others will disagree with this and say it must move without effort. In reality, portability is a compromise dissecting these two views and is carried forward by standards specifiers.

13.1 X/Open

X/Open is involved in a number of related projects in the area of standards. As well as the Portability Guides it has a Common Applications Environment specification and a number of initiatives looking at other areas like systems management, user requirements and networking standards.

13.1.1 X/Open Portability Guides

The X/Open Portability Guide (XPG) is an important part of the X/Open Specifications called *XPG Specifications*. There have been four issues of these, the latest being XPG4.

'XPG Specifications are the formal specifications which are backed by X/Open's test and verification program and by the X/Open XPG branding scheme. They are intended to be used widely within the industry for product development and pro-

---

[1] Sir Thomas Beecham, British conductor.

curement purposes. Developers who base their products on these specifications can apply for registration under the XPG branding process.'[2]

The 1990 X/Open *Open Systems Directive* states:

'X/Open objectives with the XPG Specifications include:

- portability of applications at the source level so that application porting is a mechanical recompilation process.

- connectivity of applications via portable networking services that are independent of underlying protocols, plus support for common protocol stacks to ensure that X/Open conforming systems can interwork effectively, and

- a consistent approach to the user interface with the system'.

The full range of topics occupying X/Open can be gauged by the list of X/Open publications in Appendix C.

X/Open Portability Guide 4: The XPG1 documentation consisted of a single volume, XPG2 was five volumes and XPG3 weighed in with seven. XPG3 introduced the concept of *base*, *plus* and *optional* conformance. The XPG4 Guide comprises 24 specifications covering:[3]

- complete open systems environment
- portability
- interoperability
- usability.

The XPG Guides are generally cumulative and their present status is shown in Figure 52.

Where XPG3 concentrated on portability, XPG4 enhances many of the XPG3 specifications and explores the key areas of heterogeneous interoperability.

XPG4 Components

Base Computing Platform
- Systems calls and libraries
- Commands and utilities
- C language

Programming Languages
- Cobol
- Pascal
- Fortran

---

[2] From an untitled X/Open publication, 1 November 1991.

[3] Mike Lambert of X/Open at the 1992 Xtra '92 Congress.

- Ada

Data Management

- ISAM
- Relational database (SQL and the XA Specification)

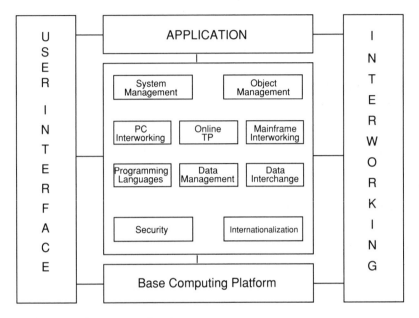

Figure 52. *XPG4 Functionality Areas*

User Interface

- X Window System display
- X Window System API
- Terminal interfaces

General Interworking

- Byte-stream data transfer(*)[4]
- X.400 Gateway(*)
- X.400 Message Access(*)
- Directory access(*)
- Network File System(*)
- Transport interface (XTI)

---

[4] Items marked (*) are new in XPG4.

Mainframe Interworking

■ Common Programming Interface - Communications (CPI-C)(*)

PC Interworking

■ (PC) NFS server(*)

■ LMX server(*)

Data Interchange (Media)

■ Magnetic media (tape, floppy disk, cartridge)

XPG4 Profiles

XPG3 included two profiles, Base and Plus, to which vendors could aspire for conformance. In XPG4, the Base profile is maintained but the Plus is not. Instead, there are extra functional profiles which are comprised of collections of brandable XPG4 components. To achieve *profile branding* a vendor must demonstrate conformance, integration and availability of all the components of the profile. These additional profiles are:

● OSI communications gateway

● Base server

● Workstation

● Database platform.

The grouping of functional areas into profiles is illustrated in Figures 53 and 54.

Figure 53. *XPG4 Profiles Structure*	
1. Base Profile	*2. OSI Communications Gateway Profile*
Systems Calls & Libraries	Systems Calls & Libraries
Commands & Utilities	Commands & Utilities
C Language	C Language
	Transport Service (XTI)
	X.400 Gateway
	X.400 Message Access
	Directory Access
	Byte Stream File Transfer (BSFT)

Figure 54. *XPG4 Profiles Structure (cont.)*	
3. Base Server Profile	*4. Workstation Profile*
Systems Calls & Libraries	Systems Calls & Libraries
Commands & Utilities	Commands & Utilities
C Language	C Language
Transport Service (XTI)	Transport Service (XTI)
X Window Systems API	Network File System
Terminal Interfaces	X Window System Display
Network File System	X Window System API
(PC) NFS Server	Terminal Interfaces
5. Database Platform Profile	
System Calls & Libraries	
Commands & Utilities	
C Language	
Cobol Language	
Relational Database	
Transport Service (XTI)	

13.1.2 X/Open Common Applications Environment (CAE)

In a nutshell, the Common Applications Environment is a set of specifications divided into ***developers' specifications***, ***preliminary specifications*** and ***snapshots***. These are separate volumes from the X/Open XPG3 Specifications or Portability Guides dealt with above, and are defined thus: 'CAE (Common Applications Environment) Specifications are the long-life specifications that form the basis for conformant and branded X/Open systems. They are intended to be used widely within the industry for product development and procurement purposes. Developers who base their products on a current CAE specification can be sure that either the current specification or an upwards compatible version of it will be referenced by a future XPG brand.'

The developers' specifications comprise:

- Protocols for X/Open Interworking;XNFS

- Indexed Sequential Access Method (ISAM)[5]
- Protocols for X/Open PC Interworking (PC) NFS
- CPI-C
- Revised XTI (X/Open Transport Interface)
- X/Open Window Management;Xlib-C Language Binding
- X/Open Window Management;X Window System Protocol
- X/Open Window Management;X Toolkit Intrinsics
- X/Open Window Management;X Window System File Formats and Application Conventions
- Protocols for X/Open PC Interworking; SMB.

The preliminary specifications equate to 'beta test' products while the snapshots are draft specifications for information and comment by developers and procurers.

13.1.3 The X/Open SYSMAN Group

This interest group, composed of major vendors, meets six times a year to discuss and advance the systems management disciplines in the OSE. The components of major interest are SNMP, CMIP and OMG. Key focus areas are management services and management applications, such as back-up/restore and licence management. It has similar interests to the OSF Systems Management SIG.[6]

On 11 August 1992 X/Open and the Open Software Foundation announced a joint initiative to integrate OSF's Distributed Computing Environment (DCE) specifications into X/Open's CAE.

The integration of the DCE interface specifications into the CAE will expand the scope of the CAE to a full distributed framework. The main focus of the OSE, and X/Open's contribution, is shifting from portability to interoperability. The incorporation of DCE in X/Open's CAE is seen as providing a base for this.

However, OSF will continue to include DCE in its Application Environment Specification (AES) which covers all the OSF technologies.

The specification for DCE will be published by X/Open in the same way as other CAE specification. The goal is to make the DCE interfaces components of the formal XPG specifications in the future.

---

[5] Extensions to the XPG3 ISAM definitions.

[6] Special Interest Group.

13.1.4 The X/Open Xtra Requirements Process

The X/Open Xtra process aims to define the market requirements for open systems. This will hopefully provide the IT industry with a consistent, single source, open systems direction free of vendor self-interest. A yearly Xtra Market Requirements Conference is held to gather data which is latterly published in the annual Open Systems Directive (OSD).

13.1.5 X/Open and Vendors

In June 1992, X/Open appointed Dataquest to carry out a survey of 'open systems' vendors. The purpose of the survey was to analyze vendor progress in delivering solutions to the requirements expressed by previous X/Open Xtra surveys of 'open systems' users and other interested, non-vendor, parties.

One of the main conclusions of the 1991 Xtra World Survey was that users found it difficult to assess the stance of vendors on important issues like those raised in the Xtra World Survey on Open Systems.

The survey covered 65 IT vendors, including 26 with no connections with X/Open. To gauge the representative nature of the vendors, you should note that their 1991 turnover was in excess of $220 billion. Four areas were surveyed:

- 'Interoperability:
    - an open approach to support applications software services to enable applications to run across heterogeneous networks
    - an open approach to enable the support by application software services of communications protocols across heterogeneous networks.
- Data Systems:
    - the open systems clients need to access proprietary DBMSs
    - uniform access to all types of data, including graphics
    - the establishment of enterprise-wide access to a single data dictionary.
- Distributed Transaction Processing:
    - transparent access to heterogeneous OLTP databases
    - portability and interoperability of transaction monitors
    - future open approaches to OLTP architecture.
- Network Management:
    - the establishment of network management to function from any platform and with the ability to manage the entire enterprise network

- the application of centralized management of distributed applications in an open manner, especially software installations, configuration and upgrades.'[7]

Compare these with the 'needs' expressed in GUIDE 82, where users were asking IBM to provide or enhance functions as specified in their cooperative processing document. It basically means that in the Dataquest survey, vendors were asked to state their position on many of the issues already recognized and being debated by proprietary IBM accounts today.

The first use of the results was as input to the Xtra Congress held in Washington, DC, on 1-2 December 1992. An overview[8] plus a full report are available from X/Open. In essence, the outcome of the survey was that there are safe areas for (IT) investment today, while in others users can drive the development and delivery of standards and specifications for open systems.

13.1.6 X/Open CoMIX Initiative

The apparent conflict between TCP/IP and OSI for mastery of the communications universe has often seemed an intractable issue. However, in 1991 X/Open announced its *CoMIX* initiative aimed at defusing this. Petr Janecek, X/Open manager of connectivity strategy, believes that although OSI will supplant TCP/IP 'in the long term, ... our primary interest is in guiding users who face considerable practical problems today.' X/Open published a guide,[9] the second on TCP/IP-OSI, which seeks to ease the transition between IPS (Internet Protocol Suite - read TCP/IP) and OSI.

'Specifically it will:

- define problems of coexistence between the two technologies
- define problems in migration
- provide implementation guidelines for solving these problems.'

This is an example of a pragmatic approach to open systems interoperability using a *de facto* standard during the development of a *de jure* standard.

---

[7] X/Open Press release, June 1992.

[8] *Overview of the World Survey of Suppliers' Plans for Open Systems.*

[9] *Guide to IPS - OSI Coexistence and Migration.*

13.1.7 The X/Open Roadmap

A 'roadmap' in the context of standards is usually taken to mean a statement of intent to deliver products with an associated timescale. X/Open does not have a Roadmap in the sense that UI and OSF do, with dates and products specified. It is rather an evolving set of requirements unearthed by the Xtra process and published in successive Open Systems Directives (OSD) which follow the annual Xtra Congress. If anything can be viewed as an X/Open Roadmap, it is probably the X/Open Technical Newsletter.[10] It provides a brief status report and update on current developments in each of the main areas that X/Open is working. The areas covered in issue 1 were:

1. Base environment
2. Data interchange
3. Data management
4. Distributed computing services
5. Distributed system management
6. Human computer interface
7. Internationalization
8. Interworking
9. Object technology
10. Programming languages
11. Security
12. Transaction processing.

The most active and key areas are 3, 4, 5, 7, 9, 11 and 12. Since the Technical Newsletter is updated monthly, the 'status', or futures, sections are volatile. Interested organizations should either join X/Open to receive the newsletter in electronic form, or obtain a copy of the quarterly printed version by contacting X/Open.

13.2 POSIX

The POSIX 1003.1 group[11] began work on standardizing the interface between C programs and the Unix operating system. This POSIX standard has its roots in that language. Today, vendors such as DEC, IBM and ICL are incorporating POSIX

---

[10] First edition January 1993 and available monthly.

[11] Base system calls.

compliance in their proprietary systems[12] to enable the huge installed base of legacy systems to partake in an open systems environment. Despite reports of the death of the mainframe, like Mark Twain's, they are greatly exaggerated. They will be with us for some time.

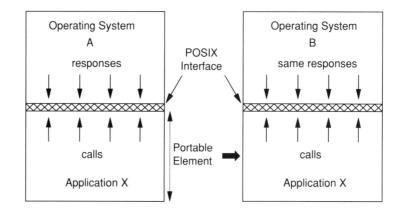

Figure 55. *POSIX Interface Schematic*

The interface is shown schematically in Figure 55. In essence, it is a set of commands and rules 'agreed' by the application and the operating system that make the application portable across operating systems which support that interface.

POSIX standards are classed as either 'approved', 'balloting', or 'working' in increasing order of the maturity of the specification.

The POSIX initiative is not just the delivery of specifications from the committees. The 1003.0 Working Group is putting together a comprehensive set of standards known as the POSIX Open Systems Environment (OSE). The POSIX OSE does not just use the POSIX 1003.xx specifications in its deliberations, but others such as ANSI and ISO standards with POSIX forming the basis. The OSE as specified by 1003.0 is therefore an evolving environment. Moreover, the POSIX model attempts to make the POSIX specifications more than a random set of standards.

---

[12] POSIX compliance in their Unix offerings is taken as read.

1003.0   *POSIX Guide*
1003.1   *System Interface*
1003.2   *Shells and Utilities (Tools)*
1003.3   *Common Test Methods*
1003.4   *Real Time API*
1003.5   *Ada Bindings*
1003.6   *Security Extensions for 1003.1*
1003.7   *System Administration*
1003.8   *Network Transparent File Access (TFA) API*
1003.9   *Fortran Bindings*
1003.10 *Supercomputing Application Environment Profile (AEP)*
1003.11 *Transaction Processing AEP (defunct)*
1003.12 *Protocol Independent Network Interfaces*
1003.13 *Real Time AEP*
1003.14 *Multiprocessing AEP*
1003.15 *Supercomputing Batch System Administration*
1003.16 *C Language Binding*
1003.17 *Directory Service API (Renumbered 1992 - see (*) below)*
1003.18 *POSIX Platform Environment Profile*
1003.19 *Fortran 90 Binding*
1003.20 *Real Time Ada Bindings plus 20a extensions*
1003.21 *Real Time Distributed Communications Services*
1003.22 *Distributed Security Framework*

1201.1 *Window Interface for User and Application Portability*
1201.2 *Graphical User Interfaces - Drivability*
1224.0 *Object Management (OM) Services API*
1224.1 *X.400 Message Handling APIs*
1224.2 *Directory Services API(*)*
1238.0 *OSI Connection Management API*
1238.1 *OSI FTAM API*
1326.2 *Test Methods for 1224.2(*)*
1327.2 *C Language Binding to 1224.2(*)*
1328.2 *Test Methods for 1327.2(*)*

Figure 56. *POSIX Specifications*

It classifies the specifications into two areas of the model:

- Those which define an Application Programming Interface (API) between the application program and the ***application platform***.[13]
- Those which define the relationship between the application platform and the ***external environment***. The external environment covers peripherals, like printers and displays, and the network.[14]

In meetings between June 1992 and January 1993, there was much progress in the submission and approval of POSIX standards outside the long-standing 1003.1.

Approved Standards

The list of approved POSIX standards at April 1993 is given below:

IEEE Std 1003.1-1990   System Application Program Interfaces
- also approved as ISO/IEC 9945-1:1990

IEEE Std 1003.2-1992   Shell and Utilities
- also approved as ISO/IEC DIS 9945-2:1992 (Draft International Std)

IEEE Std 1003.3-1991   Test Methods for Measuring Conformance to POSIX
- will be renumbered IEEE Std 2003-199x when next updated

IEEE Std 1003.5-1992   Ada Binding to 1003.1-1990

IEEE Std 1003.9-1992   Fortran 77 Binding to 1003.1-1990

IEEE Std 1224-1993	OSI Abstract Data Manipulation API
IEEE Std 1326-1993	Test Methods for IEEE Std 1224-1993
IEEE Std 1327-1993	C-Language Binding to IEEE Std 1224-1993
IEEE Std 1328-1993	Test Methods for IEEE Std 1327-1993

IEEE Std 1224.1-1993	X.400 Based Electronic Messaging API
IEEE Std 1326.1-1993	Test Methods for IEEE Std 1224.1-1993
IEEE Std 1327.1-1993	C-Language Binding to IEEE Std 1224.1-1993
IEEE Std 1328.1-1993	Test Methods for IEEE Std 1327.1-1993

IEEE Std 1224.2-1993   Directory Services API

---

[13] This normally means the operating system.

[14] See D. Richard Kuhn, *IEEE Spectrum*, December 1991.

IEEE Std 1326.2-1993   Test Methods for IEEE Std 1224.2-1993
IEEE Std 1327.2-1993   C-Language Binding to IEEE Std 1224.2-1993
IEEE Std 1328.2-1993   Test Methods for IEEE Std 1327.2-1993

IEEE Std 2003.1-1992   Test Methods for 1003.1-1990

The various specifications approved, being balloted and worked on are summarized in Figure 56. The status of work not yet approved can be found in Appendix A.

13.2.1 1003.0 POSIX Guide

This document is a management guide to open systems as defined by the POSIX 1003.0 committee. The definition of an 'open system' in this guide is the one we quoted in Chapter 2 and it has been adopted by IBM and others.

1003.1 System Interface: Since 1003.1 is the most mature POSIX specification, we will deal with it in greater depth here than the other 1003.x standard specifications, details of which can be found in Appendix A.

The 1003.1 Systems Interface Definition specifies the interface between application programs and the operating system and is based on the Unix operating system interface with the user or application.   The standardization is aimed at system calls and subroutines.   This formally defines application calls to the Unix kernel and libraries such that the application can be ported to any other operating system that complies with the 1003.1 standards. Although the standard has its origins in Unix, it does not mandate Unix and so in theory other operating systems might achieve POSIX conformance by adding function to support the calls (or requests) made to the operating system by the application program. You do not have to be a Unix variant to 'speak' POSIX 1003.1 any more than you have to be German to speak German - you just have an edge.

POSIX 1003.1 has three levels of 'conformance' to which applications can aspire:

1. Strict conformance, where no extensions to the standard are permitted.

2. Conformance, where extensions are permitted but must be ISO or national standards. These extensions must be documented.

3. Conformance using extensions which permits the addition of any documented extensions over and above those specified in item 2.

The third conformance type is obviously the least portable, although in reality, little is made of differences in levels of conformance by users or vendors. In fact, POSIX calls are almost exclusive to the Unix world and application developers on other operating systems are unlikely to use the low-level POSIX calls anyway.

The details of the functions covered by this standard are explained in more detail in Appendix I.

13.2.2 Non-Unix POSIX

We alluded earlier to the fact that proprietary operating systems are acquiring POSIX interfaces. Figure 57 shows how POSIX compliant interfaces sit alongside proprietary interfaces for various types of application.

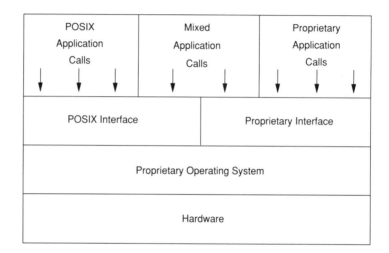

Figure 57. *Proprietary and POSIX Interfaces*

13.3 Programming Languages

The major standards for programming languages and APIs come from:
- the ANSI standards for languages, for example X3J1-PL/I, X3J3-Fortran, X3J4-Cobol, X3J9-Pascal, X3J11-C and X3J16-C++
- X/Open Portability Guide (XPG)
- vendors.

Programs written in 3GLs have always been assumed to be portable at the source level, that is, they only need to be recompiled to run on another platform.

In fact, extensions to the languages, for example Cobol, and specific operating system calls are often implemented by the major IT vendors. These impact the portability of applications and should be avoided by software vendors and purchasers alike if they wish to be considered an open systems supplier or user.

Compilers, compiler options and even hardware can sometimes cause portability problems, albeit indirectly. In the scientific world, the same program can give different results when executed on different platforms even if no errors are apparent. For commercial programs, such errors are rarer but can occur for a number of reasons.

- In floating point programs, the hardware accuracy and rounding of numbers may differ from machine to machine.

- Some compilers initialize defined fields to blanks, zeros or do nothing so that whatever is in memory when the program is loaded into main storage for execution remains there. Programmers frequently take short cuts in programming by exploiting compiler options such as defaults which may not be observed by other compilers

- Other assumptions on the part of the programmer can also cause problems.

However, you may find it difficult to persuade a software vendor who wishes only to develop and maintain a product on a single architecture to open it up to other hardware platforms. On the other hand, it is understandable for a software vendor to limit the number of platforms on which the product is supported simply because of the cost and effort of developing it, providing fixes and chasing reported problems across all known platforms. The software vendor is often the arbiter as to which platforms are open as far as portability of the product is concerned, simply because he cannot afford to own and support all known platforms.

13.4 Relational Database (RDB)

In general, the programs and associated databases from the one relational database vendor are not portable to the environment provided by another relational database vendor. Traditionally, when you bought or wrote a relational package or application, you were essentially locked into that particular RDB, although gateways to other RDBs would be available as an option.

Structured Query Language (SQL) arose out of the IBM System R project, a prototype relational database system, which spawned the 'Sequel' language. SQL, its successor, is essentially a language by which relational tables are accessed. The language was adopted by RDB vendors who, as might have been expected, added their own flavour to it. The first attempt at standardization was by an ISO/ANSI committee, formed in 1983, which produced the ANSI SQL86 specification in 1986 and a further one, SQL89, three years later. In the same year, a number of vendors formed a consortium called the SQL Access Group (SAG) to tighten up the ANSI specifications which were still considered 'liberal'. The group also aimed to accelerate the work of the ISO Remote Database Access (RDA) group.[15]

The SAG specifications are in addition to the ANSI ones, SQL86 and SQL89. ANSI had the SQL-2 specification approved as SQL92 in 1992. A further refinement, SQL-3, is targeted for delivery in the second half of the decade. Despite these standardization efforts, applications developed on one RDB system in general will not run on another RDB system, essentially since the program/4GL specifications and the database itself are inextricably linked. Today, however, there is customer pressure on RDB suppliers to separate their application development tools from their databases. In this way, purchasers can choose the best tools and the best database for their needs - the two will not necessarily come from the same supplier.

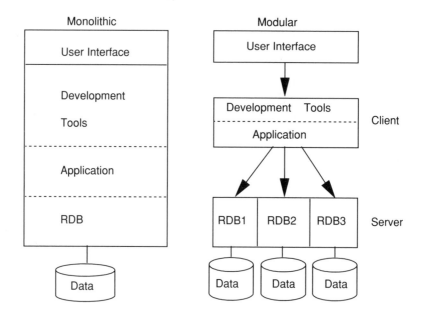

Figure 58. *Database Independent Development. The left hand part of this figure shows the single-vendor world of 'bundled' tools and database. The right shows the 'unbundled' environment.*

The major RDB vendors, such as Ingres, Sybase, Informix and Oracle, are moving to structure their tools/database offerings in such a way. Aside from these traditional RDB vendors, there are today suppliers of tools which can develop

---

[15] See Chapter 16 for a discussion of RDA.

applications to run against a number of databases. Progress, UNIFY (Accell/SQL) and TechGnosis (Sequelink) are examples from the Unix world.[16]

These front end tools often work in conjunction with an OLTP monitor such as Tuxedo, which was the first OLTP that Accell/SQL used. The back end databases can be chosen from a number available, although the list varies with each front end. The whole fits together in client/server mode as shown in Figure 58.

Programs running against the C-ISAM file structure (associated with the C language) are normally portable but are very limited in function when compared to a modern RDB.

13.5 Graphics

As a rule, graphics programs written at the primitive (machine) level will not be portable across machine architectures, and some standardization was needed to remove machine dependencies from programs.

Graphics-Device Standards

Several attempts at standardization have been made and out of these, the main standard graphics APIs to emerge and are in use today are as follows:

- Graphical Kernel System (GKS 2D)
- GKS 3D
- Programmers' Hierarchical Interactive Graphics System (PHIGS)
- PHIGS+

Silicon Graphics Inc., developed a very popular high-level graphics API known as GL (Graphics Library). Although not an agreed standard API, it nevertheless accounts today for over 75% of advanced graphics applications and is considered to be a *de facto* standard in the graphics world.

PHIGS: PHIGS is a set of graphical API subroutines and utilities, callable from languages such as C and Fortran, for:

- device-independent 2D and 3D graphics programs
- dynamic manipulation of graphical models
- interacting with a graphics picture
- storage and retrieval of models and pictures.

A *model* is a network of related structures making up an object for viewing or manipulating. It approximates to the figure of a motor car where the manufacturer

---

[16] There are also similar 'unbundled' tools available for PC/DOS users.

shows all the features and how they fit together, with pointers and dimensions. A *picture* is a view of the object after the software has traversed the data that makes it up - rather like the picture of a car from a particular angle. Structures are stored in *archive files*, while pictures are stored in *metafiles*.

PHIGS operates in non-immediate mode, which is the graphics equivalent of interpretive languages such as APL. GL works in immediate mode, which is the graphics equivalent of compiled code.

OpenGL: OpenGL is a descendant of the Silicon Graphics GL. It was the result of an effort by Silicon Graphics Inc. to make GL a standard. Its development is governed by an Architecture Review Board (ARB) which used GL Version 5.0 as its starting point. SGI are responsible for providing ARB with samples of future GL enhancements. Enhancements are then evaluated and, subject to a two-thirds majority vote, accepted. There are also test suites for verifying implementations of OpenGL by vendors.

GL works in two modes:

Immediate Mode. This is the most frequently used mode in which graphics data is sent directly to the raster subsystems, displaying it as it is generated. It is easy to learn for simple graphics programs.

Deferred Mode. In this mode, display lists are stored for later recall by the program.

The GL library routines, like PHIGS, can be used in C and Fortran programs.

GKS: GKS is an ISO standard for 2D graphics, although today many PHIGS implementations offer GKS function as part of PHIGS.

PEX (PHIGS extensions to 'X'): PEX originated with the X Consortium supported by major vendors like DEC, H-P and IBM. It is an extension to the X protocol[17] to allow the transmission of 3D data over network connection. PEX caters for PHIGS implementations and offers *immediate mode* display. PEX support for GL is being worked on by DEC.

In summary:

- PEX is a protocol for 3D graphics and is an extension of the 'X' protocols.

- PEXlib is a C API which generates PEX protocol.

- PEX Sample Implementation (SI) is a PHIGS library, implemented by Sun with code from Tektronix. It is probably only an interim implementation until PEX is fully specified.

PHIGS and PHIGS+ are ISO standard specifications, whereas GL and OpenGL are at present *de facto* standards.

---

[17] Discussed in Chapter 16.

Graphics Program-to-Program

Computer Graphics Metafile (CGM): CGM was an ISO attempt to describe 2D pictures for exchange purposes between unlike systems. It is not as comprehensive as most users would like and is not very widely used. There are other formats used to interchange pictures such as the CALCOMP plotter formats but there is no comprehensive standard yet available.

Initial Graphics Exchange Specification (IGES): IGES is a standard specification for the exchange of graphical data between unlike systems and programs, particularly CAD/CAM. IGES has shortcomings of its own but also suffers from weak implementations by some CAD vendors resulting in erroneous data exchange in many cases.

Standard for the Exchange of Product Model Data (STEP): This is the unofficial name for an ISO initiative to tighten up previous data exchange 'standards', such as IGES. It is of necessity quite rigorous and complex and beyond the scope of this book.[18]

Standards Summary

The status of standards in graphics has a parallel in the networking world where OSI is the *de jure* standard but TCP/IP is the *de facto* standard. There are far more users of TCP/IP than of OSI.

A summary of graphics standards and their relationships is shown in Figure 59, followed by a comparison of GL and PHIGS.

The main contenders for the 'best' graphics standard are X/PEX and OpenGL - although both have their supporters and denigrators. Some judgement may be made from a list of their capabilities and limitations when compared with an organization's requirements.

- *GL*
  - simple to use
  - many applications are written using GL
  - supported by the major manufacturers
  - moving towards being a *de facto* standard via the OpenGL group
  - only works for 3D adapters
  - device independence is difficult to achieve.

- *PEX*
  - device independent

---

[18] See Hans Gunter Siebert, 'STEP Inches Toward Reality', *CADENCE*, Vol. 2 No. 1, February 1993.

- supported by the major manufacturers
- implements PHIGS with immediate mode
- good for distributed applications.

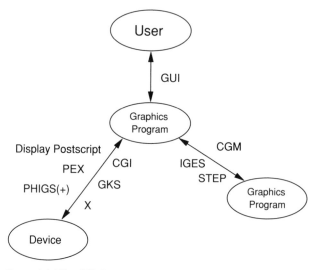

Source: Iain Elliot, IBM Germany

Figure 59. *Summary of Graphics Standards*

13.6 CASE

Computer aided software engineering (CASE) tools are employed in the design, implementation and maintenance of applications. These tools do not simply speed up labour-intensive parts of application development but employ proven development methodologies and project management techniques. Vendors offering CASE tools are unlikely to have developed them in the same way, giving the old 'shall we speak Esperanto?' problem again. The answer as always is standards. What are the emerging CASE standards?

CDIF

The increase in the number of people using CASE tools, together with the growing number of CASE tools, has given rise to the need to exchange data between tools. The standard aimed at this problem is called *CASE Data Interchange Format* or CDIF. It is being developed by an EIA committee called the CDIF Technical Committee. CDIF is a set of standards that define a neutral CASE interchange format to facilitate the exchange of data between unlike CASE tools. The standard includes descriptions, plus placement and details of text and graphics elements such as process logic and dataflow diagrams.

The CDIF committee is attempting to avoid a lowest common denominator approach by catering for functionally rich CASE environments. The work is only at the prototype stage but eventually aims to deliver an abstract information model to feed IRDS (see below) and PCTE.

IRDS

The Information Resource Dictionary System (IRDS) is an entity-relationship model which defines :

- the contents of a standard repository
- the way information is logically stored in the repository
- the methods by which CASE tools should access this information.

The design and physical implementation of the IRDS is not specified by the model.

ECMA Reference Model

An attempt was made by ECMA[19] to produce a standard environment into which development tools could be 'plugged'. The *Portable Common Tools Environment* (PCTE) is the ECMA initiative to develop a reference model for *software engineering environments* (SEEs). A SEE is 'a system which provides automated support of the engineering of software systems and the management of the software process'.[20]

A SEE essentially needs to provide information about;

- the software under development
- project resources
- organization policy, standards and guidelines.

The ECMA SEE environment is divided into functional elements called *services* as follows:

1. object management services
2. process management services
3. communication services
4. user interface services

---

[19] European Computer Manufacturers' Association.

[20] *Reference Model for Frameworks of Software Engineering Environments*, Technical Report ECMA TR/55.

5. tools

6. policy enforcement services

7. framework administration and configuration services.

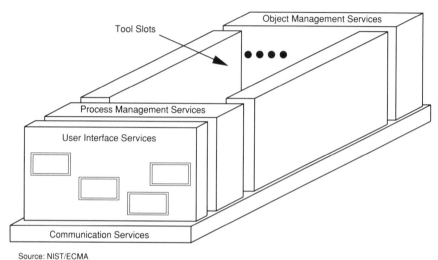

Source: NIST/ECMA

Figure 60. *ECMA SEE CASE Environment*

The framework can be modified by what are called ***environment adapters*** to produce a specific environment. One major aim of the ECMA Reference Model is 'to be suitable to describe, compare and contrast existing and proposed environment frameworks'.[21]

The standard CASE framework, as outlined by the ECMA model, is reproduced in Figure 60.

Portable Common Tools Environment (PCTE)

PCTE was an ECMA initiative adopted and enhanced by ECMA and generally accepted as a *de facto* standard. ISO are also looking at PCTE as a possible *de jure* standard.

---

[21] ibid.

The main features of PCTE are its data integration, data modelling and data sharing across different CASE tools. It deals with data and other entities with object oriented methodologies and has its own Object Management System (OMS).

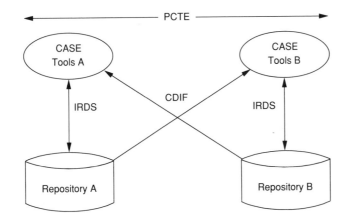

Figure 61. *Relationships of CASE Standards*

A summary of PCTE, CDIF and IRDS and their relationships is shown in Figure 61.

Other CASE Standards

Other standardization efforts relevant to CASE are:

- CASE Tool Integration Models (CTIM) - ANSI X3H6
- Reference Model for CASE Tool Interconnections[22]
- OSF/Motif and X Windows
- RDA/DRDA
- OSF/1 and System V.4
- POSIX 1003.x
- XPG3/XPG4
- OSF DCE.

---

[22] IEEE P-1175.

Since the standardization of *object oriented* technologies and *CASE* environments is at an early stage, the decision is really up to the purchaser as to which way he should go in these areas. The 1 March 1992 issue of *Datamation*[23] carried a guide to 'A World of CASE Tools'. In the introduction the author stated, 'To make the task of investigating CASE a little easier, we've compiled ... a resource list of more than 400 CASE products and the operating systems on which they run'! In terms of CASE standardization, this comment speaks for itself.

In Europe, 11 CASE tools and methodology vendors share 78% of the market, the other 22% being split between many other vendors. No one vendor has more than 15% of the market, making it difficult to choose one as a *de facto* standard.[24]

Because of the apparent difficulty in assessing single-platform CASE tools and methodologies, we seem a long way from distributed, or client/server, CASE. The increase in client/server computing though may render such CASE a necessity. There is a forward-looking article about client/server CASE in the *Datamation* edition quoted above, and called 'The Race for Client/Server CASE'.

13.7 Object Orientation

In Section 8.2.4 we identified two key areas for standardization in object oriented environments:

- a standard mechanism for messaging between objects
- a standard object oriented database API.

Rather than tackling these issues in isolation the Object Management Group (OMG) decided to develop an architecture for object management. It published this towards the end of 1990 in its *Object Management Architecture Guide*. It defined object oriented systems and established a framework for the detailed standards the Group planned to produce in the future.

The first area addressed by the architecture was a messaging mechanism, referred to as an Object Request Broker (ORB). The OMG requested submissions from manufacturers in a process rather like the OSF's Request for Technology where vendors submit their products for endorsement. A number of companies responded, including HP, DEC, Sun and NCR. The OMG's approach was to synthesize the responses rather than select a single product.

The resulting standard is set out in the Common Object Request Broker Architecture and Specification (CORBA). CORBA is a specification which defines

---

[23] Special CASE edition.

[24] *Computing*, 13 August 1992, quoting an Ovum report.

Object Request Broker implementations, services and interfaces. It has been endorsed by X/Open, the OSF and UI.

The second area we identified as requiring standardization was that of an object oriented database API. To date this has not been successfully resolved. Indeed the industry is still questioning whether there is the need for a stand-alone object oriented database or whether it should be integrated into existing relational database management systems.

This is clearly an area that needs resolution if a standard approach to object orientation is to be developed.

13.8 Conclusions

The general issue of portability is addressed by standards and specifications from various bodies. They are defined interfaces (APIs) between the application program and resources on the system to which access is required. The major bodies involved are X/Open, IEEE POSIX and ISO, covering many areas of portability. Your vendor should understand what these bodies offer and be implementing them in his products if he seeks true portability.

For example, in the case of graphics portability, you will need to ascertain at least three things for each program or supplier you may wish to deal with:

1. To which graphics API is the application written?

2. Does your operating systems supplier support that API?

3. Does the supplier support that API at the level used by the application program?

A supplier who can deliver and support most of these APIs libraries is probably the best bet for 'future-proofing' your graphics application development or purchases.

In many other areas the products delivered by vendors have a proprietary flavour. As examples, consider the 4GLs offered by the RDB vendors we have discussed. They are in the main incompatible and have many unique features which are hardly addressed by the standards bodies, which often lag market needs. It appears to be a case of the old adage 'You pays your money and you takes your choice'.

Chapter 14 User Interfaces

Mirror mirror on the wall, who is the fairest of them all?[1]

Although today Unix, proprietary and other systems have their own presentation styles, moves are afoot to standardize them. They are so different that establishing standards based on any one, or combination, of them is an impossible task. Such interfaces were designed at the whim of the programmer or specifier and the vehicle for interacting with the application was nearly always the keyboard.

The two basic screen types in operation today are:

- character-based screens utilizing dot matrix light spots to display characters. Displaying anything other than characters can be difficult, involving the creation of non-standard characters used in combination to form what is apparently graphical output.

- graphics capable or 'all points addressable' (APA) displays which are free of the drawbacks afflicting character terminals. User interfaces on such displays are referred to as Graphical User Interfaces or GUIs.

The development of standard user interfaces is attributable to sources not directly concerned with mainframe and proprietary computer systems, as we will see in the next section.

It is important to understand at the outset that a 'user interface' is not only a screen design but also a method of interacting with applications. The combination is often referred to as 'look and feel'. 'Look' refers to the appearance of an application screen to a user, whereas 'feel' refers to the way the user interacts with the screen and hence the underlying application. In an open distributed environment, a user at a workstation may wish to access applications running not only on his/her own system but on other systems in the network. Traditional user interfaces were not designed to do this, nor did the underlying software allow it.

---

[1] From *Snow White*.

14.1 Graphical User Interfaces (GUIs)

14.1.1 Why GUIs?

There are several reasons for the emergence and popularity of GUIs, not least the old saying that a picture is worth a thousand words:

- Pictures and symbols are better at conveying information than words - witness the road and hazard signs recognized internationally. They also transcend language barriers.

- Users also often need information from more than one source simultaneously, the so called 'messy desk' which needs multiple displays on the same screen. This led to the idea of separate viewing *windows* on a screen.

- Users do not like typing.

In 1990, tests[2] showed that users in a GUI environment produced 58% more correct work than those working in a character interface environment. The GUI users also suffered less fatigue and could work longer at a given level of effort.

GUIs spawned the idea of *WIMPs* as a means of interacting with the system. WIMPs stands for Windows, Icons,[3] Mice, and Pop-up (or Pull-down) menus. System interaction is achieved by pointing at icons with an arrow shaped cursor. The cursor is driven and positioned by the mouse device, a small box with a freely moving ball underneath and activated by mouse buttons. Pop-up menus are chosen via the pointer from a series of options around the main GUI screen. For example, selecting 'edit' will generate a menu of edit options overlaid on the screen. After selecting an option from the new menu, the menu can be closed and disappears from the screen.

14.1.2 Origins of GUIs

GUIs are relatively new in information technology, belonging to the PC generation. In Figure 62 we illustrate the genealogy of the better-known GUIs.[4]

---

[2] By Temple, Barker & Sloane, Inc., co-sponsored by Microsoft.

[3] Scalable pictures/symbols.

[4] For a biblical discourse on the origins of GUIs, with one GUI begetting another, see Frank Hayes and Nick Baran, 'A Guide to GUIs', *BYTE*, July 1989.

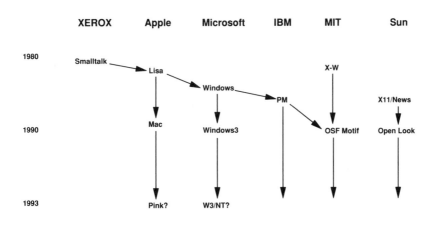

Legend: X-W X Windows, W3 Windows 3.X

Figure 62. *GUI Family Tree*

The reality of GUIs in vogue are that they all look very much the same, having, as we saw, a common ancestry. They also 'feel' the same in operation to the user so comparing one with the other at a gross level achieves nothing. Where they do differ is in:

- the underlying windowing technology
- the APIs to use them
- their availability on different vendors' systems
- their ability to distribute the user interface.

The most popular GUIs in use today, with the operating systems they access, are as follows:

- Presentation Manager (OS/2)
- Microsoft Windows (DOS and latterly NT)
- OSF/Motif (OSF/1, SVR4 and other vendor platforms, although X and Motif can be used with almost any operating system).
- OpenLook (SunOS and SVR4).

The underlying structure of these GUIs is illustrated in Figure 63.

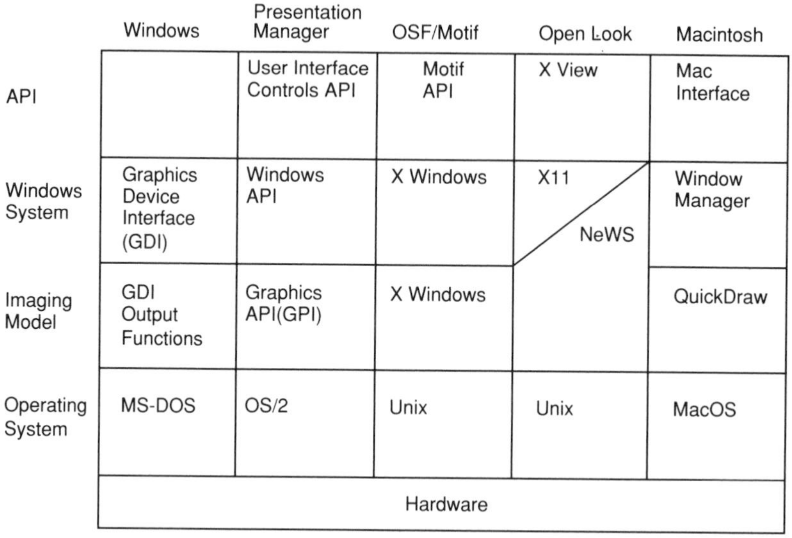

	Windows	Presentation Manager	OSF/Motif	Open Look	Macintosh
API		User Interface Controls API	Motif API	X View	Mac Interface
Windows System	Graphics Device Interface (GDI)	Windows API	X Windows	X11 / NeWS	Window Manager
Imaging Model	GDI Output Functions	Graphics API(GPI)	X Windows		QuickDraw
Operating System	MS-DOS	OS/2	Unix	Unix	MacOS
	Hardware				

Source: *BYTE* Magazine

Figure 63. *Structure of Popular GUIs. Although they may look and feel the same, the underlying windowing elements are different. This is the place to look for openness or standards.*

14.1.3 OSF/Motif

OSF/Motif is a specification and an implementation of a GUI and is based on the Common User Access (CUA) specification of IBM's SAA, and Windows-like specifications. Motif seeks the following advantages for users in its design philosophy:

- Portability of the application, via a single API, and of the user's skill, by a single style guide using a single API,[5] across all platforms supporting OSF/Motif.

- Conformance to standards to participate in an OSE. Motif is based on X Windows and complies with the Inter Client Communications Conventions Manual (ICCCM).

- Provision of a development environment via:
    - a user interface toolkit of high-level objects built on the lower-level X Windows 'intrinsics' or code

---

[5] Based on DEC's DECwindows technology.

- a User Interface Language (UIL), a specification for separately describing the visual aspects of a user interface
- a window manager which allows users to move, resize and generally manipulate windows linked to application across a network.

- Adaptability to other languages by complying with the XPG3/XPG4 standards for National Language Support (NLS).
- Support from the IT industry. Motif is supported by virtually all computer hardware and software vendors.

We anticipate Motif will be the generally accepted GUI for the Unix environment and other operating systems supporting 'X'. This is increasingly likely since COSE[6] includes it as part of its desktop environment.

14.1.4 OpenLook

OpenLook is a GUI specification developed by AT&T and Sun Microsystems and is independent of any particular implementation. OpenLook comprises:

- a style guide
- development toolkits
    - NeWS development environment (NDE), a Sun development to support a windowing system
    - XView, again from Sun, builds the GUI on top of the low-level Xlib calls of the X Windows system
    - Xt+, a toolkit built on the X Intrinsics[7]

OpenLook has more proprietary elements than OSF/Motif but is used extensively on Sun platforms.

Not all GUIs need an APA screen, however, as we will see in the next section.

14.1.5 AlphaWindow

Most GUIs operate by detecting screen interaction, usually via a mouse or other pointing device, at various positions. The GUI also associates actions with these *events* as they are called. With normal character-based screens, such positional sensitivity is not possible and interaction with an application is via the keyboard. Such screens are not designed to cater for windowing as outlined in section 16.6.

---

[6] See section 10.5.

[7] Higher level than base Xlib calls - see Section 16.6.

Attempts to widen the functions of character terminals have included:

- Software-only windowing, but these had poor performance, both in windowing and systems functions.

- Specific 'firmware' resident in a terminal to offload display work from the system. Although these addressed some of the drawbacks of the software option above, they were non-standard, vendor-specific and often of limited function.

As before, the solution to this diversity was to be found in the development of a standard for character screen windowing.

In the middle of 1990, Dataquest invited terminal and software vendors to a meeting to discuss the formation of a consortium on this topic. A second meeting six months later saw the formation of the ***Display Industry Association (DIA).*** The DIA mission was to represent users of character-based applications[8] with a charter 'to cause the creation of and promulgate hardware and software standards for display terminals'.

AlphaWindow Features

The DIA attempted to define standards for character windowing which would not require changes to existing applications. The aim was to offer, via software and terminal hardware, a windowing GUI lying somewhere between the standard terminal and the full GUIs in sophistication. The DIA standard covers five elements or specification groups to which terminals may be built:

- *windowing* - window sizing and placement via a window manager, mandatory for any AlphaWindow terminal

- *mouse support* - for 'mouse aware' programs to obtain mouse position and movement information

- *character oriented decorations* - to support scroll bars, buttons and other visual features common to GUIs today

- *communications* - to support networked windowing

- *extensions* via a communications mechanism which provides reliable flow control.

Although a defined standard, AlphaWindow does not preclude vendors differentiating their terminal products. Ways of achieving this might include increasing the number of windowed sessions, use of colour or larger screens, high resolution and in the types of pointing devices supplied. In addition, the DIA has defined an

---

[8] Santa Cruz Operation (SCO) estimates that about 80% of existing applications are character-based. In addition, Dataquest estimates that these applications generate the purchase of over 3 million such terminals each year.

AlphaWindow C program library to enable developers to write or modify applications to exploit the window capabilities defined by the standard.

14.1.6 Unix Shells

Unix shells are command interpreters for Unix (not application) users. A shell prompts the user line by line after each command entered to indicate readiness to accept the next. The three main shells in Unix (with their prompt 'trademarks') are:

- Bourne shell ($)
- C shell (%)
- Korn shell ($)

Although powerful tools for manipulating jobs, utilities and commands, they have little to do with portability and interoperability and are mentioned here for completeness.[9]

14.2 Conclusions

GUIs are the accepted way of interacting with systems, be they Unix, DOS or, increasingly, open proprietary systems. There are many productivity and ease-of-use arguments which make them the ideal means of interacting with applications, especially those on remote systems. They have a similar 'look and feel' in many cases and are all 'intuitive' so that moving from one to another is not a major issue. The differences between these GUIs are not at the visual level but in the lower layers. Some are based on standards, some proprietary and some on a mixture and this is where IT people should be looking to ensure openness.

---

[9] Refer to Appendix A for details of POSIX shell standards work.

Chapter 15 Pragmatic Interoperability

There is no such thing as a conversation. It is an illusion. There are intersecting monologues, that is all.[1]

Interoperability in heterogeneous networks is sometimes called **multi-vendor connectivity** but we will use the term **interoperability** since 'connectivity' suggests little more than the connection of two or more systems by a network.

The following classification of interoperability may be useful to you in deciding what sort of interoperability is needed in your organization:

- Physical connection only - this is essentially useless, even with the *de jure* standards available at this level.
- Simple file transfer (2780, FTP, FTAM and so on). It is perfectly feasible to link systems and applications using these techniques.
- Remote login to a system other than your own.
- Execution of commands on a remote machine without having to login to it.
- Remote file access (NFS, AFS or other RPC-based programs).
- Remote process access (NCS or other RPC-based programs).
- Remote database access (client/server RDBs).
- True distributed database (transparent to user and programmer alike).
- True cooperative processing.
- Totally transparent computing across a managed network of heterogeneous systems (a combination and enhancement of the above environments).

Before reading any further, you should ascertain at which level you think your organization would need to operate to gain the business benefit it wants from

---

[1] Rebecca West, British novelist.

'open systems computing'. You may be waiting anxiously for something you do not need.

Today, many installations are tackling interoperability issues with tactical solutions. In many cases, the wait for formally defined standards is not acceptable.[2]

15.1 LAN Interoperability

The simple fact that there are nearly 50 million PCs in the world today means that any pragmatic approach to interoperability must cater for these - with or without open standards. General LAN interoperability is outlined in Figure 64.

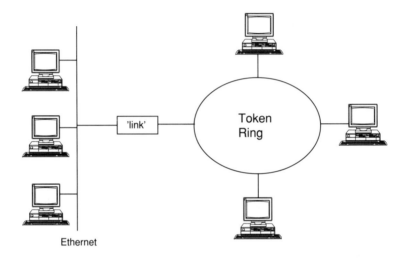

Figure 64. *LAN Interoperability Example*

The following sections outline four ways that LANs can be interconnected and, in many cases, connected to mainframes or minis. The major relevant standards in this area are OSI, Token Ring and Ethernet. *De facto* standard products such as Novell NetWare may also prove important.

---

[2] Remember the 8,000 or so ISO standards.

15.1.1 Bridges

Local area networks (LANs) can be linked together to form an extended network, sometimes giving the impression of a large LAN. The previous individual LANs are then known as subnetworks. When a set of LANs are bridged in this fashion, any workstation can share data with any other on the extended network. The bridges operate at the medium access control (MAC) level 2 in the seven-layer model and can thus join different topology LANs, such as Ethernet and Token Ring.[3] Bridges are transparent to all network-level protocols.

15.1.2 Gateways

Gateways attempt to go one step further than bridges in supporting different protocols and different LAN topologies. They are normally designed as a hardware/software combination to make them more flexible in operation. Their main function is to map the protocols of one system onto those of the other, dissimilar, system at the higher layers of the seven-layer model.

A typical use of a gateway would be to attach a LAN to an IBM SNA mainframe.

15.1.3 Routers

Routers are in essence 'clever' bridges which function one level above the MAC level that bridges use, namely the network-level. They can handle LANs of differing topologies and one or more network protocols. Each network program needs its own program - OSI or TCP/IP.

Routers can do what their name implies and evaluate different routes through which data might be passed. This is very useful if one route is unusable due to a failure somewhere in the network.

Routers can sometimes bend the rules by encapsulating non-routable protocols (for example SNA) within routable protocols (for example TCP/IP) in order to transport them from entry point to exit point. Routers are more selective than bridges and can therefore optimize the use of slower wide area links.

---

[3] As long as they have a common protocol such as TCP/IP or Novell IPX/SPX.

15.1.4 Brouters

A brouter is a hybrid of a router and bridge which performs many of the tasks of both routers and bridges. It will route data with suitable protocols and bridge data which cannot be routed.

Figure 65 summarizes the typical functions afforded by these various interconnection methods.

Figure 65. *LAN Interconnect Summary*				
Capability	*Bridge*	*Router*	*Brouter*	*Gateway*
OSI Level	Data Link (Level 2)	Network (Level 3)	Network (Level 2/3)	Network (Level 7)
Different topologies	Yes	Yes	Yes	Yes
Different protocols	No	No	No	Yes
Routing ability	No	Yes *	Yes *	Yes
Program-mable	No	No	No	Yes

Legend * - yes for routable protocols, no otherwise. SNA is non-routable, for example, as is Netbios.

15.2 Unix to Proprietary

Many Unix workstations installed today are in organizations with a large established IT infrastructure of DEC, IBM and ICL proprietary systems. The question of interoperability between the workstations and the mainframes then arises.

Interoperability between systems with different network architectures can only be achieved by agreeing on a common network protocol. Unix to proprietary links can be made by the Unix system adopting the protocols of the proprietary system. For all intents and purposes, the latter system thinks it is communicating with an identical proprietary system as shown in Figure 66.

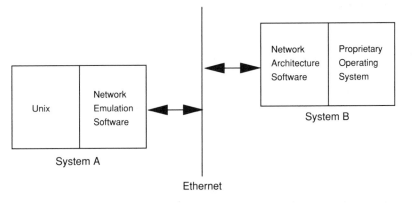

A looks to B like another proprietary node like System B.

Figure 66. *Unix to Proprietary Interoperability*

The kinds of interaction between these systems would normally be of the following types:

- terminal access to the proprietary system from the Unix system[4]
- file transfer
- program-to-program communications
- print serving.

Such products[5] also allow a Unix system to act as a gateway between TCP/IP networks and proprietary networks, for example, linking a Unix TCP/IP network to a DECNet or SNA proprietary network.

15.2.1 Unix-ICL IPA

Boldon James, a UK specialist in Unix, OSI and ICL connectivity, offers interworking facilities between Unix machines and ICL's Information Processing Architecture (IPA). An example of its products for this is IMPART/6000 which runs on the IBM RISC System/6000 with AIX. Similar functions are available for other Unix platforms.

---

[4] Similar to Telnet in TCP/IP.

[5] The description of a product does not constitute an endorsement by the authors or imply uniqueness.

- *Interactive Video* - full screen emulation enabling the AIX user to login to a remote VME system, appearing to it as an ICL terminal.

- *Direct Print* - direct printing from the ICL mainframe on the RISC System/6000.

- *File Transfer Facility* - two-way file transfer.

- *Remote Virtual Console Requester* - access to a remote ICL Unix system via a terminal attached to an AIX system.

- *Remote Virtual Console Server* - allows the above in reverse.

- *Application Data Interchange* - peer-to-peer communication between an AIX program and an ICL VME program.

- *Distributed Application Facility* - allows the building of AIX applications which can participate fully in an ICL Distributed Transaction Service (DTS).

- *Transport Router* - routing between an Ethernet LAN and an X.25 WAN.

15.2.2   Unix-DECnet

Because of the widespread use of VAXes for departmental applications, there is often a need to connect departmental workstations to them. Two products aiding this integration process are described in this section.

KiNet

One product, *KiNet* from Ki Research, allows Unix systems to participate as fully-fledged members of DECnet, MOP (Maintenance Operation Protocol) and LAT (Local Area Transport) Terminal Server Networks.

KiNet provides integration facilities such as file transfer and network programming interface for end users, allowing Unix users to take advantage of their existing DEC network resource as well as the Unix platforms. It provides the following facilities:

- Users can carry on using the DECnet protocol.

- Existing peripherals, such as LAT terminal servers and LAT printer servers, can be used by the Unix system as well as VMS host printer services.

- Immediate integration of Unix systems in the existing DECnet environment.

- Users can take advantage of the security, recovery and other features of their version of Unix.

KiNet consists of the following components which allows Unix systems to join DNA networks:

- DNA (DECnet Phase IV)

- LAT for LAT Terminal Servers

- MOP for downline loading terminal server binary code
- NETwatch for network analysis.

KiNet DNA allows the Unix system to become a 'smart' DECnet end node for:

- remote login (bidirectional)
- file transfer
- mail
- remote batch and print submission
- programming interface
- node maintenance
- X Window client and server support.

The KiNet product resides entirely on the Unix system and does not require additional software on the DEC systems to which it is connected.

TSSnet

TSSnet is an offering from Thursby Software Systems which addresses Unix-DECnet connectivity in a similar fashion to KiNet.[6] It makes a Unix system a fully functional DECnet Phase IV and node whilst maintaining TCP/IP coexistence with other systems.

By making use of DEC's Data Access Protocols (DAP), TSSnet offers a fast and comprehensive file transfer utility plus the following:

- File utility commands allowing for bidirectional, single or multiple file manipulation between remote and local nodes.
- A range of commands to exploit Unix and VMS file transfer capabilities via TSSnet.
- Support for VMS file name conventions and almost all VMS file formats. VMS applications have totally transparent access to Unix files.
- Ability to access both DECnet and LAT print services as if the Unix system were itself a VAX.

TSSnet also offers support for DECwindows and X Windows plus 'xgate', a gateway between an X Window server and DECwindows clients:

- X Window implementations that currently only support TCP/IP can be easily extended to support DECnet. This provides access to all the new DECwindows server and client routines residing on the VAX/VMS system.
- TSSnet also provides required DECwindows and fonts for X Window servers.

---

[6] We do not intend to compare the two products, but simply provide an overview.

Network terminal support is provided under both CTERM and LAT protocols, allowing for multiple inbound and outbound terminal sessions over both local and wide area networks:

- Using familiar mail commands, whether the mail originates from a Unix or VMS system.

- Taking into account the differences in mail systems.

TSSnet provides both LAT host and terminal services for a Unix system.

- LAT services.

- The Unix system can serve as a LAT host and a LAT terminal server on the network.

- TSSnet provides a LAT to TCP/IP Gateway Service. A LAT terminal can login to any Unix system running TCP/IP through a gateway on the Unix system.

- LAT users can offer their own applications as LAT services allowing direct access to them from LAT terminal servers.

- The Unix system is provided with direct access to LAT-based print resources on the network.

TSSnet also offers a set of network management utilities.

15.2.3 Unix-SNA

Systems Network Architecture (SNA) is what it says - an architecture. The IBM implementation of that architecture is often called SNA as well but is actually a set of software products and APIs running across the ES/9000, AS/400 and PS/2 platforms. SNA functions form part of the SAA architecture which spans these platforms.

AIX V3, IBM's version of Unix for the RISC System/6000, implements SNA functions to allow a RISC System/6000 to operate in an SNA environment. It should be noted here that other Unix vendors also offer SNA connection functions on their platforms.

IBM's SNA Services/6000 licensed program allows a RISC System/6000 application:

- to communicate with a host application. An example is connection to CICS[7] applications using LU 6.2[8] over a Token Ring or SDLC network. This is

---

[7] Customer Information Control System.

[8] Logical Unit 6.2, an SNA protocol for program-to-program communication.

essentially an implementation of program-to-program communications or interprocess communication (IPC).

- to connect, via a variety of data link topologies, to non-host applications on AS/400, other RISC System/6000s or PS/2s. Again the 'IPC' mechanism is LU 6.2.

- to use other SNA services and protocols.

There are related AIX products which allow RISC System/6000s to emulate 3270 terminals and conduct multiple sessions with host system applications.

15.2.4 Unix-PCs

All the proprietary-based architectures we have mentioned so far are usually, though not exclusively, based on mainframe or mid-range computers. Hence the move to put applications onto Unix machines, which are usually much smaller, is referred to as downsizing. However, there are nearly 50 million PCs in the world and many will need to move from being stand-alone machines to being networked into a wider system. This may be just so they can interoperate with the other systems on the network. It may be so that applications currently running on them may be migrated to larger machines - which might be termed upsizing.

Linking PCs to Unix-based machines is very popular for upsizing and there are a variety of methods of doing this. All require additional software on top of DOS, Windows or OS/2. The choice of methods depends on the degree of function and of interoperability required but two classifications of PC interoperability emerge:

- At the simplest level a PC can act as a terminal connected to the Unix system. Depending on how this is done the PC may emulate an ASCII (character) terminal or an X station (graphics) terminal. The PC can still switch out of this emulation mode and run as a normal PC.

- If the PCs are linked together on a LAN then it is possible to use the Unix machine as a file server for the PCs. In other words the Unix machine allocates a portion of its disk to DOS or OS/2 files and acts as a server to a connected network of PCs. Depending on the function required and the choice of networking protocol this can be done in a variety of ways.

X-Terminal Emulation for PCs

Several products are available to turn a DOS PC into an X Windows display terminal or even a simple ASCII terminal like a VT100. These emulation products allow the PC user to access Unix applications on another machine.

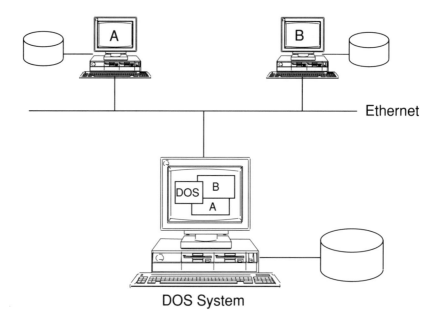

DOS System

Figure 67. *Unix-PC Interoperability*

We outline below some of the X-Terminal emulation products:

- PC Xsight (Locus Computing), sometimes called X on DOS. It runs on TCP/IP-based Token Ring or Ethernet networks and allows PC users to access multiple X-based Unix applications while maintaining access to the DOS applications.

- XVision (Visionware) is a Microsoft Windows 3.x-based display server. It supports i386/i486 systems in displaying X-based applications alongside local DOS programs, with the ability to cut and paste between DOS and X application windows. XVision can use Microsoft Windows or the standard X Windows manager to manage client applications.

- PC-XView (Spectragraphics) is a DOS application providing X-Terminal emulation and support for window managers such as OSF/Motif and OpenLook.

- X11/AT (Integrated Inference Machines) allows concurrent access to remote X applications and local Microsoft Windows (3.0) applications with a cut and paste facility between them. It too supports OSF/Motif and OpenLook.

- DESQview/X (Quarterdeck Office Systems) makes DOS into a multi-tasking systems for all Intel-compatible processors, allowing multiple applications to appear simultaneously in a number of windows. It also permits the use of the screen by Unix X Windows clients and supports OSF/Motif and OpenLook.

- HCL-eXceed (Hummingbird) turns PCs and PS/2s into X-Terminals by providing X server function on the DOS machine and X Window client support on Unix hosts. DOS and Microsoft Windows users can access DOS facilities as well as applications (including graphics) on Unix hosts via separate windows on the PC screen.

Server Connections for PCs

Another reason for interest in PC-Unix connections is access to many of the more desirable resources available on Unix systems. The main resources which PC users would like to share are files, printers and applications. Some of the resource-sharing products available to PC users are:

- TCP/IP for DOS. This is the basic protocol needed to implement resource-sharing and is available from a number of vendors, but standard TCP/IP functions can also be used.
- PC-NFS (Sun Microsystems) allows DOS PCs to share files on non-PC systems which support NFS, for example, Unix systems and some mainframes. It is basically a DOS version of NFS and provides many of the functions of NFS, such as file and record locking and the Network Information Service (NIS).[9]
- Netware NFS (Novell), a Netware 3.11 option that supports NFS filesharing, print queue support and file/record locking. It also allows the mapping of Unix files into 'namespaces' such as OS/2, DOS and Apple Macintosh.

A number of major vendors such as DEC and IBM offer their own (or badged) versions of similar resource-sharing products for DOS, often with extensions like APIs for DOS applications.

The drive to integrate PCs into the corporate network has produced some very interesting interoperability products. For example, there exist SQL connect products which enable PC applications to make SQL calls to an SQL database on the network. The SQL database is then the server to a PC client. An example might be a spreadsheet of monthly sales data with a cell that requires the sales figures from a particular business area. The accountant puts an SQL call into that cell requesting the specific piece of information from the sales figures database held on another machine. Each time the spreadsheet is 'run' the cell is updated directly from the sales database.

The size of the PC market, and the levels of interoperability now demanded, mean that suppliers are constantly providing more exciting PC interoperability products. Indeed, developments seem to be limited only by the imagination of the

---

[9] Previously known as Yellow Pages or YP.

user. Furthermore, the unit cost of such products is remarkably low and hence the case can often be made for them, even with a relatively small business benefit.

15.2.5 Unix-Macintosh

Apple machines can run their own version of Unix, A/UX, but for System 7 users, there are a variety of tools to allow access to other Unix environments in a similar way to the PCs discussed above.

15.3 Proprietary to Proprietary

The separate development of networking architectures has compounded the problem of heterogeneous interoperability. Because many organizations had large investments in SNA, DNA and other proprietary architectures and OSI was relatively immature, there had to be some way of accommodating these existing architectures.

Some approaches to the problems of interoperability are:

- Everyone adopts SNA (or DNA or IPA or ...).
- Convert the protocols of one architecture to the semantic equivalents of another.
- Envelope the protocols of one system inside those of another which treats them simply as data.
- Implement layers of one architecture in another architecture, for example, part of the SNA stack in DNA or OSI in SNA. This is often the pragmatic approach used today.

The last method is illustrated in Figure 68.

While mapping, enveloping or emulating protocols may offer the interoperability functions required, there are often issues like the following to be taken into account:

- performance[10]
- network management
- problem determination
- software change management.

---

[10] A ratio of 1:4 was observed by one of the authors in the time taken to transfer a file from SNA to SNA in native mode, and SNA to another architecture via protocol mapping.

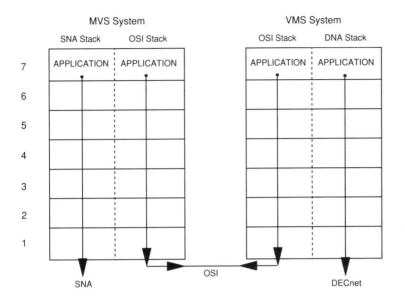

Figure 68. *Pragmatic Interoperability*

15.3.1 DECnet/SNA

IBM MVS/VM-DECnet Connectivity

Interlink Computer Sciences, Inc. markets solutions for connecting IBM System/370 or 390 processors and SNA networks to Digital DECnet networks.

The Interlink SNS/SNA Gateway addresses DECnet-SNA connectivity requirements including the following:

- cross-system bidirectional file transfer
- database extract and distributed database access
- peripheral device sharing
- electronic mail exchange
- program-to-program communications (LU 6.2 and Digital Task-to-Task)
- centralized data storage
- record-level access to IBM sequential data
- bidirectional full-screen terminal emulation
- centralized network management of DECnet networks and NetView
- interconnect remote DECnet networks across an SNA Backbone
- back-up of DEC system disk files to IBM tape drives

The IBM 3172 provides a means of attaching a LAN to a 370/390 channel, which allows the connection to DECnet.

DECnet-SNA from DEC

The DECnet SNA-Gateway[11] supports communication between VAX nodes and MVS hosts. With the exception of the MicroVAX, where the gateway is a pure software implementation, the DECnet SNA-Gateway consists of a gateway processor plus several software components (gateway management, protocol conversion, server modules). It allows users to exchange information bidirectionally and to share resources between the DECnet and the IBM SNA environments. In essence, it makes any VAX or PDP in the network look like an SNA node to IBM SNA nodes.

Architecturally the DECnet/SNA Gateway looks like a DECnet Phase IV node to DECnet and a PU Type 2 to SNA. It connects directly to an E-LAN and provides SNA connectivity to every other Phase IV node in the network which installs the necessary Gateway management and access routines. Functionally it makes no difference whether these nodes are physically connected to the E-LAN or logically connected through either the DECnet router communication server or the host routing facility.

The following set of gateway access routines, programming interfaces, and facilities can be installed 'on top' of the Gateway:

- Remote Job Entry (RJE)
- 3270 Terminal Emulation (3270TE)
- Distributed Host Command Facility (DHCF)
- Data Transfer Facility (DTF)
- Printer Emulation (PrE)
- Application programming interface (API)
- APPC/LU 6.2 Interface
- 3270 Data Stream Programming Interface
- DISOSS Document Exchange Facility (DDXF)
- EDE with DISOSS
- VAX-IBM Data Access (VIDA).

You should bear in mind that emulation of SNA functionality does not necessarily bring the performance and management benefits of a native implementation. This applies to other emulations too.

---

[11] Announced in 1982.

15.3.2 Tactical Network 'Standards'

There are networking products from various sources which enable certain levels of interoperability, for example:

- Novell Netware
- Banyan Vines
- LAN Manager and LM/X
- Appletalk

However, they offer interoperability at a level lower than the one we discuss in this book and we do not intend to cover them. These are essentially network applications based on mainly proprietary layers at level 3 in the OSI Basic Reference Model. Incidentally, we do not cover Windows/NT in this book either, the reason being that it does not conform to any of the standards outlined in it. If you remember the arguments in Chapter 2 which accompanied Figure 1, you will understand why. Although NT has POSIX 1003.1 compliance it does not seek to match the POSIX 1003.2, 1003.4, XPG3 or X Windows standards and specifications, which severely limits the portability and interoperability of applications.

We will conclude this chapter with a look at two unique systems which have attracted a large following over the last twenty years - PICK and MUMPS. Initially totally proprietary, they have taken steps to join the OSE community.

15.3.3 PICK

The PICK operating system[12] was aimed at data oriented environments and was never a full-function operating system. It is over 25 years old and runs on over 260,000 installed CPUs, including PCs;[13] the value of the PICK market was expected to reach $3 billion in 1992.[14]

PICK is not what one would normally expect of an operating system since it has no graphics or communications abilities and is in essence a database machine for end users. The PICK database organization and access tools account for its continued and growing popularity. The main strengths of PICK can be summarized as follows:

---

[12] Designed by Dick Pick, the founder of PICK Systems, along with Don Nelson, and initially implemented on an IBM S/360.

[13] Datapro Research 1991.

[14] InfoCorp Inc.

- It has a built-in relational database capability based on a four-dimensional way of representing the data. The data is not stored in conventional relational tables with fixed relationships but in a form that can be envisaged by an end user. The database model in PICK makes extensive use of data dictionaries where data is described and located by metadata in the form of files, items, values and attributes.

- PICK programs and the database can be logically separate. There are variable length fields which can be shortened or lengthened without having to reload/reorganize the database. PICK simply changes *attributes* which describe the data, rather than moving the data around.

- It has a powerful *ad hoc* report generator called Access which boasts an English-like language.

- PICK has implemented a single-level storage view of data with integrated database and query (rather like AS/400).

- PICK can appear as a relational database but generally can outperform 'true' relational databases.

There are varieties of PICK, some running in native mode on certain hardware platforms, others under an operating system such as DOS. Names like Evolution, Sequel, UniVerse, Reality, Revelation and Ultimate may not sound like operating systems but they are in fact variants of PICK.

How could PICK (and its variants) possibly have a place in the OSE without any communications and with a proprietary database and query language? The answer was to remove certain operating systems functions from PICK and rely on another operating system to host PICK as an application in its own right. The applications under PICK were no concern of the mother operating system; neither was the interface between PICK and its applications.

PICK Systems introduced a version of PICK that ran under IBM's AIX and called it Blue PICK. Subsequent versions, also with a colour associated, ran on other versions of Unix such as Ultrix. In the meantime, clones of PICK moved towards Unix to take advantage of the respected position of Unix in the OSE. Sandra Grant of Gartner recently concluded 'The marriage of Pick and Unix has rejuvenated the Pick market'. PICK users can take advantage of the graphics and communications features of Unix and Unix users have access to the 4,000 or so PICK business applications.

PICK is no longer considered by most people as a viable open operating system but its database, *ad hoc* query and reporting facilities make it worthy of consideration as a Unix database application.

15.3.4 MUMPS

MUMPS is a versatile programming system developed as the Massachusetts General Hospital Utility Multi-Programming System. Since its development in the late 1960s, the MUMPS language has spread throughout the medical community and is now also used in general financial management, process control, order entry, and many other areas of information processing. It is now an ANSI standard with implementations on many platforms, such as DEC PDP11 (Digital Standard MUMPS) and IBM VM Systems (MUMPS/VM). MUMPS is also hosted by Unix systems.

MUMPS basically comprises:

- a high-level programming language (MUMPS language)
- a comprehensive database management facility
- a flexible operating system
- an I/O supervisor.

Each one of these plays a key role in the execution of a MUMPS program. The MUMPS language is procedural (like Fortran and Cobol, for example), and it includes capabilities that make it useful for the development of conversational applications, rather like OLTP. One major difference is that the language is interpretive and not compiled into executable modules as Fortran and Cobol are, for instance.

The MUMPS system, like the PICK system, is basically self-contained and proprietary and its ability to run under the Unix operating system offers it similar advantages to those available to PICK under Unix.

The main purpose of the MUMPS operating system element is to act as an interface between the MUMPS application and the host operating system. Recently, MUMPS has acquired its own version of program-to-program communication which reduces its reliance on Unix and possibly renders it closed.

15.4 Conclusions

Many organizations are developing interoperability solutions using their own code and hardware and software from vendors. This is perfectly legitimate. It can be a good solution for an individual organization but a mix and match method can become a tangle as new connections are made to solve problems in earlier connections. The standards for physical interoperability (layers 1, 2 and 3 of the seven-layer model) are quite mature. However, the standards for interoperability at higher levels are emerging slowly.

A 'big bang' approach, going from existing pragmatic solutions to a totally standards-based environment, is not feasible. The gradual migration to standards-conformant products seems the way to go as long as they fit the needs of the business. Unless you code your own applications, then the onus is on the vendors to show allegiance to relevant standards affecting their products. Even in this mode, a piecemeal approach using a multitude of vendors to construct your own standards-based systems can bring problems. Most organizations do not have the resources to resolve these issues. They become reliant on consultants and vendors to help them integrate the products. The number of organizations requiring assistance makes one wonder if creating a complex environment, and then benefiting from the difficulty of resolving it, is the hidden agenda of some vendors.

There can be only one sensible approach. To work with vendors and consultants wherever necessary but to ensure that they take responsibility firstly, for the success of the project and secondly, for the training of staff so next time, outsiders may not be required.

Chapter 16 Standards for Interoperability

Ideal conversation must be an exchange of thought, and not
  ... , an eloquent exhibition of oratory or wit.[1]

This chapter is not a technical exposition on the various implementations of network and interoperability standards - there are many very good books written by people who know far more than we do about the detail. This chapter is written for people who know less than we do, and less is not enough if they intend to embrace open systems as a strategy.

It aims to give an overview to complement the concepts, architectures and standards discussed previously, particularly in the area of distributed computing. It will also put the implementations in the context of the all-pervasive seven-layer model.

In our discussion in Section 8.2.4 concerning where standards are needed, we listed distributed computing in heterogeneous and the management of heterogeneous networks. They are discussed in this chapter, but also see Chapter 18.

16.1 Security

In Chapter 8, we examined the need for security and discussed the key concepts. Security is often thought of in terms of passwords and database access on a single system. It is wider than that, however, since open heterogeneous networks of systems add another dimension to the security issue.[2] Although security standards

---

[1] Emily Post, US writer.

[2] Fink's Fifth Law: 'The complexity of the system is proportional to the square of its components'.

are complex, we will review them briefly here in keeping with our philosophy of 'reality'.

16.1.1 ISO Security Model

ISO/IEC Joint Technical Committee (SC21) is charged with[3] providing an overview of security-related work, ensuring coherence of other security-related work and producing documents that can act as a 'roadmap' for other security work inside and outside SC21. It was recognized that there was need for security elements in the OSI Basic Reference Model (BRM) and such a standard[4] was published in 1989 as an 'architectural document'. The standard:

- provides a general description of security services and related mechanisms.

- defines where in the BRM such services and mechanisms might fit.

The SC21 work, although focusing on the OSI BRM, recognizes that 'wherever possible, the broader Open Systems perspective is considered ... whether or not this is possible will not be apparent for some time ...'.[5] This means in reality that it is not possible today to assess whether a vendor's security mechanism matches the ISO model. However, one aspect of the security which holds promise for the purchaser is evidence of layering in the security mechanism being considered.

Aspects of Security

In the ISO/IEC document referred to above, there is a detailed discussion of some aspects of security within the scope of the SC21 work. We summarize these now since some of them have a bearing on other standards areas discussed in this book.

- Security Frameworks. This covers the areas of authentication, access control, confidentiality, non-repudiation and key management.

- Security Models. This applies the concepts detailed in the security frameworks to specific areas of open system architectures but concentrates on the OSI Basic Reference Model.

- Security in Data Management. This section is concerned with controls in the following areas:
  - database data
  - Information Resource Dictionary Systems (IRDS)

---

[3] ISO TC97/SC21/N - November 1991 Draft.

[4] ISO 7498-2.

[5] *Ibid.*

- ▪ Remote Database Access (ISO RDA)
- ▪ Database language SQL.

- ● Security in OSI Management Standards. This addresses areas in CMIS (Common Management Information Service) such as audit, alarms and various directory security aspects.

- ● Security in OSI Applications. Applications in this context include security in OSI FTAM, transaction processing, terminal security and presentation cryptography. The models in this area are still quite new.

Other elements of security have been covered elsewhere is this book but are listed again for completeness:

- ● POSIX 1003.6 (see Appendix A)
- ● TCSEC (US Department of Defense Orange Books - see the Glossary)
- ● Kerberos (see Chapter 18)
- ● SVR4 ES (see Chapter 17).

Whether you understand security or not, rest assured you should be looking at it carefully, especially in distributed environments.

16.2 Database

The benefits of mainframe, departmental and desktop computing have brought other, possibly unforeseen problems with them. One of them is consistent and accurate data access across the platforms. In the emerging heterogeneous environments, data access across dissimilar databases, local or remote, is an expectation of many users. However, such distributed databases are not simple to specify or implement without rigorous standards for all to adhere to. It was said in 1991 that 'the state of the art today is that you can drop SQL calls into a network and it is possible they will disappear'.[6] Although progress has been made to date, distributed database technology is still in its infancy.

As in every sphere of interoperability, installations with an immediate need have constructed tailored solutions for themselves. They are still keen that standards for distributed database be developed since *ad hoc* solutions can be costly to create and maintain. In today's RDBs, there are gateways that allow access to remote, dissimilar database systems but they are unique to that RDB. In the true distributed database environment, the same code in *any* RDB will access *any* other database on the network which complies with the relevant standards for distributed database.

---

6 George Zagelow, IBM: see *Datamation*, 15 August 1991.

16.2.1 Why Distributed Database?

There are several reasons why distributed databases are being developed. The most important is that data in most cases is **already** distributed. Many enterprises or companies have more than one single processor or DBMS. Since all these environments contain data, distributed data is a fact. The main objective of a distributed database is to facilitate the access to and management of existing distributed data.

There are a number of ways of providing access to remote and local data by replicating data at locations or sending update 'snapshots' of data to them. These methods involve data currency issues and potential problems of maintenance. Distributed database seems to be the most elegant and efficient solution provided it is rigorously defined and implemented.

There are other important reasons why an organization might require distributed databases.[7]

Organization: Most corporations are logically divided into divisions, departments, projects and so on and often physically distributed as well into plants, factories, warehouses, branch offices. A distributed database may describe more naturally the structure of the organization and local needs for data access. Many companies today are moving from monolithic hierarchies to organizations using matrix management with the ensuing need for access to data across traditional organization boundaries.

Capacity: Another common reason for installing a distributed system is that the requirements of many applications and databases, constantly expanding, exceed the storage capacity of a single site. The cost of several smaller machines is becoming competitive with the cost of large mainframes on which database management systems have traditionally relied. Additionally, the cost of communication links between computers is decreasing while their speed is increasing. Distributed database management systems can provide the single system image required for data processing integrity, similar to a single database management system in a non-distributed environment.

Growth: Once installed, a distributed system may grow more gracefully than a non-distributed system. If it becomes necessary to expand the system because the volume of data has expanded or the volume of processing against it has increased, then it may be easier to add a new site to an existing distributed system than to replace an existing centralized system by a larger one. Such additions may be made in small increments and typically result in less disruption of service to the users than in the non-distributed case.

---

[7] See IBM publication GG24-3200 and references in it.

Local Autonomy: Local autonomy is another aspect of logically or physically distributed systems. Distributing IT systems allows local control and accountability of data. Such autonomy, however, does not isolate that system since distributed database allows those local groups to access data at other locations when necessary.

Availability: The distributed database approach, especially with redundant (replicated) data, can also be used to obtain higher availability. In a distributed environment, the impact of the failure of one machine, or the link to it, is reduced. The localization of failures should enhance availability. Conversely, by replicating data and programs, systems may act as back-up for one another during periods of maintenance or failure.

Cost and Performance: If the application has geographic locality, then distribution may also reduce communication costs and response times by placing the data and the computing power nearer to the users.

It may occur to you to ask why relational databases seem to be the basis of distributed database technology. Simply because a single SQL statement from a client can initiate a complex search on a server site and deliver just the requested data across the network. In the case of navigational databases, such as hierarchical or network, the return of records in the access path to the client is needed, resulting in a much less efficient architecture.[8]

In an article,[9] Chris Date stated what he called the *fundamental principle of distributed database*:

> To the user, a distributed system should
> look exactly like a nondistributed system.

To support this principle, Date lists what he calls 'The twelve rules for Distributed Systems':

1. Local autonomy
2. No reliance on a central site
3. Continuous operation
4. Location independence
5. Fragmentation independence

---

[8] International DB2 Users Group (IDUG) Globe, 'Distributed Relational Database Architecture: What's It All About?', January 1992.

[9] Chris Date, *Relational Database Writings 1985-1989*, Addison-Wesley, 1991, ISBN 0-201-50881-8.

6. Replication independence
7. Distributed query processing
8. Distributed transaction management
9. Hardware independence
10. Operating system independence
11. Network independence
12. DBMS independence.

It was noted that the rules are not necessarily equally important or independent of each other. To have any hope of achieving the functions behind these rules we come once more to our old friends - standards.

16.2.2 Distributed Database Standards

Accepting the requirement for distributed databases and the by now obvious need for standards, we will look briefly at their status. There are two main specifications covering the area of distributed relational database:

- Remote Database Access (RDA), an ISO specification with additions from the SQL Access Group (SAG).
- Distributed Relational Database Architecture (DRDA), an IBM specification.

Before discussing these specifications, we will outline some of the important concepts and terminology associated with distributed databases.

There are five main terms used when talking about distributed database access:

- *Unit of Work* is the work that occurs between the start of a transaction to the commit point or between commit points in large transactions or jobs. It is considered to be an indivisible unit (or processing entity) where all changes made by it are completed or none are.

- *Remote Request* where an application program sends a single SQL statement to be executed on a remote system containing the required data. It is technically a unit of work although it can be a single statement.

- *Remote Unit of Work* (RUW) is an interface implemented on a local systems allowing several SQL statements to be submitted for execution on a remote system against a single database. Remote Unit of Work must ensure that all recoverable resources are changed completely or not at all.

- *Distributed Unit of Work* (DUW) is a set of database access requests which are allowed to access multiple database sites, although it is limited to one database per SQL statement.

- *Distributed Request* is similar to the RUW except that the unit (or transaction) can request access to multiple databases which can be located on
  multiple systems.

The last three of these somewhat esoteric terms are illustrated in Figure 69. Figure
70 shows what they mean in terms of numbers of databases which can be accessed
using each of the types of 'units of work' in a program.

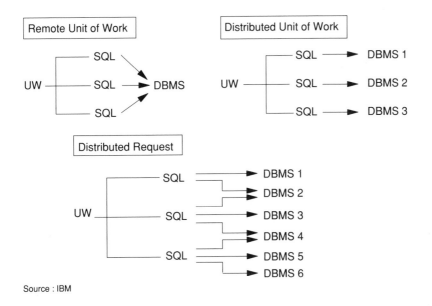

Source : IBM

Figure 69. *Distributed Database Terminology*

The function of distributed database architectures is to allow an application
program to make SQL calls to many tables as if they were all local to one system.
This is similar in concept to NFS (Network File System), covered in Chapters 7
and 16. The implementation of the architecture handles access to remote databases and the translation of data between machines of dissimilar architecture. It is
also responsible for synchronization of multiple updates to several databases since
they may be 'seen' and accessed by the programmer as a single table.

Both RDA and DRDA are defined sets of protocols, translation mechanisms
and software services to enable applications to access remote databases. The goals
of both architectures are similar - access via an SQL API to remote relational
databases. At the SQL interface the differences are marginal, but in the distributed
aspects there are some differences. We will review some of these differences later
in this section.

Figure 70. *Distributed Database Access Terminology*			
Terminology	*Number of SQL statements/UOW*	*Number of Databases/UOW*	*Number of Databases/SQL statement*
Remote Request	1	1	1
Remote UOW	> 1	1	1
Distributed UOW	> 1	> 1	1
Distributed Request	> 1	> 1	> 1

RDA Overview

ISO RDA work started in 1986 and was based on ISO SQL specifications as the API and OSI as the communications vehicle for remote access. A Draft International Standard (DIS) was issued in June 1991 covering:

- Part 1: Generic Model, Service and Protocol
- Part 2: SQL Specialization Protocol.

RDA supports RUW but calls it a Remote Transaction and DUW using the ISO OSI TP standard for two phase commit. It uses standard functions[10] in performing remote access and control of data:

- OSI as the general network environment
- OSI TP conversational mode for communications
- Canonical form for data representation when moved
- Security using OSI ACSE[11] and SQL Access functions.

DRDA Overview

DRDA was initially designed to provide interoperability between IBM's four major SAA relational databases - DB2, SQL/DS, SQL/2 and SQL/400.

There are three participating elements in DRDA, illustrated in Figure 71:

---

[10] Compare the list in the DRDA discussion.

[11] The Association Control Service Element which assists in establishing and terminating program-to-program associations.

- Application Requester (AR) - which allows users and applications to access remote databases from a system that may or may not have a local database.
- Application Server (AS) - an element that performs database access on behalf of the requester (user or application). The AS can access local databases and reroute requests for non-local databases to the appropriate Database Server(s).
- Database Server (DS) - a relational database server.

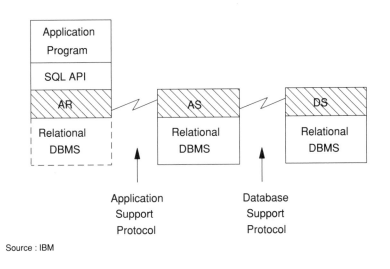

Source : IBM

Figure 71. *Flow of Work in DRDA*

There are two protocols involved in the interaction between these three DRDA components:

- Application Support Protocol between ARs and ASs.
- Database Support Protocol between ASs and DSs.

These protocols are also illustrated in Figure 71.

DRDA protocols specify the interchanges between an application or its agent such as an AS and a remote database. In performing its work, IBM DRDA uses the following IBM architectures:

- SNA for the general network environment.
- Logical Unit Type 6.2 (LU 6.2).

- Distributed Data Management (DDM). DDM provides DRDA with an overall command and reply structure across participating systems.

- Formatted Data Content Architecture (FD:OCA) which describes the layout and data type[12] for exchanges between an AR and an AS.

- Character Data Representation Architecture (CDRA) which supplies integrity for characters transmitted. As an example, it caters for conversion between ASCII and EBCDIC representations. It also handles the case where the same character has different representations in systems participating in DRDA exchanges.

16.2.3 Summary

If you plan to implement true distributed relational database then your questions to the supplier or vendor should cover the aspects of RDA and DRDA. It should be remembered that RDA contains many elements of DRDA, and other parts of the architecture have been offered by IBM to the RDA developers. The similarities between RDA and DRDA include:

- SQL support
- client/server relationship
- conversational programming model
- basic application context
- RUW concept.

It is likely that each can be made to interoperate with the other.

You should also be aware that the RDA model developed by SAG does not match that developed by the ANSI group on several counts. They are both referred to as RDA as if they were one and the same standard. There are some notable differences between RDA and DRDA as well, including the following:

- DRDA uses the LU 6.2 conversational model for communications whereas RDA uses the OSI TP model.

- DRDA supports static SQL which has performance advantages over dynamic SQL.

- DRDA performs data conversion at most once.[13] RDA converts all data into a canonical[14] format each time it traverses the network.

---

[12] CHAR, NUM, BIT.

[13] Receiver makes it right.

[14] A prescribed standard format.

- DRDA supports problem determination[15] and different SQL 'dialects'.
- RDA does not at present support DUW, which is necessary for ensuring data integrity.
- The range of character and international language support.

It is not clear whether RDA (ANSI or SAG) or DRDA will become *the* standard for distributed database. Many software vendors support one or the other, while others support both. The situation is a little more confused when you realize that X/Open has published a 'snapshot' of SAG RDA Formats and Protocols (FAP) as part of its documentation.

16.3 OLTP

Frost and Sullivan estimate that by 1995 some 60% of commercial applications will be OLTP-based. In the late 1980s, nearly half the OLTP work was done by banks and other financial institutions. The percentage is expected to drop by 1995, indicating that other sectors are moving towards OLTP. The use of OLTP in the retail and distribution sectors is growing at 36% CGR (Compound Growth Rate) against the average of 13% CGR.[16]

It is estimated that decentralized OLTP revenue, which overtook centralized OLTP revenue in 1991, will grow at twice the rate of centralized OLTP.[17]

As a result of this burgeoning activity, the issue of open OLTP will assume greater importance in the OSE.

OLTP Systems

Examples of transaction processing systems in use today are:

- Tuxedo from USL
- TopenD from NCR
- Open ACMS from DEC (VMS) with DEC Rdb or RMS
- CICS from IBM (MVS) with DL/I database (hierarchical) or DB2 (relational)
- CICS/6000 from IBM (uses Encina)
- Open/OLTP from Unisys

---

[15] Use of more 'SQLSTATES' and recommended actions.

[16] Source: Gartner Group Inc. Others surveys from the Aberdeen Group, Yankee Group, Hambrecht and Quist, Digital Consulting, DataQuest and Infocorp support these figures in the main.

[17] About 24% CGR versus 12%: Gartner Group.

- B.O.S./TP from Bull
- Tuxedo/Encina from Hewlett Packard
- TPMS (VME) and Open System Transaction Management system (OSTM) from ICL
- VIS/TP from VISystems
- Encina from Transarc
- UniKix from Integris.[18]

The most mature OLTP system is IBM's CICS, with Tuxedo the most mature Unix-based OLTP. However, now that CICS is available with AIX and planned for other Unix platforms,[19] CICS/6000 can possibly claim the Unix maturity title on ancestral grounds.

As we have seen, the Database Manager/Resource Manager (RM) is charged with handling database requests from the transaction program API and for recovery, concurrency, data consistency and so on. The Transaction Manager looks after the transaction programs and the user terminal. Although the TM and RM are important, what is more important in an OSE is how they interact in OLTP systems. There are three important and OLTP-related standards in the process of development:

- OSI Distributed Transaction Processing (OSI TP) model
- X/Open Distributed Transaction Processing Model (X/Open DTP or XTP)
- POSIX 1003.11 Transaction Processing Application Environment Profile (AEP).

The OSI and X/Open OLTP models are being evolved to enable:[20]

- portability of OLTP applications
- the development of client/server OLTP
- the use of distributed transaction processing
- the use of different SQL database systems.

Distributed Transaction Processing is really a generic term used in different ways. The common theme across most interpretations is the splitting of work across more than one system.

---

[18] Formerly from Unicorn.

[19] For example, HP-UX on Hewlett-Packard's 3000 and 9000 series machines.

[20] OSI TP has interoperability as its goal, X/Open has portability in the context of OLTP.

16.3.1 OSI Distributed Transaction Processing Model (OSI TP)

The OSI Distributed Transaction Processing Model[21] is 'one of a set of standards produced to facilitate the interconnection of open systems ... it defines an OSI TP model, an OSI TP Service and specifies an OSI TP protocol within the Application Layer of the OSI Reference Model'.[22]

At present, the OSI TP model does not specify the interface to local resources or an API within the local system. It is merely concerned with the interaction between Transaction Managers and the transactions under their care.

The OSI TP model is concerned with semantics and protocols and forms the basis of the X/Open Distributed Transaction Processing (DTP) model. The X/Open DTP model assumes OSI TP protocols but addresses the interfaces and interactions within an OLTP system, which the OSI TP model does not.

The OSI TP Model is a transaction processing model and a specification of the supporting communications mechanisms. An associated specification is the OSI TP Service and Protocols.

OSI TP Model

The model defines a transaction as 'a set of related operations characterised by four properties: atomicity, consistency, isolation and durability' and addresses the following:

'definition of mechanisms for partitioning into transactions the interactions between application processes of two or more open systems. In particular, these mechanisms provide for:

1. indication of the completion status of a transaction

2. support of transactions which do not require the full distributed commitment mechanisms to ensure the ACID properties: the application is responsible for ensuring the ACID properties; and

3. flexibility in order to match the choice of data transfer method to the semantics of the transaction

4. specification of mechanisms to use the services of the (OSI) Presentation Layer

5. procedures that have acceptable performance and efficiency; and

6. procedures that cover a wide variety of needs (short or long, simple or complex transactions).'

---

[21] ISO/IEC 10026.

[22] OSI TP Model (3 April 1992) - Review copy of Project JTC 111.21.34.

The model then defines entities which cover dialogues and transactions, both local and distributed. Dialogues can be used to transfer data, notify errors and commit or roll back transactions. The X/Open DTP model builds on this part of the OSI TP Model to define practical usage and interfaces for distributed transaction processing systems.

OSI TP Service

In a nutshell, the OSI TP Service pertains to the services provided by TMs and the transactions running under their control. The TMs, by using an appropriate protocol 'guarantee' that all resources they control obey the ACID properties. In addition, they include recovery mechanisms to re-establish a consistent state among resources involved (for example, a database) and, if possible, re-establish transaction processing from the point of failure. The X/Open DTP model supports the OSI TP Service.

16.3.2 X/Open Distributed Transaction Processing Model (X/Open DTP)

Distributed transaction processing across heterogeneous systems and a variety of databases is not feasible without some rigorous standards for the construction of such systems. In most other areas of proprietary development, there have been elements of standards, or accepted codes of practice, to follow. Since OLTP will dominate commercial applications from the mid-1990s and beyond, an OSE needs standards urgently.

X/Open is developing a software architecture for DTP. According to X/Open[23] the DTP model 'allows multiple application programs to share resources provided by multiple resource managers, and allows their work to be coordinated into *global* transactions'.[24] The key *resource managers* of relevance to OLTP are:

- Transaction Manager
- Database Manager
- Communications Manager.

All OLTP systems have these three elements but the APIs to them, and the interfaces between them, are totally different. The X/Open DTP Model addresses this issue via a set of specifications covering three software components:

---

[23] X/Open Guide (1991), Company Review Draft (Draft reading RM2) - Distributed Transaction Processing Model.

[24] X/Open DTP model uses this instead of the word 'distributed'.

- An application program (AP) providing the business logic for a transaction, which accesses resources such as databases. It can make the decision as to whether the transaction completed successfully (allowing a 'commit') or not, perhaps issuing an error code signalling the RMs to roll back the action taken.

- RMs, like database or communications systems, which manage shared resources on the system.

- A TM which identifies transactions (via tables as we discussed), monitors their progress and takes responsibility for commit or roll back of changes. The TM might also invoke recovery action by another RM, such as a database manager.

There are also interfaces between these functional components which are considered in the X/Open DTP model:

- The AP-RM interface giving applications access to shared resources, such as database. The X/Open DTP model 'imposes few restraints on the native RM API'.

- The AP-TM interface (TX in Figure 72) which allows the application to start and end global transactions. The TM will then liaise with other RMs on behalf of the application before passing control and status information back to it.

- The TM-RM interface which is the basis of the X/Open XA specifications.

- The TM-CM interface which is the basis of the X/Open XA+ specifications.

The model then goes on to discuss the functions of these information interfaces and flows, which is really addressed to the developer of OLTP and database systems.

The model does not address all transaction processing issues, for example, security, systems monitoring or the internals of RM communications.

16.3.3 How Do X/Open DTP and the OSI TP Model Relate?

The OSI DTP model is more abstract than the X/Open model and does not specify details of the interfaces between applications and resource managers or between resource managers. The X/Open DTP model is concerned with the details of these interfaces. However, it does use the OSI TP specification for communicating between CMs.

The X/Open DTP (XTP) model in summary concerns itself with the following interfaces and APIs:

- Application programming interfaces

- the Resource Manager[25] API
- the Communications Manager API
- the Transaction Manager API
- Resource Manager Interfaces
  - the TM to RM Interface (XA interface)
  - the TM to CM Interface (XA+ interface).

Protocols are not defined by the X/Open DTP but are assumed to conform to the OSI TP model protocols. The relationship between OSI TP and the X/Open DTP is outlined in Figure 72.

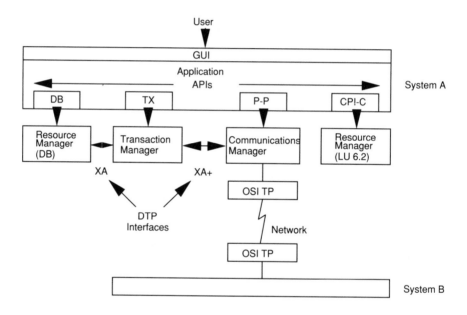

Figure 72. *OSI TP and X/Open DTP Relationship*

OLTP Standards Summary

Although there appear to be usable standards for OLTP systems (see Figure 73), in reality there is little or no portability or interoperability between implementations of transaction processing systems and programs.

---

[25] Usually a database manager.

Figure 73. *Standards Relating to OLTP*

Function	Relevant Standards
Program Development	None
Client/Server Development	X/Open DTP, OSI TP, XA/XA+
User Interface (Character)	AlphaWindow
User Interface (Graphical)	X-Windows
Language APIs	ANSI X3Jxx, POSIX, XPG
Database APIs	SQL, RDA
Network APIs	CPI-C, POSIX, TCP/IP, OSI P-to-P
Recovery	None

16.3.4 OLTP with Encina

Encina[26] is different from other OLTP systems in that it was not developed by a hardware vendor. CICS came from IBM, Tuxedo from AT&T, ACMS from DEC and had nothing in common except they were OLTP systems. Encina, on the other hand, was developed expressly to tackle *open OLTP* at the Carnegie Mellon University (CMU). The development team formed a separate company, Transarc, to develop and market Encina and announced the technology for open OLTP in January 1991. They stated that Encina would be based on the OSF Distributed Computing Environment (DCE). The Encina product had the benefit of the DCE technologies and other modern programming techniques with the result that it has a highly modular architecture. IBM and Hewlett Packard are two major vendors who have endorsed Encina and plan to make OLTP products available on their Unix platforms using Encina as the base.

What is Encina?

One is often faced with terminology in the open systems world which makes it difficult to assess whether what is being discussed is hardware, software, an architecture or a concept. It is often difficult, even if you understand what something is

---

[26] Enterprise Computing in a New Age.

in concept, to find out what it actually does. Encina presents this barrier to many people.

Encina is, first and foremost, a set of coded products which make use of the facilities of the Open Software Foundation's Distributed Computing Environment, such as the Remote Procedure Call, threads and so on. DCE by itself does not do anything - it is there to be used and this is what Encina does. It provides these products to ease the development of distributed OLTP systems while maintaining integrity of key resources. It was the result of research carried out at CMU, MIT, IBM and other laboratories and brought to the market by Transarc Corporation.

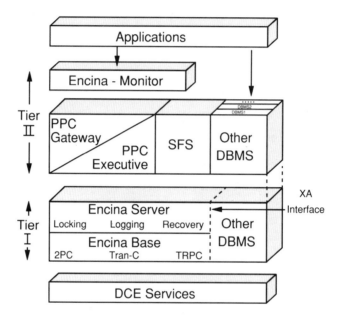

Figure 74. *Encina Family of Transaction Processing Products*

In addition to research, lessons were learned from existing successful OLTP systems to produce Encina. The structure of Encina shows detailed internal modularity and a layered approach to external users and systems. This is to allow for long-term growth and adaptation to new technologies.

The Encina architecture has two tiers:

- *Tier I* - an expansion of the DCE base to include services to support distributed transaction processing and the management of recoverable data. Tier I is referred to as *Base TP Services.*

- *Tier II* - a set of high-function transaction processing services based on Tier I and called *Extended TP Services.*

The structure is shown in Figure 74.

Base TP Services

Encina Toolkit Executive: These DCE extensions take the form:

- Transactional C, a high level API that provides transaction demarcation,[27] control and exception handling. It is basically an extension of the C language.
- Extensions to the DCE Remote Procedure Call (RPC) to ensure integrity across distributed processes in a transaction. It is called a Transactional RPC.
- Transaction service which supports two-phase commit.

Encina Toolkit Server Core: These are extensions to the Executive:

- Locking library to serialize access to data.
- Recoverable storage system using write-ahead logging.[28] Write-ahead logging ensures a copy of a changed record is logged before committing. If the system fails before commit, the change is 'rolled back'.
- An X/Open XA Interface to allow access to XA-compliant database systems.
- A common change log, on recoverable storage, used by the recovery service in rolling back the changes made by a failed transaction.

Extended TP Services

Encina Monitor: This monitor provides the OLTP developer:

- A sophisticated *development environment* which supports the programming and integration of distributed OLTP programs for front end PCs, ASCII terminals and Unix workstations. This allows the development of client/server OLTP applications.
- An *execution environment* offering load balancing and scheduling across heterogeneous systems[29] for optimum performance and transaction integrity. It employs DCE security via authentication (Kerberos) and access control lists (ACLs).

---

[27] Extensions to C to inform Encina of the start and end of code to be treated as a transaction.

[28] This was implemented in IBM's IMS product and was initially known as 'WALT'.

[29] Via a random scheduling algorithm.

- An *administrative environment* for the configuration and management of the distributed OLTP systems. This environment assists the monitoring of active clients, server load and availability, and a variety of exception conditions.

Encina Structured File Server (SFS): For high performance, OLTP systems often use simple files in preference to other types, such as relational. Relational databases are also sometimes unsuitable where knowledge of the physical layout of the data is needed by the programmer. IBM's CICS initially used VSAM[30] as its file access method. The Unix file system is byte-oriented, that is, a file is simply a string of bytes with a beginning, an end and no structure. OLTP systems need record-oriented file structures with recoverability and this is what Encina's SFS provides. The main features of SFS are:

- VSAM-like, recoverable file system
- designed for two-phase commit
- uses the transaction services of Encina and DCE
- can be shared between Encina and a coexisting OLTP system (see below).

Encina Peer-to-Peer Communication (PPC) Services: These are designed to provide enterprise interoperability via transactional CPI-C[31] peer-to-peer communication over both TCP/IP and SNA. PPC has two components:

- The *PPC Executive* which allows Encina clients and servers to carry on CPI-C conversations over TCP/IP.
- The *PPC Gateway/SNA* service which permits systems using the PPC Executive to communicate via SNA LU6.2 to other systems which support the LU6.2 protocols.

The PPC services are complementary to the Transactional RPC and both can be used in a single transaction program.

Encina Recoverable Queueing Service (RQS): RQS[32] provides queueing of transaction data and tasks so that system failures result in the minimum loss of data and processes.

Encina Cobol: Cobol support for the Encina monitor was announced in the third quarter of 1992, making it easier to migrate existing Cobol programs to Encina. The support allows the use of Cobol for client or server, where Cobol clients can access non-Cobol servers.

Existing Cobol programs can transparently access the Encina Structured File Server (SFS). In addition, Encina Cobol server programs automatically have

---

[30] An indexed file structure which replaced ISAM in CICS.

[31] Common Programming Interface - Communications, a part of IBM's SAA.

[32] It is independent of the rest of Encina and is available in 1993.

X/Open XA support, allowing them to access third party RDBMSs. Such applications can use the Encina PPC services if necessary.

Nested Transactions

Another useful feature of the Encina suite is the ability to use ***nested transactions***, similar in concept to nested procedures or subroutines in standard programming.

When coding a multi-threading application, the programmer must ensure that concurrent threads do not clash in their access to data. For example, thread 12 cannot run at the same time as thread 25 if the latter expects data from thread 12 at its completion. This can be avoided in OLTP by using a transaction hierarchy with a single parent where subtransactions contend for the resources of the parent. By breaking what would have been a monolithic transaction into smaller units, the programmer can ***nest*** these sub-transactions (children) under the parent transaction. Failures can be limited in scope by this means since a failing child does not cause roll back of the parent activity. Failure to a parent however, causes roll back of all the children.

The isolation of failures is helped by nested transactions. As OLTP transaction applications become more distributed, a failure in part of the transaction might cause a global roll back. To avoid this, nesting allows parts of the distributed transaction to isolate locally and either complete or recover without affecting the global outcome of the transaction. Without this, the developer would be faced with some *ad hoc* recovery mechanism and possibly multi-phase commit.

16.3.5 OLTP with Tuxedo

Tuxedo originated in work done by the Bell operating companies before the break-up of AT&T and it has been available outside AT&T since 1984. Tuxedo enjoyed a monopoly of Unix OLTP until about 1991 when NCR's TopenD became available. Since then, Encina and CICS/6000 have entered the arena as competitors to Tuxedo. Tuxedo is about 10 years old and 'supports over 100 applications ... which cover 1500 machine nodes'.[33]

Tuxedo Structure

The Tuxedo product has two main components:
System/T: the TP Monitor which coordinates transactions and provides client/server links. We will look first at the elements of System/T and then examine how it operates:

---

[33] *Distributed Transaction Processing Environment - A Competitive Analysis*, UI, 1992.

- Services *mapping scheme*. Multiple services may operate on a single server and a single service might be offered on multiple servers. System/T attempts to optimize scheduling and routing of services to balance system loads and maximize throughput. Another optimizing feature are the *multiple server, single queue sets* which allows identical servers to read client requests from a single queue.

- *Symbolic naming* of entities such as queues and services with meaningful names to aid administration.

- Administrative and programming *user interfaces*.

- *Resource administration*. Entities such as services or servers can be assigned certain characteristics and parameters which control their behaviour in the system. These include placement and scheduling information, recovery criteria and time-out periods, plus tools for graceful shut-down or start-up of the OLTP system.

- *Dynamic reconfiguration*. Servers can be dynamically started and stopped, while services can be made selectively available. Operating parameters, such as those outlined for resource administration, can be changed dynamically.

- *Availability*. System/T includes a number of features to enhance system availability such as time-out checks (set by resource administrator), viability checks, server automatic restart procedures and process recovery procedures.

- *Load balancing*. By means of the service load factor parameters, plus checks on outstanding work, System/T will deliver a 'work' request to the server best placed to handle it.

- *Statistics and audit logs*. These can be used for system auditing and tuning purposes.

- *Recoverable data services* (queues).

Tuxedo uses the term *server* for an application and *services* for the facilities offered by a server. A feature called the *Bulletin Board* enables client processes to look up suitable servers advertised on the Bulletin Board.

System/D: A network model database management system for use with /T, as System/T is often written. It consists of two major parts:

- a File System called FS
- a Record Manager called RM.[34]

The following features apply to System/D and but not necessarily other database systems that System/T can host:

---

[34] Not to be confused with RM - Resource Manager - as used in the OLTP standards discussion.

- Consistency, as understood in the ACID concepts explained in our OLTP discussion.

- Concurrency control via the usual serialization methods of database access.

- Backup. The copying of an entire database for archival storage, which can be done while the system is operational.

- Recovery is assisted by logging updated database records.

- Performance features. System/D offers the following aids to database performance:

  - use of a raw I/O file system, bypassing System V's UNIX file system if needed

  - file placement and direct, sequential or keyed access to records

  - caching of data and files in main memory[35]

  - file placement across different disks to increase the number of disk actuators available to access data

  - multi-threaded commits whereby multiple transactions may be committed concurrently instead or serially (not the same as Encina transaction nesting).

The /D database is an option with Tuxedo and may be replaced by other RDBMs if desired. Other components of Tuxedo are:

/HOST: A Tuxedo peer-to-peer host gateway to aid communication with transaction programs on non-Unix host systems, such as MVS CICS. It provides code for both sides of the link. The Tuxedo ATMI[36] is used to access mainframe-based services as well as Tuxedo /T services.

/WS: A gateway for workstations and PCs to access /T applications. It is supported on DOS, OS/2, Windows and UNIX System V operating environments. The purpose of /WS is to reduce the load on the /T node caused by many users trying to access the Bulletin Board.

DES: A data entry subsystem. It is forms-based and includes data validation and forms navigation for multi-screen applications.

16.3.6 Coexistence with Encina

It is possible for Encina to 'host' another OLTP system such as CICS or Tuxedo. We will illustrate this with CICS/6000, which has the lower layers of the Encina

---

[35] This has serious implications in the event of a operating system failure.

[36] Application Transaction Manager Interface.

technology as prerequisites. We will compare this with mainframe CICS to show where Encina performs some of the functions done by the mainframe CICS Monitor. The Encina/CICS partnership is shown in Figure 75.

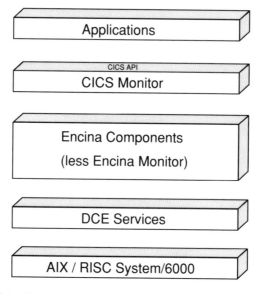

Figure 75. *CICS in the Encina Environment*

Tuxedo and H-P's OLTP would also fit with Encina in a similar fashion.

16.4 Network File System (NFS)

NFS is a term used to cover several functions developed by Sun Microsystems to enable machines on a network to share files. NFS is designed to be independent of hardware, operating system or transport protocol. It uses an implementation of the RPC mechanism and is another example of client/server computing where there are client and server parts to NFS.

The remote access mechanism is transparent to the application as is the RPC, although applications can use the NFS RPC directly if they so wish. The way the RPC works is shown in Figure 76. <1> represents a call by an application for data which is on the local System A. <2> represents a call for data by the application for data it assumes is on System A but is in actual fact on System B. System B is remote from System A but connected in some way over a network.

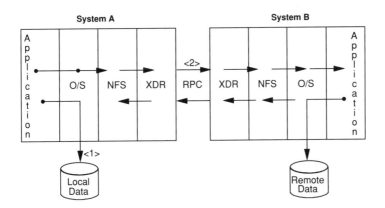

Figure 76. *NFS Remote Procedure Call*

The sequence of events when the application on System A requests data from a file is as follows:

- Prior to needing access to data on System B, the part of the filesystem on System B is made available to System A via a 'mount' command. System A then 'sees' its own filesystem plus the sections mounted from System B. In Unix, these filesystems are structured like the roots of a tree, emanating from a single point called the 'root'. Parts of a remote filesystem can be made available to the local systems by using a remote 'mount' command, usually by a systems administrator. That part of the remote filesystem is logically appended to the local filesystem hierarchy. For all intents and purposes, this part of the remote filesystems resides on the local system as part of its 'root' structure and the programmer accesses it as such.

- The I/O request is intercepted by the part of NFS residing on A (the client element), who decides whether the filesystem is local or remote. If the file is remote, the request is passed to the server part of NFS on the relevant remote system.

- If the client and server have different hardware architectures, then the data representations on the two systems will be different and some conversion will be needed.[37] In NFS, this is done by a feature called External Data Representation (XDR) which converts the RPC and its data to a special XDR format which is translated at the receiving end in a manner appropriate to its architecture. This is especially important for numeric data since the representation of numbers varies from architecture to architecture. For example,

---

[37] See Chapter 4 for discussion of binary incompatibility.

some treat the lowest-order bits of a number as the least significant whereas others treat them as the most significant.[38]

- An NFS server application retrieves the data requested by the program on System A and returned (via RPC and XDR). In general, data about resources on a network (files, user and group identifiers and network information) are stored on Network Information Service servers (NIS)[39] for querying by clients.

As a tool for making remote files appear local, and thus create a client/server environment, NFS has proved to be remarkably popular. Indeed for many sites this is as far as they have gone towards creating a truly distributed system. However, as we saw from the table at the start of Chapter 15 remote file access is only one step along the way - and the next is to allow for remote process access which is usually done with the slightly more advanced NCS. That is the subject of the next section.

16.5 Network Computing System (NCS)

NCS is a series of functions, sitting on top of TCP/IP, which provide remote access to 'objects'. NCS is an implementation of part of what was Apollo's Network Computing Architecture (NCA) which was designed as an object oriented framework. However, the most popular use of NCS today is in accessing remote processes or subroutines from a local application. The major components of NCS are:

- the RPC mechanism
- the Network Interface Definition Language (NIDL)
- the Location Broker.

We will discuss these elements very briefly now.

16.5.1 NCS RPC

The NCS remote procedure call is similar in concept to that found in NFS but the details of its implementation differ considerably. Firstly, it is easier to code than

---

[38] The so called 'big endian, little endian' problem.

[39] Used to be called Yellow Pages but this clashed with a British Telecom service of the same name.

NFS RPC; secondly, it uses UDP/IP and not TCP/IP for transport; and thirdly, it uses a different philosophy for handling network data.

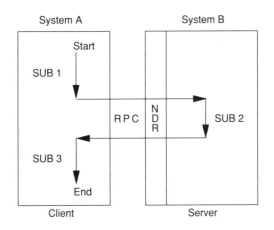

Figure 77. *NCS Remote Procedure Call. NDR is the Network Data Representation. NDR does no data translation when the systems are identical. It performs only one conversion, at the receiving end, when the systems are dissimilar ('receiver makes it right').*

The NCS RPC is coded using the NIDL compiler described below. The use of UDP instead of TCP as the transmission part of the TCP/IP protocols makes it more efficient, as does the sparing use of data translation on the network.

The NCS remote procedure call is shown in Figure 77, where the calls shown are schematic since they go through other stages, such as accessing a runtime library and locating the relevant procedure on the network.

16.5.2 NCS NIDL

The coding of the network interface part of an application calling a process on another system is aided by the Network Interface Definition Language. The part of the application trying to link to another process or subroutine is written in this C-like language. The NIDL compiler transforms the code into headers and either C or Pascal source code files and then compiles them to link with the processing logic on the client or server to form an executable, distributed, program. In NFS, much of this work has to be performed by the programmer.

16.5.3 NCS Location Broker

This feature of NCS provides information about resources on the network. It allows clients to locate special resources such as as databases or processors with special functions.[40] NCS does not itself provide remote data access as NFS does but provides an API to achieve this.

The Location Broker consists of three elements:

- A Local Location Broker (LLB), which runs on each server host to advertise its own 'wares'.

- A Global Location Broker (GLB), running on one or more chosen hosts, which allows clients to locate resources without knowing their location beforehand.[41]

- A Location Broker Client Agent, a set of routines which allow application programs to access the LLBs and GLB directly. This would for example, help a client who knew what host he/she wanted to use but needed to know what resources are available and to find the information without accessing the GLB.

A version of the NCS RPC (V2.0) is the RPC mechanism chosen by the OSF for the Distributed Computing Environment (DCE).

16.6 X Windows

It may seem odd to discuss X Windows under 'interoperability' and not under 'graphics'. This will become clear when we unfold the story of 'X', as X Windows is often abbreviated.

A little booklet called *Windows Primer*[42] gives a useful list of things that 'X Windows' is **not** which help clarify what it **is** very effectively. X is not:

- a piece of hardware although hardware is obviously a prerequisite

- an operating system

- limited to Unix although it was developed on it

- a graphical user interface (GUI)

- only useful for graphical applications.

---

[40] An example is a large Cray for numeric-intensive work.

[41] They would have to know the location if they used the LLB in such a case.

[42] This is available from Tektronix Inc.

16.6.1 Origins of 'X'

Like many technologies adopted by Unix, X began as a research project at Xerox PARC[43] about 1980 using bit-mapped screens. The concept centred on the notion that the interface between the user and the computer could be pictorial as well as keyboard/character-based. The idea of pointing at pictures to interact with the computer instead of hitting keys was born and was given the name PARC Smalltalk. The technology was adapted by Apple which subsequently incorporated windowing and pictures in the Apple Lisa, and then the Apple Macintosh. The pictures became known as *icons*.

Another windowing project, known as 'W', was being worked on at Stanford University and had similar aims. In 1983, the Massachusetts Institute of Technology (MIT) inaugurated Project Athena which was funded by themselves, DEC and IBM. The project aimed to develop a network-independent graphics protocol to provide cross-network services in the MIT, mixed vendor, environment. Many of the Smalltalk ideas and elements of the Stanford W project were incorporated in the new project which jumped one letter in the alphabet to become 'X' or 'X Windows'.

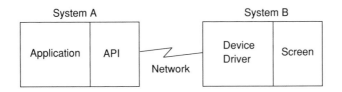

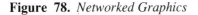

Figure 78. *Networked Graphics*

X[44] is a client/server protocol with portions of the code residing on different systems. If you remember Figure 33 on page 90, it showed a graphics application, an API and a graphics adapter (or device driver) combining to draw pictures on a screen. They were all part of the same system. However, if we split the functions up, leaving the application and API on one system but putting the device driver and screen on another, we have a networked graphics application. This is illustrated in Figure 78.

---

[43] Palo Alto Research Center.

[44] As we will refer to it from here onwards.

System A is a client of System B which provides a display service to the application on the client.[45] There may be more than one server displaying results from a single client or several clients displaying their data on a single server. To achieve the latter, it is necessary to section the server screen into viewing areas or 'windows', and this and the network aspect are what X is all about.

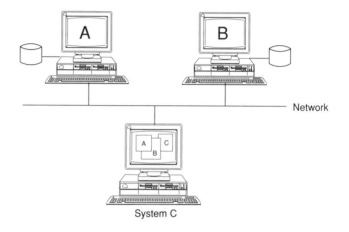

Figure 79. *X Windows in an Applications Network. The client machine C is attached to a LAN which has two other systems, A and B, attached. C has three windows visible on its monitor, one accessing an application on C, the others applications on A and B.*

X has two major parts:

- X protocol for inter-systems communication.[46] This normally uses TCP/IP as its base transport mechanism. X protocol is, in essence, an 'X' RPC.

- Xlib or X library, a library of low-level functions, written in C, to aid development of windowing applications. In fact, the libraries are very difficult to use so 'aid' is somewhat euphemistic.

Applications may either create their own windows or simply be passively 'windowed' themselves without being aware of it. Because of the difficulty of using Xlib, other tools called toolkits, widgets and gadgets can assist in the creation of a windowed application environment. Figure 79 shows how X Window spans

---

[45] This application may also be a server to some other client, which often causes confusion in the use of the terms 'client' and 'server' in X.

[46] Or Interprocess Communication (IPC) if client and server are on the same system.

machines and applications, while Figure 80 shows the underlying structure of X Windows.

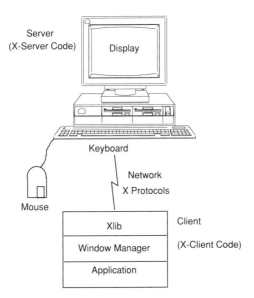

Figure 80. *X Windows Structure*

X is still under development at MIT under the auspices of the X Consortium and is thus essentially vendor-neutral. As a result it has received tremendous acceptance both by vendors and users and is very widely used.

16.7 TCP/IP

Transmission Control Protocol/Internet Protocol (TCP/IP), previewed in Chapter 5, is a set of gateway and networking functions built with layered protocols. The suite of protocols which comprise TCP/IP are designed to be system-independent, although not all vendor implementations are identical.

First we will address some of the terminology. A collection of networks interconnected by TCP/IP is called an ***internet***. A router, bridge or gateway is used to connect networks so that each node in the internet can communicate with any other node as if it was on the same network. Several networks, connected via such connections can appear as one large virtual network.

The TCP/IP architecture, like others we have discussed, is layered as shown in Figure 87. In concept, the architecture, which is peer-to-peer, comprises the following:

- Application layer, where some of the applications are part of TCP/IP.
- Transport layer, which provides end-to-end data transfer via TCP[47] or UDP (User Datagram Protocol).
- Internet layer, using IP (Internet Protocol) and Internet Control Message Protocol (ICMP) to provide packet delivery across the virtual network. IP hides the underlying physical interconnected networks.
- Network and hardware layer, which does not concern TCP/IP since it does not specify any protocols at this level.

This section outlines some of the TCP/IP related applications which complement others such as NCS and NFS discussed earlier in this chapter.

16.7.1 Telnet

Telnet provides a remote login facility that allows a user attached to one system to access applications on another system on the network. The local machine acts as a client to the remote (server) host on which the application lives. Some implementations of Telnet have extensions called TN3270 to allow Telnet full screen support for IBM 3270 terminals.

16.7.2 SMTP

Simple Mail Transfer Protocol is an electronic mail feature of TCP/IP in which sending and receiving ends can be client or server. In operation, some form of electronic mail software, such as DEC's All-in-1 or IBM's PROFS Extended mail, is used to create the mail which is forwarded by SMTP.

16.7.3 FTP

The File Transfer Protocol (FTP) allows users to access files and directories on remote hosts and to initiate file transfer, with ASCII/EBCDIC conversion if necessary. Properly authorized users with read/write access can

- display
- define
- delete

---

[47] Connection-oriented.

files and directories on a network. Trivial File Transfer Protocol (TFTP) is a subset of FTP with less function and security.

16.7.4 Networked GUIs

The X Window system, discussed in section 16.6, allows a user at a single screen to view output from several applications across a network. This takes place via X client and X server functions which use TCP/IP as the communication protocol between them.

16.8 OSI

This section is not a tutorial on OSI but a series of simple overviews to complete the brief look at *de facto* and *de jure* standards in networking protocols. To learn about OSI you should consult one of the many books on the topic.[48]

16.8.1 Virtual Terminal

The OSI Virtual Terminal Protocol (VTP) is a specification to accommodate access to applications by different terminal types. The other methods available, for example protocol mapping, can be an unending task for the many terminal types on the market today.

VTP confines itself to certain *classes* of terminal:

- *Basic Class* - simple character terminals, both synchronous (like IBM 3270) and asynchronous (like DEC VT-100)

- *Forms Class* - allows mapping of fields to the basic class terminals above

- *Graphics Class* - for vector graphics devices

- *Image Class* - for bit-mapped screens, like those used to support GUIs

- *Text Class* - for word processing displays

- *Mixed Class* - for combinations of the other classes.

A schematic of how the Virtual Terminal concept operates is shown in Figure 81..

---

[48] Cypser, referenced in Appendix C, for example.

16.8.2 Message Handling Services (MHS)

Message handling is similar in principle to the Message Queueing we outlined in Chapter 7 in that it represents a store and forward mechanism. As such, the receiving systems need not be active as the shipped data can be held at some intermediate point for later shipment.

The OSI MHS recommendations are known as **X.400**. The outline of X.400 MHS is shown in Figure 81 and introduces the following concepts:

- The *User* who wishes to send or receive messages.

- *User Agents*. These are a set of services to allow the *User* to edit and compose messages, check for message arrival and perform message filing and retrieval.

- The *Message Transfer System*, a collection of *Message Transfer Agents*.

- *Message Transfer Agents* whose job is to act as a store and forward station, accept responsibility for message delivery and deliver messages to *User Agents*, and hence to the actual user.

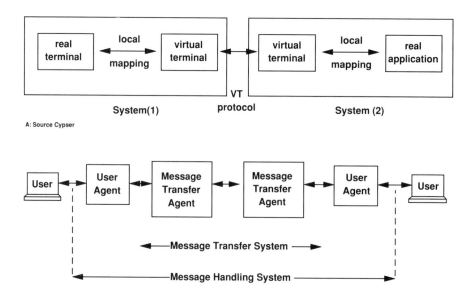

Figure 81. *Virtual Terminal Model and Message Handling Services. The top figure shows the flow of VTP and the bottom one the end-to-end flow of Message Handling Services (MHS).*

16.8.3 File Transfer Access and Management (FTAM)

OSI FTAM[49] resides in application layer 7 of the OSI Reference model (see Figure 82). FTAM caters for hierarchical, flat and unstructured files, using an intermediate structure to render its functions independent of the file structures and access methods.

It offers three basic functions:

1. transfer of files or parts of files between participating systems

2. read, write, replacement or deletion of files

3. file management function for the creation and deletion of files and the examination and/or alteration of their attributes.

7	Application Services	VT FTAM X.400 JTM TP RDA X.500 Security	Systems Management (OSI Management)
6	Presentation	Data Syntax Mapping Data Encryption	
5	Session	Synchronize Data Exchange	
4	Transport	End-to-End Flow Control	
3	Network	Routing and Topology (X.25)	
2	Data Link Control	Link Recovery, Flow Control	
1	Physical	Media Interfaces (LAN, WAN etc)	

Figure 82. *Overview of the OSI Layers and Functions*

16.8.4 X.500 Directory Services

In our discussion of MHS, it was not evident how the messages found their way unerringly to the destination. To locate any entity or resource, a ***directory*** is used. Such services revolve around the use of names, addresses and routes in locating and identifying resources.

---

[49] ISO 8571.

16.8.5 OSI Management

Given that OSI specifies functions for the various layers in OSI networks, who or what is responsible for managing the network at the various layers? In addressing the needs of catering for changing networks, security and predictable communications behaviour, OSI Management introduces five categories for the various management functions:

1. fault management, covering detection, isolation and correction of OSI network errors
2. configuration management for the monitoring and control of network status (configuration)
3. performance management to gather, store and analyze network performance
4. accounting management for allocation of resource usage to users of the network and assign costs
5. security management allowing the creation and control of security mechanisms as well as the reporting of security 'events' such as illegal access attempts.

CMIS and CMIP are dealt with in the following section.

16.9 Network Management

It is taken as fact that there need to be management disciplines applied to a large systems supporting many users and applications. In the area of distributed systems of any level of complexity it is an absolute necessity if a controlled and acceptable level of service to the end users is envisaged. A management discipline which can detect and identify faults and initiate corrective actions is acceptable to end users in the absence of error-free perfection. Untraceable faults which leave the user's screen blank or displaying the message 'ERROR' are not. In addition, performance, security and the ability to react to physical change in a network are also requirements.

We outlined the seven-layer network model in Chapter 6 in the discussion about transmission of data. A monolithic single-layer management model for such networks therefore has little appeal since the benefits of layered architectures would then be lost in the network management scenarios. The seven-layer model is sometimes reduced to three layers, as shown in Figure 83.

In the same way that applications can be built on top of TCP/IP, vendors usually build higher function network management software on top of standard management protocols.

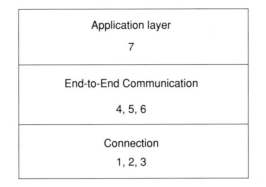

Figure 83. *Network Management Layers*

These fit into the three-layer model as follows:

- Applications - DEC Enterprise Management Architecture and DECmcc Director, Sun SuNet, IBM Netview/Systemview and HP Openview
- End-to-End Communication - OSI CMIP and TCP/IP SNMP
- Connection - IEEE 802.3, 802.4, 802.5.

16.9.1 TCP/IP SNMP

Simple Network Management Protocol (SNMP) is a set of network management protocols for managing a network of Unix systems. It was designed by four people[50] to perform the following network tasks:[51]

- monitoring network performance
- detection and analysis of network faults
- configuration of network devices.

The philosophy of SNMP is the management of systems on a TCP/IP network from a focal point so that users need not manage the network aspects of their machines. To this end, SNMP introduces two types of network 'device', *network management stations* and *network elements* which implement between them the three elements of the management architecture:

- the SNMP protocol itself
- the structure of management information (SMI) specification

---

[50] Jeffrey Case, James Davin, Mark Fedor and Martin Schoffstall.

[51] See *Data Communications*, 21 March, 1990.

- management information base (MIB).

Each network element has its own MIB, structured according to the SMI specification which allows queries to be made on it. Such a setup in an SNMP environment is called an *agent* and the source of the queries is a network management station more commonly called a *manager*.

In brief, SNMP network management is achieved by the manager interrogating the agent's MIB to determine the status of that system. The agent can also send what is called an *event* to the manager as an unsolicited piece of status information for the manager to interpret. SNMP is a protocol and vendors implement software to complement this simple query/answer mechanism to perform more detailed analysis and perhaps take corrective actions. The environment we have discussed is outlined schematically in Figure 84.

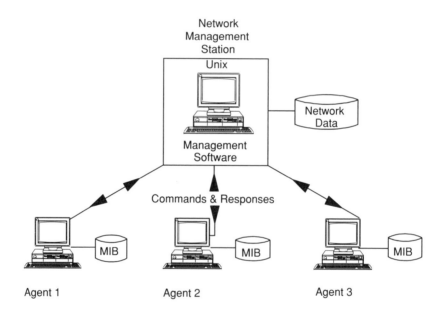

Figure 84. *SNMP Managers and Agents*

SNMP is still under development and emerging enhancements include SMP (Simple Management Protocol) which will support:

- other network protocols, such as OSI, as well as Novell Netware and Appletalk
- communications between management stations
- management of applications as well as devices
- Secure SNMP (S-SNMP).

It should be noted that S-SNMP is not compatible with SNMP and if you need to run SNMP then security functions will have to be added to SNMP. The alternatives are to migrate totally to S-SNMP from SNMP or run them side by side.

16.9.2 OSI CMIP

Common Management Information Protocol is the OSI counterpart of SNMP. SNMP is controlled by the Internet Activities Board whereas CMIP is an ISO OSI initiative. Similar concepts to the network management station, network element (agent) and MIB in SNMP are to be found in CMIP. The management of OSI networks using CMIP is very similar in concept to SNMP although it is a richer specification and uses different terminology beyond the common ones we mentioned above.

16.9.3 LAN Management

Since open systems should be independent of the lower layers of any communications protocol, we do not intend to cover them here. However, for the sake of completeness we list some of the areas needing consideration in the planning, installation and control of network elements at layers 1, 2 and 3 of the Reference Model.

- Token Ring
- Ethernet
- FDDI
- WAN Protocols
- Frame Relay
- X.25
- T1, T2 etc.

16.10 'Open' Printing and Standards

Printing standards follow the pattern of graphics and communications in that existing *de facto* standards have more relevance than the *de jure* standards. One obvious reason is that people want to print today and not tomorrow when all the necessary standards are defined. The subject is very fluid and open to interpretation by various vendors but we will attempt here to outline the various standards related to printing, either single-system or client/server. The issue can become a little confused since it overlaps with other standards concerned with office information interchange. We will include such standards in our discussion only where physical printing is a key requirement.[52]

Figure 85 lists the important *de facto* and *de jure* standards germane to documents and printing.

Figure 85. *Printing Standards*	
De facto	**De jure**
IBM Advanced Function Printing (AFP)	Office Document Architecture (ODA) ISO 8613
Adobe Postscript	Standard Generalized Markup Language (SGML) ISO 8879
Adobe Type 1 Fonts	Standard Page Description Language (SPDL) ISO DIS 10180
H-P Printer Control Language (PCL)	Font and Character Interchange ISO 9541
IBM Proprinter-II ASCII Data Stream	Distributed Printing Standard (DPA) ISO 10175
	MIL-STD-1840A CALS
	Document Style Semantics and Specification Language (DSSSL) ISO DIS 10179

MIL-STD-1840A CALS means Computer Aided Acquisition and Logistics Support. It is a US Department of Defense standard which includes SGML, IGES, CGM, ODA, and SPDL.

16.10.1 ISO Distributed Printing Standard (DPA 10175)

This standard defines protocols for distributed printing and uses the concept of printing *objects* with attributes, for example, to differentiate between character and laser printers:

- jobs

---

[52] And not, for example, the online retrieval of image and text or, indeed, multimedia.

- printers
- print parameters

DPA also specifies rules for printing operations like:

- submit
- query status
- modify
- cancel print

with the aim of allowing print interoperability between heterogeneous systems - 'print anywhere'.

16.10.2 DME Palladium

The DME technology accepted by OSF for distributed printing is another spin-off from Project Athena called *Palladium*. The research project was a joint effort between DEC, HP, IBM and MIT.

The systems uses client/server architecture and is built on top of the OSF DCE. It supports the ISO Distributed Printing Standard (DPA).

Palladium does not generate print files or print anything - it manages resources such as print jobs and print device servers. It can be driven either via an API or commands from a user and its management function is designed to extend across different systems.

The Palladium commands are 'Unix-like', for example:

- send file to a printer (*pdpr, lpr*)
- modify print job (*pdmod*)
- other user and management commands.

Key features of Palladium are that it:

- uses the DCE remote procedure call (RPC), Directory and Security Services
- does not interfere with print data streams in any way
- has its own spooling function
- manages the transfer of print files to the target system on the network.

The structure of Palladium is shown in Figure 86. The figure shows the client/server nature of Palladium and the Command and program API methods of accessing Palladium functions.

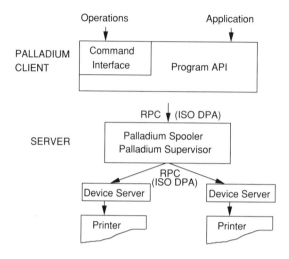

Figure 86. *Structure of the Palladium Print System*

16.10.3 Network Printing Alliance (NPA)

The NPA, founded in 1991, is a group of printer companies - Insight Development, Intel, Lexmark and Texas Instruments - and in 1993 had over fifty other members, including IBM and Unisys. The NPA has developed a specification defining a standard protocol, NPAP[53] for communications between PCs and printers on a local network. The specifications are not cast in concrete but will be continuously refined and developed.

In many respects, it is a competitor to H-P's Printer Job Language. NPAP is said to be independent of Page Description Language (PDL), the printer technology and its communications interface. Such information is carried by NPAP information packets around the network and can be of various types:

- Request Device Characteristics, or information about the printer.
- Request Interpreter containing information about PDLs and fonts.
- Job Control to start and stop print jobs as well as querying their status.
- Request Device Status used by the 'host' to detect error situations.
- Printer Configuration Control.
- Device Status Alert, which are unsolicited messages sent to the host when the printer itself detects errors.

---

[53] Network Printing Alliance Protocol.

- Interpreter Message Alerts, unsolicited messages from the PDL interpreter to the host when errors are detected.

16.10.4 Summary

Printing is one area where standardization is desperately needed. For this reason it has been the focus both of manufacturers and standards bodies. The result of this focus unfortunately has been a proliferation of standards addressing the same problems and as a result no standards at all. The only solution for users is to 'guess' the direction in which the market will move, whether the *de facto* or the *de jure* standards will emerge as the most popular. As authors, we have no crystal ball and to offer guidance would be nothing more than guess work. We have laid the facts before you as we see them, your guess would be as good as ours. You will be forced to live with your decision so we leave it to you - not an ideal state of affairs but, we believe, a realistic view of the situation.

16.11 Conclusions and Summary

We have examined seven-layer models in a fairly abstract manner so far in this book. Figure 87 shows how many of the network applications fit into the layers of the OSI, TCP/IP and SNA architectures.

The SNA part of the figure illustrates the IBM DISOSS office software at layer seven, using the CICS OLTP software to access the network of other DISOSS users. In turn, CICS makes use of VTAM to isolate it from the physical aspects of the network and terminals. The TCP/IP part shows the Telnet, file transfer (FTP), and mail (SMTP) elements of the TCP/IP suite of protocols using TCP and IP to access the network. NFS and its translation (XDR) and remote procedure call (RPC) elements also use TCP and IP in a similar way.

OSI is shown with mail (X.400), file transfer (FTAM) and virtual terminal (VTP) protocols using an OSI stack to communicate with other systems.

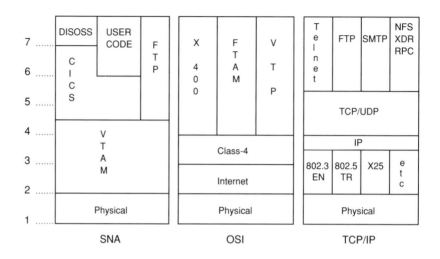

Figure 87. *SNA, OSI and TCP/IP Application Examples. The figure shows practical software products spanning and using the architectural layers of SNA, OSI and TCP/IP.*

16.11.1 Standards Summary Matrix

We have dealt with a number of standards for portability, interoperability and user interfaces in the last few chapters and a review is perhaps called for.

The matrix shown in Figure 88 summarizes which bodies have input to the areas which we have discussed and we classified as needing attention in the full open systems environment. The table is not exhaustive since there are various related initiatives in the areas listed being undertaken by a variety of bodies, for example X/Open, POSC, SPAG and COSE. It indicates the variety of issues involved in using and managing systems in a heterogeneous network. You should note that although the POSIX 1003.11 work group appears in the transaction processing row, the body disbanded voluntarily in April 1993 and there is as yet no POSIX replacement.

	ANSI	ISO	POSIX	X/Open	Other
Portability	Lang.		1003.1 1003.2	XPG XTI	
Interoperability		OSI	1224.1 1003.12 1238.0 1238.1	XPG XTI	AES
User Interface			1201.1 1201.2	XPG	MIT, UI DIA,OSF
Security		SC21	1003.6 1003.22	CAE	DoD DCE etc.
Data Base	SQL	SQL RDA	1003.1 1003.8	XPG	SAG DRDA
Graphics		GKS PHIGS		X-W	OpenGL
OO Functions			1224.0		OMG
Transaction Processing		OSI TP	1003.11	XTP	CICS Encina Tuxedo
Program Development					PCTE AD/Cycle
Dist. Computing			1003.6 1003.12	XTI	UI DCE
Dist. Management					DME UI

Figure 88. *Standards Summary Matrix. We have not included ODP since it covers many areas in the chart below and would render it confusing.*

16.11.2 Interoperability - The Task Ahead

Most of the interoperability standards discussed in this book so far have been 'either or' choices. For example you use either TCP/IP or OSI or DECnet and so on as your communications model. It is obviously desirable to devise standards at levels in the seven-layer hierarchy such that lower levels become increasingly transparent to programmers and other IT personnel.

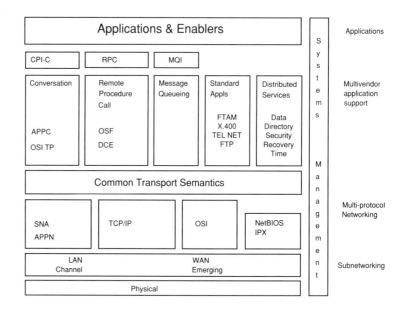

Figure 89. *IBM Network Blueprint*

For instance, sending data from a system without the sender knowing what the underlying protocols are (TCP/IP, SNA or OSI, for example) would be ideal. The X/Open Transport Interface (XTI) goes a long way towards this goal but still has some limitations. XTI is based on the old sockets interface and the SVID Transport Layer Interface (TLI) and aims to give a program independence of the underlying OSI or TCP/IP protocols.

The IBM *Networking Blueprint*[54] among other things, generalizes the transport layer interface with a Common Transport Semantics, aiming to cater for transport protocols SNA, OSI, TCP/IP, NetBIOS and IPX. The architecture is outlined simply for reference here in Figure 89.

---

[54] See IBM publication GC31-7057: *Networking Blueprint, Executive Overview.*

The point of mentioning it here is to reinforce the idea of moving APIs to higher levels to allow more options to be used at lower levels. This will then mean that more systems and architectures will be able to fit into the OSE. For example, the IBM Blueprint defines APIs above the level of Interprocess Communication where there will be a choice of the conversational, RPC and message queueing methods of communication. Again, refer to Figure 89 for an illustration of this.

Until standards properly address the higher levels and provide APIs at those levels interoperability will be difficult. It is a constant theme of this book that open systems should only be strived for if they provide a business benefit. The difficulty of creating an interoperable environment might be thought to tip the balance against attempting it. However, as we saw in Chapter 2 most organizations want open systems primarily for interoperability, so in fact the balance is unlikely to be tipped sufficiently for most users to give up. It is therefore beholden on vendors committed to open systems and to standards bodies to focus in this area. Some are starting to do so, but undoubtedly more could. Until this takes place many businesses will struggle to create a beneficial OSE.

Chapter 17 Open Operating Systems

The future is made up of the same stuff as the past.[1]

There is no doubt that open systems are growing in popularity in commercial computing. However, the majority of businesses have a significant investment in proprietary systems, including the investment in software, applications and skilled staff. The situation was well summed up by X/Open in their 'Open Systems Directive': 'The unstoppable force, open systems, has met the immovable object: one trillion dollars of installed, proprietary age systems.'[2]

The manufacturers of proprietary systems have realized the size of the investment in their computers makes it difficult for companies simply to abandon them. At the same time they have realized that these companies, their customers, are anxious to gain the benefits of open systems. Many have therefore embarked upon a programme to open up their proprietary architectures, and we will look in this chapter at four examples:

- DEC's VMS operating system
- IBM's operating system MVS/ESA
- IBM's mid-range operating system OS/400
- ICL's VME operating system.

In addition to opening up their proprietary systems, a number of manufacturers have taken the step of offering Unix on them. While this might at first sight seem like a method of maintaining a role for the mainframe, with customers migrating from proprietary operating system to Unix, the reality is slightly different. The main interest in mainframe Unix has come from companies with voracious

---

[1] Simone Weil, French philosopher.

[2] 1992 X/Open Open Systems Directive - Executive Summary.

requirements for storage, data management and data processing. In this chapter we shall look at two examples:

- Amdahl's UTS implementation of Unix
- IBM's AIX/ESA implementation of Unix.

Offering Unix on the mainframe might be thought of as the ideal solution to the problems of combining the demand for open systems with the investment in proprietary architectures. However, many IT professionals are still wary of Unix. They see it as a backward operating system, developed for technical rather than commercial environments and not suitable for running a business's mainstream applications.

Vendors of Unix systems have recognized this and have striven over the last few years to improve Unix in a number of ways. We shall look in detail at how this has been done by the two different Unix groupings we discussed in Chapter 5, namely:

- The Open Software Foundation's OSF/1
- Unix System Laboratory's System V Release 4.

17.1 Proprietary but Open

17.1.1 DEC and VMS

The cornerstone of DEC's computing strategy is the VAX architecture - a family of machines ranging from desktop to mainframe size. Every member of the family runs the VMS (Virtual Memory System) operating system.

In July 1992 DEC announced the latest version of its VMS operating system - Version 5.4. It announced that in future the operating system would be known as OpenVMS to reflect its openness. OpenVMS complies with POSIX 1003.1, is branded XPG3 compliant and can communicate using TCP/IP. DEC has announced its intention to offer the Open Software Foundation's DCE on VMS in the future. Figure 90 shows the VMS adherence to a range of open systems standards.

17.1.2 IBM and MVS/ESA

IBM mainframes can run a number of operating systems and each is targeted at particular environments. The flagship of IBM's operating systems is MVS/ESA - Multiple Virtual Storage/Enterprise Systems Architecture.

IBM has stated that it plans to make MVS/ESA POSIX 1003.1 compliant. It already offers TCP/IP and NFS[3] and will contain elements of the Open Software Foundation's DCE in the future. Refer again to Figure 90 to see how MVS adheres to a range of standards.

17.1.3 IBM and OS/400

There are over 200,000 AS/400 machines - IBM's proprietary mid-range computer. The AS/400 was a successor to the System/36 and System/38 and there are a further 100,000 of those in the world. The AS/400 runs the OS/400 operating system.

IBM have stated that it plans to offer a POSIX 1003.1 compliant version of OS/400 in the future and also offer NFS and elements of the Open Software Foundation's DCE. The OS/400 can run TCP/IP but the ability to manage it using SNMP is something that IBM plans to offer in the future.

17.1.4 ICL and VME

ICL's proprietary operating system is VME. In line with ICL's commitment to open systems, VME implements POSIX 1003.1 and is branded XPG3 compliant. ICL has no plans to offer the Open Software Foundation's DCE and though it implements TCP/IP there is no ability to manage systems using SNMP.

17.1.5 Summary

Figure 90 shows where the platforms discussed in this chapter meet the standards, both *de facto* and *de jure*. The table was accurate at the time of writing but you should consult the respective vendors to check the latest position before making major decisions.

In the table, you will note that XPG3 is not listed. This is because XPG4 compliance assumes XPG3 compliance.

---

[3] Server mode.

Figure 90. *Non-Unix Standards Position of Major Vendors*

Standard	*OS/400*	*MVS/ESA*	*VMS*	*VME*
POSIX	Future	Future	Y	Y
DCE	Future	Future	Future	N
SAA	Y	Y	Future	N
XPG4	Future	Future	Y **	Y **
NFS	Future	Y	Y	Y
NCS	N	N	Future	N
TCP/IP	Y	Y	Y	Y
SNMP	Future	Y	Y	N
Ethernet	Y	Y	Y	Y
Token Ring	Y	Y	Y	Bridge
ASCII	Y	Y	Y	Y
BSC	Y	Y	Y	Bridge
X.25	Y	Y	Y	Y
OSI	Y	Y	Y	Y
OSI-NM	Future	Y	Future	Y
X.400	Y	Y	Y	Y
EDI	Y	Y	Y	Y
C	Y	Y	Y	Y
Cobol	Y	Y	Y	Y
Fortran	Y	Y	Y	Y
X-Windows	Future	Y	Y	N
SCSI	Y	Y *	Y	Partial
SQL	Y	Y	Y	Y

    * = Via PS/2   ** Layered onto operating system

17.2 Mainframe Unix

Unix, despite its popularity and widespread use on a wide range of machine power, is not designed for very large-scale computing or controlling and allocating the resources demanded by it. There is almost an order of magnitude difference between the provision of computing resources on the large Unix machines and that supplied on the large mainframes, for example:[4]

- main storage - 1Gb versus 8Gb on mainframe
- DASD storage - 100Gb versus 1000Gb on a mainframe
- 500 users versus 5000 on a mainframe

In addition, the housekeeping and administration associated with large numbers of users is different. The two mainframe implementations outlined here (Amdahl's UTS and IBM's AIX/ESA) have added significant 'scalability' features to the Unix implementations on which they are based (UNIX SVR4 and OSF/1 respectively).

The key requirements addressed by mainframe Unix are:

- Numerically intensive computing (NIC), particularly jobs with very large storage requirements, both main or auxiliary, or which are very long running. Major additions have been made to the mainframe Unix environment to reflect the scaling-up of UNIX to large mainframes, especially in the areas of reliability and recovery which are important for long running jobs.

- Data server. Mainframe environments have a high-quality storage environment, developed over several years, and it makes some sense for distributed or multi-site installations to take advantage of this.

- Academic (or campus) server. Most people in Universities have access to a terminal or workstation of some sort and a central server is a very secure, cost-effective way of offering extra function or power without having to upgrade or replace each person's workstation or screen.

Amdahl and IBM have developed versions of Unix to run on mainframe systems and these are our next two topics.

17.2.1 IBM's AIX/ESA

In 1988, just before the Open Software Foundation was formed, IBM announced AIX/370 to cater for people who needed Unix function in mainframe environments. It was designed to run as a 'guest' operating system under Virtual Machine facility (under VM/SP HPO, VM/SP or VM/XA SP). It also supported the Vector

---

[4] These are typical numbers.

Facility on System/370 machines and was therefore a good candidate for those who needed a NIC environment.

In September 1991 IBM unveiled a new product for mainframe UNIX - AIX/ESA. Unlike AIX/370, AIX/ESA is based on OSF/1. It can run as a VM guest or in a partition (PR/SM) under MVS/ESA. Most importantly it can run native on ESA machines.

The revised structure of AIX/ESA is outlined in Figure 91.

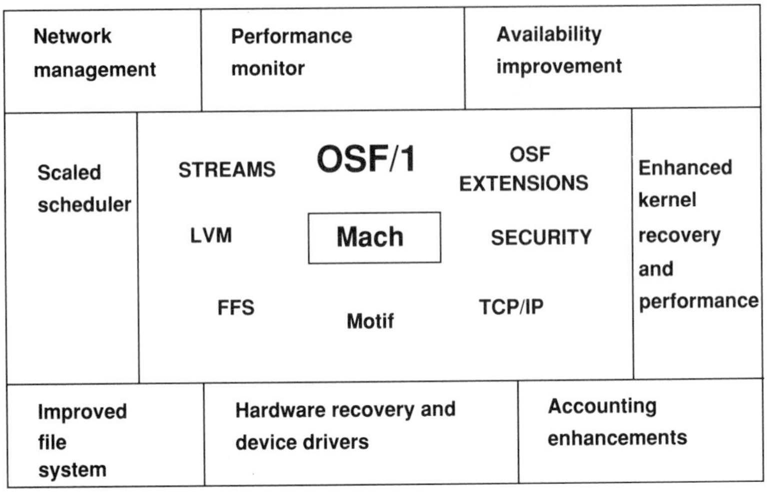

Network management	Performance monitor	Availability improvement	
Scaled scheduler	STREAMS **OSF/1** LVM **Mach** FFS Motif	OSF EXTENSIONS SECURITY TCP/IP	Enhanced kernel recovery and performance
Improved file system	Hardware recovery and device drivers	Accounting enhancements	

Figure 91. *AIX/ESA Extensions to OSF/1. Legend: LVM - Logical Volume Manager, FFS - Fast File System.*

The core of the AIX/ESA system is the Mach kernel from CMU, with symmetric multi-processing extensions from Encore Corporation. It is a full multi-processing UNIX making use of the multiple processors of the ESA mainframe range. It also offers:

- commands and libraries from IBM and BSD
- OSF/Motif
- TCP/IP
- The OSF/1 file system based on the BSD fast file system
- Logical Volume Manager from IBM
- Portable STREAMS from Mentat
- Security features from SecureWare

- UniTree/ESA.[5]

In the standards area, AIX/ESA includes support for:[6]

- SVID 3
- BSD 4.3
- POSIX 1003.1
- XPG3
- C, Cobol and Fortran
- NFS and NCS
- DCE and OSI are planned.

17.2.2 Amdahl's UTS

Amdahl introduced the Universal Timesharing System (UTS) in 1984 as a large-scale implementation of Unix System V. UTS can run on IBM System/370 processors in native mode or as a guest under the VM Operating systems on System/370 or System/390 and Amdahl processors. In October 1992, UTS Release 4 was announced, based on UNIX V.4 ES (Extended Security). UTS R.4 carries forward features from UTS 2.1 and 2.1.3, announced in October 1991:

- support for 3270 and ASCII terminals
- channel-to-channel interface to IBM's Network Job Entry (NJE)
- extended file system allows files to span multiple volumes allowing for files up to 6,000 Gb (6 terabytes)
- adheres to Sun's Open Network Computing (ONC) specifications
- disk (file) striping as in R.A.I.D. 0[7]
- Advanced Program to Program Communication (APPC) support via SNA LU6.2 and support for other SNA LU types
- Extended File Support (EFS) to aid back-up and recovery operations and cater for long file names
- multi-byte character support and multi-language message handling.

UTS R.4 itself adds System V.4 conformance and a workload scheduler that allows workloads to be assigned to groups which are allocated specific percentages

---

[5] Based on General Atomics/Discos UniTree version 1.6.3.

[6] See 'AIX/ESA Reference Guide' GX11-6210.

[7] Redundant Arrays of Inexpensive Disks, Level 0.

of the CPU capacity. In the area of OLTP, UTS R.4 supports Tuxedo from UNIX International. Other major standards features of UTS R.4 are:

- OSI support
- support for X11.4, OSF/Motif and OpenLook
- ANSI compliant C[8] and Fortran, and C++
- XPG3 compliance
- SVID3[9] conformance
- POSIX 1003.1 base system compliance
- includes many BSD capabilities and features.

Of course UTS supports the standard features expected of a Unix system such as uucp, TCP/IP and so on. Amdahl has announced plans[10] to enhance UTS in the following areas:

- Amdahl UniTree,[11] a data management and archiving product
- Amdahl Huron application systems environment, aimed at application development
- Amdahl Cobol, available in the fourth quarter of 1993
- XPG4 branding
- UK GOSIP, OSI X.400 MHS (1988) and the X.500 Directory Service
- X/Open Transport Interface (XTI)
- Simple Network Management Protocol (SNMP)
- UNIX Measurement Architecture (UMA), a performance measurement system driven though an interface based on X Windows
- 3490 Tape Compression and Improved Data Recording Capacity (IRDC).

17.2.3 Summary

The market for mainframe Unix is currently a small one. Should this alter in the future it is likely that the ambitious plans of the manufacturers of RISC- and Intel-based Unix systems will enable the requirements to be met by far less expensive

---

[8] ANSI X3159-89.

[9] System V Interface Definition Release 3.

[10] Under the heading 'Directions' in the Amdahl publication EM001225.

[11] Developed by General Atomics/Discos.

systems. It is therefore unlikely that the current mainframe offerings will become popular amongst buyers of new systems.

The important issue is whether the existing mainframe sites install Unix either alongside or instead of their established proprietary systems - that is IBM MVS, VM or VSE. So far this has not happened widely but the Unix bandwagon is such that it is certainly a possibility.

The key difference between IBM and Amdahl's offering is that the former is based on OSF/1 and the latter on SVR4. We shall conclude this chapter by looking at these core operating systems from the OSF and USL respectively.

17.3 OSF/1

OSF/1 is the Open Software Foundation's UNIX-like operating system. As we explained in Chapter 5 it was originally developed as a competitor to AT&T System V (five) Release 4 (SVR4) which was seen by a number of vendors as being developed and licensed in a way that unfairly favoured Sun Microsystems in which AT&T had bought a holding.

OSF/1 combines the basic functions of System V and Berkeley UNIX with a number of new functions to create what has been described as a new, redesigned, UNIX-like, operating system. OSF/1 is not a competitor to UNIX in the sense that OS/400 from IBM or VMS from DEC is. Rather OSF/1 is an alternative to, and, the OSF would claim an improvement on, USL UNIX. It is UNIX-like in its look and feel and has all the functions a UNIX user would expect. It also matches the key industry standards for operating systems - POSIX 1003.1 and XPG3. In addition OSF/1.1, the second release of OSF/1, is SVID 3-compliant. SVID 3 is the Systems V Interface Definition for System V Release 4. The last point is of particular importance because it effectively neutralizes the myth that there are two entirely different Unix camps. In reality the differences between the two are not great and they both match the SVID 3 definition.

OSF/1 does have some important features and facilities not traditionally found in UNIX-like operating systems. These have tended to be over-emphasized by the advocates of OSF/1 to the extent that many feel OSF/1 is not really UNIX-like at all. OSF/1 combines a number of existing offerings from a range of vendors in a structured fashion. In Figure 92 we show the components of OSF/1.

17.3.1 The OSF/1 kernel

The kernel in OSF/1 is not the traditional UNIX kernel but the UNIX-like Mach kernel from Carnegie-Mellon University (CMU). Mach was chosen for a number of reasons - not least the fact that CMU licenses it to the OSF at no cost. Mach was designed for parallel and distributed environments. A parallel environment is one in which there are multiple processors working in parallel - usually in the same machine. A distributed environment is one in which computing tasks, either at file or process level, are distributed across the network and spread among a number of machines.

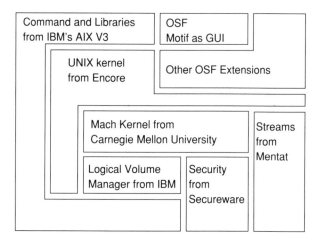

Figure 92. *Components of OSF/1*

Mach works efficiently in these environments because it uses multi-threading which enable processes to be run on several processors at once. These processes may be parts of the application or of the kernel of the operating system. An application has to be coded to be multi-threaded and OSF/1 uses a POSIX 1003.4a compliant programming interface. Such an application can be broken up into very small units, called threads, which can execute on different processors, thereby significantly improving the throughput of the system in many cases. Threaded applications also work well in distributed environments because a server can handle requests from several clients at once - each request being a different thread of work.

A threaded kernel allows multiple threads in the operating system to execute simultaneously on multiple processors. Unlike application threads it is not necessary to make any changes to applications to take advantage of the benefits of a threaded kernel.

17.3.2 Systems Management in OSF/1

One feature of UNIX that receives constant criticism from those familiar with more mature proprietary systems is the need to take the system off line for routine systems tasks. This is because traditional UNIX cannot load and link kernel function dynamically, that is, as the system is functioning. Traditional UNIX does not separate the kernel from other operating system functions cleanly so the inability to dynamically link and load the kernel means the system has to be taken off line for many system tasks. OSF/1 does offer the ability to bind kernel function dynamically so device drivers, streams modules and file systems can all be accessed, altered and re-linked while the system is active. In addition, OSF/1 allows the system configuration to be changed dynamically, enabling physical devices to be added or removed while the system is running.

The original UNIX file system had a number of problems and various alternative file systems had been developed - the Andrew File System developed at CMU being a leading example. OSF/1 needed to be able to offer the new more advanced file system types and at the same time allow users to use the traditional UNIX file system. The method chosen was for the operating system to offer a Virtual File System - an interface between the kernel and the selected file system. As part of this Virtual File System there is a switch within the software which allows users to select between file systems. The Virtual File System in OSF/1 supports both the traditional UNIX file system and the most popular modern file systems.

17.3.3 The Logical Volume Manager

OSF/1 implements a feature called the Logical Volume Manager (LVM). In UNIX, physical disk space is allocated to groups of files called volumes, in other words a volume is allocated an amount of hard disk space. In traditional UNIX systems the partitions which together make up the volume could only reside on one disk. The LVM allows the partitions to span multiple volumes - they appear to be volumes but physically are not. Hence the name 'logical volume manager'. As well as allowing for spanning, the LVM allows for mirroring too. With disk mirroring some or all of the files held in one volume are held in an exact copy, a mirror, on a second disk. In the event of a disk failure the second copy can be used instantly. The LVM supports duplicate and also triplicate mirroring of disks.

The LVM also improves disk management because it allows the amount of disk space allocated to any particular volume to be increased while the system is on-line. Previously it was necessary to back up the volume, edit the file allocation table in the kernel of the operating system, reboot the system and restore the volume from tape.

17.3.4 Security

OSF/1 offers three security options: standard UNIX security, C2 level and B1 level.[12] The security options are selected at compile time from a range of modules all of which are shipped. This has two advantages. Firstly, it allows system vendors to work with one source code base rather than having the expense of supporting several. Secondly, as a rule the more secure the system the slower it runs. With module options administrators can select their optimum mix of security and performance and even have a different mix on different machines on the same network. The security for OSF/1 comes from SecureWare, Inc. and utilizes its Trusted Application Programming Interface - a popular API for secure systems already widely used within the industry. Applications already written using the Trusted API can be ported easily to OSF/1.

17.3.5 The Application Environment Specification (AES)

An important feature of OSF/1 is that it is possible to create an OSF/1-like environment without taking all of the operating system. Both Hewlett-Packard and IBM are keen not to adopt the current kernel of OSF/1 but still to have the non-kernel based features of OSF/1 and to offer users a consistent OSF/1-like environment for their applications. The OSF offers the opportunity to do this through the Application Environment Specification.

The AES, simply described, is a specification of a common environment presented to applications. So an application written to the specification will be portable between any AES compliant system.

In providing a consistent environment across platforms AES is like POSIX 1003.1 and XPG3. Indeed AES includes both POSIX and XPG3, and more besides. Where accepted standards and specifications exist, AES incorporates them sometimes with additions and extensions. Because emerging standards are incomplete (by definition), AES attempts to give pragmatic additions to create a working environment.

AES itself is evolving and the complete AES volume set will define stable APIs[13] in the following areas:

- operating system
- user environment services
- network services
- graphics services
- database management services

---

[12] For a discussion of these security levels, see the Glossary.

[13] These are described as full, trial or temporary depending on maturity.

- programming languages.

AES integrates functions from other sources such as *CAE* from XPG3, *ANSI C* and *POSIX*. A summary of AES is shown in Figure 93.

Figure 93. *AES Standards List*	
Area	*Specifications*
Operating System	POSIX, XPG3 Base
Languages	C, Fortran, Pascal, Ada, BASIC, Cobol, LISP
User Interface	X Windows V11, ANSI X3H3
Graphics	GKS, PHIGS
Networking	ARPA/BSD, TCP/IP set, some OSI protocols

The reason why AES is important is that if it develops sufficiently to provide a complete environment, such that an application could be written entirely to AES, then there will be total portability across AES compliant systems. If there was total portability of an application between systems, with only a need to recompile for the particular hardware, this would be a considerable advance. The OSF would have met a major customer requirement. If it happened, many customers would see matching AES as more important than providing an OSF/1 based environment. If this were to happen the whole *raison d'être* of the OSF would have altered. An organization that had set out to develop a competitor to System V Release 4 would have developed a solution that made compliance to SVR4, or any other implementation of UNIX, irrelevant.

17.3.6 The Future

Version 1.1 of OSF/1 was shipped in 1992 with enhanced internationalization support, dynamic configuration[14], POSIX 1003.1 (1990) conformance and DCE integration. OSF/1 V1.2 will be available in 1993 in 32- and 64-bit versions, removing some old UNIX restrictions via:

- alternate scheduling policies
- priority-based scheduling for OLTP

---

[14] To enable kernel modules to be loaded when needed without having to reboot the system.

- support for large files and large commercial file systems
- further standards compliance such as XPG4 and POSIX beyond 1003.1.

The longer-term future of OSF/1 is potentially even more exciting than the present. This is because the OSF is planning to introduce microkernel technology into OSF/1 - it currently uses the 'macro-kernel' Mach 2.5. To understand this, it is important to say a few words about microkernel technology.

Traditional operating systems consist of a 'core' set of code that controls the system hardware and other basic operations such as paging and memory management. In UNIX, the core is called a kernel, while in MVS and other operating systems it is known as the nucleus. The rest of an operating system consists of layers of services and application functions.[15] If the interface to this core is precisely defined, then application programmers and software vendors can write programs to run against it.

The kernel of any Unix operating system is small when compared with the other functions layered on it.[16] The layering avoids a monolithic operating system with its attendant update and maintenance problems. The notion of a microkernel modifies the idea of a kernel to offer a minimal set of code, independent of operating system or architecture, which performs the very basic functions of:

- device drivers (tapes, disks, network adapters and so on)
- task (process) management
- memory management in virtual memory environments
- interprocess communication (IPC).

You might almost say that the microkernel concept in operating systems parallels the RISC concept in hardware architectures.

The structure of a microkernel in shown in concept in Figure 94.

A compact kernel, with efficient thread support, can serve a number of functional layers and requirements, for example real time and massively parallel computing. An agreed and thoroughly tested microkernel might even be implemented in hardware or, at worst, microcode. However, the key advantage of the microkernel is that it is small enough to allow a guest operating system or systems above it - thus offering the possibility of multiple operating system environments on a single machine. In Unix these guests are called personalities.

The OSF has been working with two microkernels, Mach 3 (from CMU) and Amoeba (from Vrije Universiteit in the Netherlands). The work is still continuing at the OSF Research Institute but the basic idea of a microkernel which will allow multiple personalities is accepted.

---

[15] For example security and APIs.

[16] Typically 60,000 to 100,000 lines of code compared with 2 to 4 million.

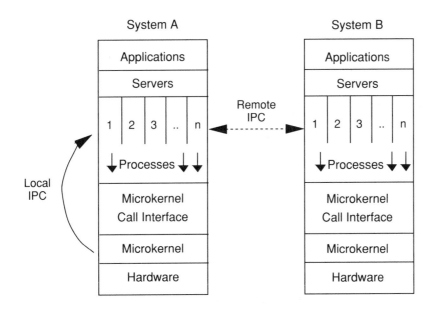

Figure 94. *Microkernel Structure*

The multiple personalities will use a single microkernel through a well defined API, as shown on the right hand side of Figure 95.

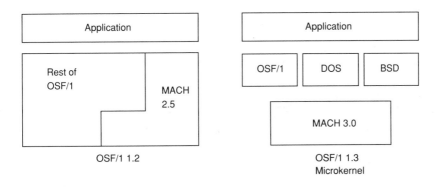

Figure 95. *OSF/1 Microkernel Migration*

The complete OSF/1 operating system Roadmap is summarized in Figure 96. The timescales should not to be assumed to accurate to the month, however.

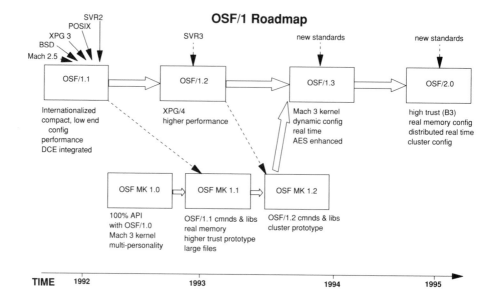

Figure 96. *OSF Roadmap 1992-1995 Summary*

17.3.7 Summary

OSF/1 is a UNIX-like operating system that provides the features and functions commonly associated with UNIX, matches the key industry standards and also offers some significant enhancements. It has enhanced UNIX in the areas of kernel functionality, systems management, storage management and security. The fact that so few vendors today actually ship it means that other implementations of UNIX have established themselves already. The success of OSF/1 will therefore depend on how many vendors ship it in the future, whether it is a significant improvement on what is available and the degree to which applications are portable between OSF/1 implementations on different hardware. This last point may be resolved by the Application Environment Specification - which may overtake OSF/1 in importance and prove to be the more lasting solution. AES provides a common definition of programming interfaces on which applications can rely.

17.4 System V Release 4

As we discussed in Chapter 5, UNIX is now developed by Unix Systems Laboratories rather than AT&T. The latest version of that software is System V Release 4 (SVR4) which brings together the previous release from AT&T, SVR3, and Sun's

BSD-based operating system SunOS. It also seeks to integrate Microsoft XENIX. The object in bringing together the three most popular UNIX variants was that they would offer a single platform and provide a clear direction. In doing so they hoped to dominate the UNIX market.

SVR4 is not a new UNIX, in the way that OSF/1 is, rather it is the next step in an evolutionary development process that began in Bell Laboratories in 1969. It looks both forward and back. By that we mean that it has to ensure compatibility with what has gone before and yet provide a platform for future development and improvement. It would be wrong, however, to think of SVR4 as *just* a new release. USL has resolved many of the problems most associated with UNIX and provided a greatly improved operating system. They have managed to do this while retaining compatibility with what has gone before.

The method used for doing this is by restructuring the kernel of the operating system to be more modular. By having a kernel that is modular new components can be added alongside older ones, thus maintaining compatibility with older versions and allowing new advances to be made. That is not to say that the *whole* of the kernel is modular, only that some components are. It is not yet possible for modules of the kernel to be dynamically loaded (that is, during operation) or linked - i.e. the system still has to be rebooted to add or remove modules.

17.4.1 SVR4 enhancements

When SVR4 was first announced there were several other key improvements - to the file system, to the development tools available and to the support for various national languages. Since the original announcement there have been additions to the system - most notably the announcement of Multi-Processing and Enhanced Security version and the addition of the Veritas File System.

We explained when looking at OSF/1 the need to offer file systems other than the basic UNIX file system. Like OSF/1, the developers of SVR4 decided to use a software switchable Virtual File System. The key difference between the two implementations is that SVR4 supports the /proc and Fifo file systems. The /proc system allows a process owner to look at the address space of a process. Fifo is, as its name suggests, a first in first out method of prioritization.

One of the key developers tools in UNIX is the Common Object File Format (COFF). COFF defines how binary and object files are formatted but is not well suited to high-level languages like Ada and Cobol. As a result Sun developed, and offered in SunOS, the Extensible Link Format (ELF) which is ideal for high-level languages. However, because COFF has been available for a long time, and because it is used for C programming, there are a large number of utilities that use it. COFF could not therefore be abandoned, but developers needed to be encouraged to migrate to ELF. The answer, as with kernel features, was to support fully both the old and the new. SVR4 fully supports both COFF and ELF. In addition, there are a range of tools available to migrate from COFF to ELF.

UNIX support for languages other than English was not something in the minds of the original developers. Clearly if SVR4 was to be come widely used and profitable it needed to offer this National Language Support facility. To reach the widest market it needed to offer support for ideographic languages such as Japanese, Chinese and Korean, which is significantly more complicated than supporting Roman alphabet based languages. The basic method for support of multiple foreign languages has been to implement an interface between systems services and national languages, an API, that allows you to set up libraries of phrases in the appropriate language with are then called up at the appropriate point. Users can select which language libraries they wish to use and a single system can use several. This facility, called Multi National Language Supplement (MNLS) is available as an option to base SVR4. In addition, SVR4 supports Extended UNIX Codes (EUC) which offers ideographic language support and is based on the relevant ISO standards. (It also matches the X/Open XPG4 draft specification for wide-character interfaces.)

17.4.2 Security and Multi-processing

The Virtual File System, the Extensible Link Format and the Multi-National Language Supplement were all part of the original SVR4 announcement. Since that first announcement USL has announced multi-processing and enhanced security versions known as SVR4 MP and SVR4 ES respectively. Multi-processing is a method of delivering higher-performance computing. Quite simply instead of a single processor forming the central processing unit of the computer several processors are used. There are various ways of linking these together but the most common, certainly among the mid-range UNIX machines, is symmetric multi-processing. In this the processors share a single, common, memory and address spaces are shared between all the processors. The processors then take turns to get their 'slot' in the address space.

The advantage of symmetric multi-processing is that in a single machine there is the power of many machines. Clearly this requires a level of sophistication that is not present in traditional UNIX systems. Not only does the kernel of the operating system have to be capable of supporting multiple processors but so do many of the system services - the device drivers and job schedulers are two areas that clearly need major modification. For USL all this had to be done while at the same time supporting the single processor environments that are still widely used.

USL resolved the problem in the short term by offering both SVR4 and SVR4 MP - the MP version being designed specifically for use by multi-processing machines. Depending on the exact hardware used the MP version can be used in a single-processor machine but the basic version is likely to work more efficiently. The future MP/ES release discussed above will remove the need to have a non-multi-processing version as well as it will better cope with the issue of backward compatibility.

Traditional UNIX is not a very secure operating system and over the years various methods have been used to improve security. For USL security was an important requirement from the start. There were essentially two reasons for this. Firstly, the popularity of UNIX in the government environment meant that success in this market was vital to USL's overall success - and government now demands high levels of security. Secondly, the move towards open systems environments, an area in which UNIX has led the way, has created a very large security threat which would make many customers wary of moving to this environment if the operating system offered was not quite secure.

USL's first high-security product was not based on SVR4 but on a high security version of SVR3.2 - called UNIX System V/MLS (Multi-Level Secure). MLS offered B1-level security. A high-security version of SVR4 called SVR4 ES is now available, offering users B2-level security with some B3 features.

We discussed earlier the importance of kernel modularity in allowing the coexistence between new and old UNIX facilities. Kernel modularity has also allowed for improved security through compartmentalization of facilities - an important requirement at the higher levels of security. Of course the modular kernel will allow new, even more secure, features to be added in the future.

So today users may opt for base SVR4, SVR4 MP or SVR4 ES. The plan for the future is to offer a single SVR4 - a SVR4 MP/ES version which will be available to licensees in mid-1993 - and presumably available in products during 1994. See Figure 97 for a schematic of this transition.

17.4.3 The Veritas File System

The most recent addition to the facilities within SVR4 is the Veritas VxVM file system. Veritas offers a number of advanced features including advanced disk management facilities and increased resilience. The advanced disk management primarily relates to the management of file volumes. As we explained earlier, in UNIX, physical disk space is allocated to groups of files called volumes, in other words a volume is allocated an amount of hard disk space. Veritas allows any volume to span several hard disks rather than being limited to a single disk. More importantly, it allows the amount of disk space allocated to any particular volume to be increased and decreased while the system is online. (The OSF logical volume manager only allows for increasing volume size in the current release.) As we explained earlier in our discussion of OSF/1, without volume management it is necessary to back the volume up, edit the file allocation table in the kernel of the operating system, reboot the system and restore the volume from tape.

Veritas offers increased resilience in two ways. Firstly, through disk mirroring. Some or all of the files held on one hard disk are held in an exact copy, a mirror, on a second disk. In the event of a disk failure the second copy can be used instantly. Secondly, resilience to power or system failure. Because of the way files are accessed and held in cache it was possible, in traditional UNIX, to be unable to rebuild the file system following a power or system failure. Veritas resolves this problem by holding information about files in a different way. Thus in the event of a power or system failure the file system can now be easily rebuilt.

17.4.4 The Future

The future of SVR4 can be divided into two areas. The first, the technical area, seems relatively clear. The second, which one might term the business area, is far more complex, being inextricably bound to the future of AT&T, Novell and the owners of SVR4, USL.

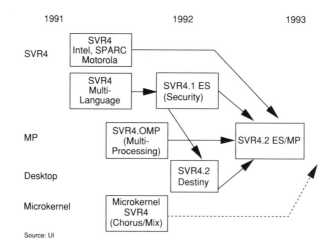

Figure 97. *SVR4 Development Plan*

The technical future of SVR4 and UI-ATLAS is shown in Figure 97, and in Figure 98.

Feature	1992			1993				1994				1995	
	Q2	Q3	Q4	Q1	Q2	Q3	Q4	Q1	Q2	Q3	Q4	1H	2H
Basic System Enhancements													
Asynchronous I/O	+		●→	→	→		■						
Internationalization Enhancements			●			+	■	→	→	→○	□		
Localization Packages			■	→	→	→	■	→	→	→			
Multiprocessing Enhancements	●			→	→		■						
Performance Management Enablers					+		■		→	→	→		
XPG4 base Conformance Enhancements		+	●	→	→		■						
XPG4 Commands and Utilities						+		→	→	→○	□		
DCE Support Package													
DCE Call Directory Service				■			→	→	→				
DCE RPC				■			→	→	→				
DCE Security (Kerberos)				■			→	→	→				
DCE Time Service				■			→	→	→				
Distributed System Management Framework	+		●	■		→	→	→					
Distributed System Management Basics													
Backup and Restore Management				+	●	■→	→	→					
Device Management					●	■	→	→	→				
Network Management									□				
Print Management				+●		■→	→	→					
Software Installation and Distribution Management				+●		■→	→	→					
Software License Management					●	■→	→	→					
Startup and Shutdown Management	+				●		→	→	→				
User and Group Management			+		●	■→	→	→					
ONC + Distributed Computing Services													
Phase 1				+■●		→	→	→					
Phase 2						●	+■	→	→	→			
Phase 3							+●		■	→	→	→	
Transaction Processing Environment Basics													
Enhanced CICS Interoperability							+				□	→	→
Support for the OSI Transaction Processing Standard					●	■	→	→	→				
Support for X/Open Transaction Processing Specifications			+		●		■		→	→	→		
Transaction Processing Environment Enhancements			+		●		■	→	→	→			

Legend: + Technology specification available ● Early Access begins
■ Technology available →Technology expected to be broadly deployed
Hollow figure means date is estimated

Figure 98. *UI Technology Availability Matrix*

In the longer term, just as the Open Software Foundation is looking at a microkernel for OSF/1, so similar technology seems a likely route for SVR4. Some of the original work was done with the Chorus microkernel from Chorus Systems. However, in January 1993 it was revealed[17] that USL was looking at the Mach 3 microkernel from CMU - just like OSF. The two organizations supporting the same microkernel, providing they were similar implementations and not just using the same basic technology but producing a different product, could at last offer a common operating system.

The business future of SVR4 is far from clear. At the end of 1992 Novell and AT&T issued a letter of intent in which AT&T announced that it would sell its USL stock to Novell.

The background is that in 1991 AT&T spun off its Unix System Operations division into a wholly owned subsidiary, Unix System Laboratories (USL). Towards the end of that year AT&T sold 23% of its USL stock - 5% to Novell and the other 18% among 11 other companies. In the letter of intent Novell proposed to buy USL outright and paying with Novell shares. AT&T agreed to the sale prior to the announcement, the 'in principle' agreement of the other eleven shareholders followed soon after. The contractual side of the agreement is still being finalized (as of June 1993).

This seems relatively clear - but what is to become of USL and UNIX? We can only speculate. However, we can think of only one reason why Novell wants USL - to increase its profits. But both when it was part of AT&T and since, the UNIX line has been remarkably unprofitable.

There appear to be two possible outcomes of the purchase:

- By increasing the royalties on SVR4, Novell can make USL profitable - the demand for SVR4 is relatively inelastic (i.e. an increase in price will not cause a fall in demand) and most hardware manufacturers could not easily stop licensing the product. They would probably absorb any price increase themselves and thus leave the end user price unaffected.

- By integrating into Novell Netware some parts of SVR4 - filling the gaps in Netware but making SVR4 redundant once it is done. This scenario could be combined with the first - with the added likelihood that further development of SVR4 would be stopped if significantly higher royalties where not achieved.

Neither scenario is particularly healthy for USL, SVR4 or the companies that depend on them for their products. However, it is only speculation with very few of the real facts known. It will be interesting to see if our predictions turn out to be correct.

---

[17] Roel Pieper, Chief Executive of USL quoted in *Computergram*, No. 2091, 22 January 1993.

17.4.5 Summary

UNIX SVR4 is a good implementation of UNIX, bringing together the three most popular implementations. Since it was originally announced significant improvements have been made in a number of areas and as a result SVR4 is firmly established as the base for a number of companies' UNIX implementations. The fact that, almost without exception, these companies seek to make enhancements to SVR4 means no two implementations are identical. On the other hand the differences are now so slight that for most users and systems managers the various 'flavours' are still SVR4.

17.5 OSF/1 and System V Release 4 : a Comparison

In Chapter 5 we looked at the emergence of the two UNIX 'factions' - the OSF faction and the SVR4 faction. We discussed how vendors were now developing their UNIX-like operating systems on one of these two bases. We have now reviewed the major features and facilities of OSF/1 and SVR4. The question for users is whether one is any better than the other. Are there any advantages, any additional function that you get, in opting for a hardware platform that runs OSF/1 rather than one which runs SVR4?

We would argue that while the question is a sensible one it should not be the first question to be asked. Before functionality is addressed it is vital to ask whether the implementation you are considering matches the standards.

In reality both match the completed standards fully. However, where standards are still emerging OSF/1, being a later implementation, sometimes has a slight lead (matching X/Open's X Transport Interface and POSIX 1003.4 threads for example). We believe that this should not influence the decision too strongly; the standard is only worth having when it is matched by multiple implementations.

If both OSF/1 and SVR4 match the agreed standards then should you be making a decision for one or the other? Our firm belief is that you should not. If you have a policy which says 'only OSF/1' then why not extend that and say 'only AIX' (IBM's implementation of UNIX) or 'only HP-UX' (HP's implementation of UNIX).

The whole point of open systems is to give you the widest choice possible. OSF/1 and SVR4 can coexist and both can participate in an open systems environment based on all the major standards available. The most often heard argument to limit yourself to one is because users, or more likely systems administrators, will find it easier to gain familiarity with one environment. However, given that all OSF/1 implementations, and all SVR4 implementations, differ slightly the whole argument can be logically carried on to, say, the equivalent of adopting a policy of 'only AIX' or 'only HP-UX'.

Quite simply, open systems is about matching standards. Neither OSF/1 not SVR4 are standards in themselves. They both match standards and both are acceptable UNIX choices. To opt for one or the other, even on the basis of some perceived functional difference, is to limit your choices and we could never recommend that.

It thus follows that the question of whether OSF/1 is better than SVR4 is really irrelevant. Decisions made on that basis would be bad decisions. But people will still ask the question. Our answer is the same as that reached by the respected consultants Patricia Seybold's Office Computing Group in the February 1992 issue of their monthly report *UNIX in the Office*. They carried out a very detailed evaluation of both OSF/1 and SVR4 and concluded 'the two technologies appear to stack up very evenly'. There really is no great difference between the two. OSF/1 might have originally had a number of advanced features but USL have significantly enhanced SVR4 since it was first announced. These enhancements have meant that it is now difficult to choose between the two.

Chapter 18 Open Interoperability

I have always depended on the kindness of strangers.[1]

Much of what we have said in the preceding chapters has focused on two major trends in IT, namely:

- distributed computing
- open systems.

We saw earlier that these two are often linked, though they need not be. We have also seen that they have foundered on a major obstacle - the installed base of proprietary systems.

It is also a fact that these proprietary systems may well be distributed and that they may well take part in an open systems environment based on the POSIX standard. However, the reality is that this is not sufficient to create an open, distributed, environment - that requires interoperability rather than portability.

There is a requirement for a distributed, networked, environment which will interoperate using open systems standards. Furthermore, this environment must combine both legacy systems, open proprietary systems and Unix systems.

The first steps to the creation of such an environment were taken by the Open Software Foundation with its Distributed Computing Environment (DCE). DCE has been extended by Unix International into its Atlas Environment. In addition to DCE, the Open Software Foundation has created a set of management tools specifically for distributed environments - the Distributed Management Environment (DME). These are the subject of this chapter.

---

[1] Tennessee Williams, *A Streetcar Named Desire.*

18.1 Distributed Computing Environment (DCE)

The Open Software Foundation's DCE promises to resolve many of the problems associated with interoperability. In addition, 'computer vendors representing over 70% of the market in PCs and workstations are incorporating DCE software in their products'.[2] Furthermore, X/Open has said that it intends to 'integrate the OSF's DCE specifications into X/Open's Common Applications Environment'.[3] If the majority of companies in the industry do offer a product that actually achieves its goal of providing for interoperability amongst heterogeneous systems and it is adopted as an agreed standard then we may well be able to talk about open systems being a reality.

In Chapter 15 we talked about the various levels of interoperability - from physical connection through to totally transparent computing. Most sites moving towards open systems tend not to have progressed beyond the remote file access level - for many this is a network that runs Sun's Network File System (NFS). DCE is basically a toolkit that provides the building blocks to move beyond that to remote process access. In addition, it provides tools for security, structured naming and time services which can provide a very elegant environment, significantly better than one just running NFS. However, it is not in itself the solution, rather it is an enabling technology from which distributed environment can be created.

OSF defined DCE in their original documentation as 'a single software technology that will let computers from a variety of vendors transparently work together and share resources such as computing power, data, printers and other peripheral devices'.[4]

If DCE were to deliver this then it would be a major step forward and provide users, software vendors and systems vendors with considerable benefits. Users would be provided with an open, vendor-neutral environment which both allowed them access to all their computing resource and used that resource more effectively. Software vendors would be provided with the tools to create distributed applications which they could sell into any DCE network no matter what system or operating system it was based upon. Systems vendors would discover that network environments previously closed to them could now be sold to and that DCE enabled them to open up their proprietary architectures.

---

[2] Source: Douglas Hartman, 'Unclogging Distributed Computing', *IEEE Spectrum*, Vol. 29, No. 5, May 1992.

[3] Source: *OSF Open Line*, Vol. 4, No. 3, September 1992.

[4] 'The Distributed Computing Environment Request For Technology', reproduced in *OSF DCE Rationale*, 14 May 1990, from OSF.

An overview of the DCE technologies can be found in Figure 99.

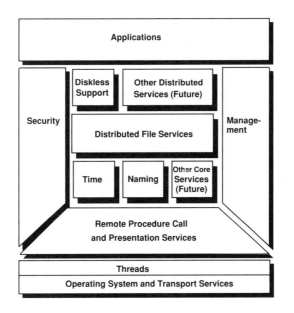

Figure 99. *The DCE Technologies*

The DME Services fit in the 'Other Distributed Services' block in Figure 99. You should note that the interface between the Operating System and Transport Services section and the rest of DCE is clearly defined so that non-Unix systems can support DCE.

To understand DCE we will look at each of the individual blocks in turn and describe what they contribute.

18.1.1 Operating System and Transport Services

DCE works across a network, WAN or LAN, which can be made of heterogeneous machines running a range of operating systems. The only requirement is that the platforms involved run the DCE software package.

18.1.2 Threads

Traditional computer programs are single-threaded - that means that they have a single stream of execution. For example, a program with ten subroutines will execute them sequentially.

Some programs lend themselves to being multi-threaded - that is, having multiple streams of execution where several parts of the code can be executing simultaneously. This multi-threading can exploit the multiple machines on a DCE network because the individual thread processes can be sent to a different processors. In a client/server environment, this enables the server to cope with multiple clients - it can be processing data from one client while waiting for another piece of data from a second client.

Some operating systems already support threads, in which case the DCE threads may not need to be implemented on the platform. However, for those that need threads DCE provides a user-level threads library based on the POSIX 1003.4a *pthreads* draft standard. This provides programmers with an API to allow them to create and manipulate threads. The last sentence is fundamental - applications have to be written to make use of the threading, it does not happen automatically.

18.1.3 Remote Procedure Call

We have already explained in Chapter 16 what a remote procedure call is - and we looked at two examples, NFS and NCS. We saw that NFS was file-based and NCS was process-based and both implemented their own versions of the RPC mechanism, The OSF selected the NCS remote procedure call because it was implemented at a higher level than the NFS RPC, was therefore easier to code and did not carry the overhead of XDR translation between like systems.

Basically the RPC provides the ability to create distributed applications. These distributed applications allow individual procedures in an application to run on another computer in the network. This has advantages in terms of efficient use of processor resource - it makes the old phrase 'the network is the computer' a reality.

Like threads the RPC must be coded in - programmers must actually use it. In reality it is not much different from writing programs making use of local calls, which is very much business as usual for programmers. However, it does use a special Interface Definition Language (very similar to ANSI C) which is then compiled. The output of the compilation includes a client stub and a server stub which together make the operation of the call transparent to the user.

18.1.4 Distributed Time Services

A large mainframe computer has a single clock and everything runs according to that clock. In a multi-machine network each individual machine will have its own clock. If these machines have to interoperate, as in a client/server environment, then confusion can arise in processes and programs that are time-dependent if the clocks do not all show the same time.

DCE resolves this problem by providing groups of machines with one or possibly a number of time servers. Time servers are machines that hold the time that all other machines in the network must synchronize with. There may be one or more time servers on a network but all will show the same time and will ensure that they, and the clients, keep together.

The distributed time service operation uses the following:

- time providers which take the time from the universal time clock (UTC)
- global time servers and couriers (carrying the time) across LANs
- local time servers on LANs (they feed off the above)
- time clerk responsible for time synchronisation
- time adjustment for out of line clocks (this has to be done in small stages since a sudden change of time will upset time-stamped activities such as logging and recovery).

Typically, time administration is a task for the systems administrator rather than for programmers, but even so programs have to be modified to use the new timing system. Administrators simply have to set the system up correctly initially - from then on administrative maintenance is infrequent.

18.1.5 Directory and Naming Services

One of the central ideas of DCE is the concept of a cell. A cell is a group of users, systems and resources that share common DCE services. While the systems in the cell may all be located together geographically (such as in a LAN) it is more likely that the membership of a particular cell will be influenced by a common purpose as well as by administrative and performance considerations. So it is quite possible for a single cell to include machines in London, Paris and New York; while the other machines in the London office are in a second cell which is just local to that office.

Users will want to access the resources of the cell of which they are a member, but may sometimes wish to access resources external to the cell. Given that a complete DCE network could consist of many hundreds or thousands of machines, with peripherals to match, finding a specific resource, such as a particular printer, could be problematic. Therefore this type of information is held in a central database within each cell (which can be replicated for resilience) and DCE provides a mechanism to interrogate both the local cell directory and a global directory. This directory service is based on the already established X.500 (ISO 9594) standard and programmers building applications can, in the unlikely event they need to, use the API defined in the X/Open Directory Service (XDS).

To hide the complexity of the network, both resources and users have to have names that are both constructed logically and the same all over the network. DCE provides a distributed naming service to enable this. It is the administrator who sets these names up and manages the directory service. The administration of a cell directory, and for at least one administrator a global directory, is business as usual for the administrator - though the methodology may be different from current practice.

18.1.6 Distributed File System

Today most sites that offer a distributed file system use Sun's Network File System (NFS) - it is undoubtedly the *de facto* standard. NFS, like any other distributed file system, makes remote files appear local. However, as NFS networks grow, and in reality this means above ten machines, they become difficult to manage. In addition, there may be performance problems, reliability issues and doubts about data consistency. As a result the OSF did not adopt NFS as the distributed file system in DCE but chose the Andrew File System (AFS) developed at Carnegie Mellon University and marketed by Transarc Corp. OSF has made some modifications to AFS to enable it to fit in with the other parts of DCE; to avoid confusion we refer to it here as DFS - Distributed File System.

In an ideal world a distributed environment would be managed and seen as one massive file system. In reality, though it can be seen as such, it is impractical to manage it this way - it has to be broken into manageable units. The Distributed Computing Environment has exactly such units - cells. The DFS copes with cells and uses distributed databases to keep track of file locations, access control listings and so on.

With DFS users can access files anywhere on the network with the result that in very large networks there can be a degradation in performance due to the volume of network traffic. NFS resolves this by caching some of the data onto the local machine. However, it caches relatively small amounts. In contrast, DFS caches large amounts of data. Thus the client makes fewer requests from the file server reducing server and network load.

The main problem associated with cached data is that clients work with the cached version not the server version. Another client requesting the same data would have no knowledge that the server has already issued a copy. This is important because the client with the copy might already have amended it - making the server version in effect out of date. NFS keeps no record about clients which have copies of the data - it is described therefore as stateless. By contrast DFS allows the server to keep such records - it is therefore described as stateful. It allows users to have read-only access to files, and when a write access is issued and the file amended the users who have read only access have their permission revoked and have to request a new, up-to-date, copy.

To improve resilience DFS supports replication of all its network services - in other words, it supports multiple servers. This has clear advantages in terms of reliability and while possible with special configurations of NFS is generally difficult to administer.

That is not to say that administration of DFS is not a significant task but there are tools provided to enable the administrator to make full use of the varied and flexible configurations available. The down side of this is that the administrator has the additional task of designing and evolving a configuration that best exploits the needs of the users.

Application programmers use DFS transparently by making POSIX file system calls. DFS can be used on its own without the RPC element of DCE if applications requiring distributed files rather than distributed processes are required.

DFS provides an easily managed, high-performance, consistent and reliable distributed file system which is generally seen as being superior to NFS. However, NFS has a much larger installed base. Therefore the OSF has done two things. Firstly, it has constructed the whole of DCE to run on either NFS or DFS. Secondly, DCE provides gateways that allow NFS clients to operate with DFS file servers. These gateways provide a migration path to DFS for sites already using NFS. The benefits of DFS are such that we imagine it will establish itself very quickly.

18.1.7 Security

The aim of DCE is to provide an open, readily accessible network. This does not mean that security issues are abandoned. On the contrary, security in such an environment is vital. In the case of a single machine, the operating system can be trusted to protect resources from unauthorized access - in a distributed system it cannot. The network is open by definition so mechanisms are needed to detect and report on unauthorized attempts to access resources. There are three important services which help to achieve this:

- an authentication service to enable two processes on different machines to be certain of one another's identity
- an authorization service that grants privileges with respect to resources
- a secure messaging service to check both that a message has arrived intact and unaltered and, when required, that it is protected by encryption from eavesdroppers.

See Section 8.3.1 for a discussion of the concepts of authentication and authorization on a network.

DCE provides such a complex security requirement, based on the Kerberos system developed as part of Project Athena at MIT. (Kerberos, or more usually Cerberus, was the three-headed dog that guarded the gates of hell!)[5]

It authenticates users at logon and provides each one with a ticket containing information such as their name and location. Access control lists are then to used to check whether the holder of the ticket may access a particular resource. The security details, access control listings and so on, are held on a security server which should be kept physically secure to avoid it being tampered with.

It should be noted that Kerberos does not control access to resources on nodes in the system. That task is still performed by the security system peculiar to that node as long as it can operate with Kerberos. This, as we now know, is called *authorization*.

DCE provides a comprehensive secure environment that can also be used in combination with any security mechanisms found in the base operating system. Programmers who use the RPC within DCE will automatically make use of the security as this is integrated with it. In addition, programming interfaces direct to the security service are available. Administrators will have to change their method-ologies to administer a new security system but the system is relatively simple to administer. Users should see no difference - they login only once and DCE does the rest.

18.1.8 Diskless Support Service

To keep costs down many sites with distributed machines opt for diskless or dataless machines. These machines hold no data, or operating system, which is downloaded from the server at start-up. In the case of a dataless machine, any disk is used as paging space to increase the efficiency of the system and lessen the network traffic to the server. It would be a major weakness in DCE if such machines could not participate in the system. DCE provides a range of diskless support services which offer the four basic functions that local disks traditionally support:

- booting up with the operating system kernel
- obtaining configuration information
- remote file system support
- remote swapping support.

---

[5] For a full description of Project Athena, one of the first attempts to produce a truly distributed computing environment, see George Champine, *MIT Project Athena* (Digital Press 1991).

Most of this is transparent to the programmer. The systems administrator merely needs to set up the system initially to allow heterogeneous clients to boot from the same server. After that the diskless system runs without any need for further involvement.

18.1.9 Building a Distributed Computing Environment

It is important to realize that DCE is not the solution to distributed computing - it is merely the enabling technology. It provides programmers with a range of tools to create distributed applications and administrators with other tools to administer a distributed environment. A traditional application will not benefit fully from DCE though it may run in a DCE environment and use such functions as the security service and the distributed file system.

One example of how DCE can be used by higher-level software is demonstrated by the overview of Transarc's Encina online transaction processing system shown in Figure 75.

It is also important to realize that DCE technology is scalable. A single DCE cell can be just a single client and a single server - though in reality that is most unlikely. Certainly DCE cells with fewer than ten clients are quite conceivable. By contrast a complete environment might consist of many hundreds of cells spread across the whole world - all taking part in a single Distributed Computing Environment.

One can imagine a two-cell environment, one cell consisting of a single server and a handful of clients, the other of a multiplicity of different types of servers each replicated for resilience together serving potentially thousands of clients spread across the globe. DCE provides for both and offers the advantages of truly distributed computing to every user.

18.1.10 DCE Technologies

DCE was developed by OSF after it had issued a Request for Technology and selected from the numerous submissions the components it felt would best meet the requirements. (For a full description of the OSF RFT process see Chapter 10.) There is therefore nothing new in DCE - all the individual components are already proven to work. What is new is bringing them together into a coherent integrated package - a task that was contracted to IBM despite the fact that none of the original technologies came from that company. Figure 100 shows the origins of the various technologies.

Figure 100. *Origins of the DCE Technologies*		
Function	*Selection*	*Origin*
Remote Procedure Call	RPC	HP & DEC
Naming Services	DECdns (distributed naming services)	DEC
OSI X.500 Directory Server Interface	DIR-X	Siemens
Security Authentication	Kerberos	MIT & HP
Time Services	DECdts (distributed time service)	DEC
Threads	CMA (Concert MultiThread Architecture)	DEC
Distributed File	AFS 4.0 (Andrew File System)	Transarc
Diskless Operation	AFS and BOOTP	Transarc & HP

Early press comment on DCE produced mixed reactions. However, its inclusion in X/Open's Common Application Environment will increase its acceptance as the *de facto* technology base for distributed computing.

18.2 Distributed Management Environment (DME)

One of the biggest problems associated with computing today is the management of distributed systems. The trend towards distributed computing has meant that network and systems managers are faced with the task of managing large networks often made up of heterogeneous machines. This is the issue the Open Software Foundation set out to tackle with its Distributed Management Environment.

The OSF DME Request for Technology was issued in July 1990 in the form of 5,000 copies of the RFT, announcements in academic and trade publications and postings to electronic bulletin boards. The 21 September deadline saw 42 letters on intent to submit technology. The 25 submissions which materialized by the 15 December deadline were evaluated by ten OSF personnel and ten outside experts and technology selections made.

In addressing the manageability problems, OSF has taken into account the existing management protocols - CMIP (the Common Management Information Protocol) which works over OSI, and SNMP (the Simple Network Management Protocol) which works over TCP/IP. However, they have advanced distributed management significantly further than these essentially rather basic protocols.

There are two things that should be said about DME before going any further. The first is that DME is not just the management side of DCE. Initially it was independent of DCE but recently DCE has been made a requirement. Secondly, unlike DCE it is not just an enabling technology. When you implement DME you can implement a specific solution rather than simply the building blocks for developing your own. However, as well as providing specific solutions DME prescribes a model for future management software that can integrate into the modules already included within DME. As a result DME is in some senses prescriptive but it is expected that software developers will produce additional management packages that fit into DME.

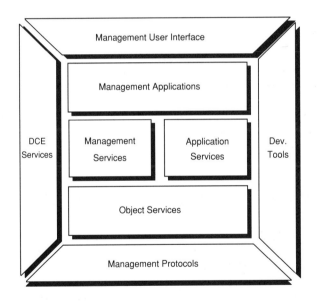

Figure 101. *The Structure of DME*

Like the other OSF products DME was developed from software selected through the RFT process. The integrator of the different components for DME is a team of developers from the OSF - originally based in Munich and now based at OSF's main offices in Cambridge, Massachusetts. They issued the original RFT in July 1990 and announced their selection in September 1991. A final product will probably not be available until the end of 1993 at the earliest. The difficulty with this is that solutions to the problem of managing distributed environments are needed now. As a result different vendors are coming up with different interim, and in some case longer-term, solutions. At this time it would seem sensible to select only those solutions that will migrate easily towards DME - leaving the choice open in the future to stay with your initial selection or migrate to DME. There are a number of current offerings from vendors, most of whom claim a migration path to DME of some sort.

Figure 101 shows the DME model in picture form.

18.2.1 Management User Interface

The interface provides a standard access method to all management applications. There will be both a graphical, Motif-based, and a non-graphical version. The idea behind the interface is to make familiar and non-familiar tasks work in roughly the same way so that a systems administrator or manager can carry out all the tasks with relative ease.

The interface has the following properties:

- consistency across systems and network management operations
- single point of access to all management information
- simple development facilities
- no programming knowledge is needed.

18.2.2 Management Applications

As well as providing a general framework for the development of distributed management tools and applications, DME provides four management applications itself:

- Distributed Printing and Management
- Host Management
- Distributed Licensing and Management
- Software Distribution and Installation.

The reason why OSF has opted to provide these is that they are sensibly provided the same way in every case. Take, for example, printing. If all printers are managed in a similar way printer management would be a much simpler task. Secondly, from the user's point of view if the way printing is accessed is the same in each application it is much simpler to learn new applications and use them efficiently. Thirdly, from the software developer's point of view the availability of common print management tools is a major advantage. Most applications depend on printing but it is not a special benefit of the system - but the developer still has to develop a complete printer management function within the application. It would be far more efficient and cost effective to be able to do that by simply slotting in a module of pre-written code that handled all the printing tasks in a way familiar to the user.

This functionality is a key part of DME and covers management applications, management services and application services. The management application part is the portion which the user sees, the screens written to the management user interface standard, which present the tasks. In other words, management applications reside in the user application and provide an API into the services beneath.

18.2.3 Application and Management Services

Application services are the actual pieces of code that carry out the management applications. Management services are where management policies are defined. For example, the distributed printing application: the screens which are in the user application and present printing choices are management applications. The actual code which drives the printers and allows what the management application requested to happen is the application service. The policies such as 'printer X can only be used by certain specified users' are set out in the management services.

18.2.4 Object Services

The application and management services are built on the foundation of object services. However, DME has significantly enhanced the object oriented ideas contained in CMIP and SNMP. In simple terms what DME does is provide a methodology so that devices can be seen as objects and these objects can contain software. So, for example, a router vendor who provides a router box now also provides a DME router object containing the management information base (MIB) and also software for interacting with the router. The software, part of the basic object, will allow DME applications to interact with the router to perform functions such as downloading software and analysing network traffic in the standard DME way. It will also provide the icon so that the object is displayed on the management user interface. Everything is bundled in one package and, like traditional objects, can be invoked by other objects in the system.

18.2.5 Management Protocols

The traditional management protocols are SNMP over TCP/IP and CMIP over OSI - DME supports both of these. However, they are seen as rather insecure - there is no authentication, for example. By contrast RPC is seen as a good management protocol as it is location-transparent, secure and efficient. So, in addition, DME supports the RPC within DCE.

Though to date there have been no announcements there is nothing stopping vendors of proprietary systems announcing implementations of DME over their own proprietary protocols.

18.2.6 Application Development Tools

These are the tools within DME with which to develop new management applications. They provide a set of APIs to access objects and protocols - two APIs are provided, one for objects and one for protocols, both ANSI C-based.

18.2.7 DME Technologies

DME was developed after OSF had issued a Request for Technology and selected from the numerous submissions the components it felt would best meet the requirements. There is very little new in DME - the individual components are already proven to work. Integrating them, a task the OSF had initially given to its own developers, is now a joint OSF member venture, headed by IBM.

The components and their sources are shown in the following table. As can be seen they are divided into the framework and the applications that sit within the framework.[6]

The Ingredients of System Management

Because of the size and complexity of the constituent DME technologies, the delivery of DME needs to be phased. In July 1992, OSF announced that it would deliver DME technology in a two-phase process starting in 1993:

- Distributed Services Release to provide key distributed management services to DCE
- DME Framework Release, delivering the integrated DME framework, development tools and selected framework applications.

The details of the application services (Phase 1) and the framework (Phase 2) are outlined in the table below.

---

[6] *UNIX World*, Interoperability Supplement 1992

Application Services

- HP's distribution utilities for software installation, distribution management over networked systems;
- Palladium, a printing system developed by MIT in conjunction with IBM, DEC, and HP to provide distributed management of print services;
- software for licence service, management, and administration from HP and Gradient Technology Inc;
- Tivoli's distributed host management software, known as HUGS, for host/user/group subnet, services.

Framework

- HP's Openview Windows, for the graphical user interface which includes pulldown menus and maps;
- HP's Openview Network Manager Server, which supports network management protocols like the simple network management protocol and the common management interface protocol;
- Groupe Bull's CM-API, an application programming interface that lets network management protocols talk to interprocess communications;
- other higher-level APIs from Tivoli Systems and IBM Corp., used to hide the complexity of communication protocols;
- software from HP and Tivoli to handle routing, address resolution, and address authentication;
- software from Banyan Systems Inc., to handle event management, logging, alerts, alarms, auditing and reporting.

18.2.8 OMNIPoint

It is convenient to look now at a standard model for the management of complex heterogeneous networks. OMNIPoint stands for Open Management Interoperability Point, a project completed in 1993 with US (NIST) and UK (CCTA) backing as well as support from user groups and consortia. In essence, OMNIPoint is a description of the processes and systems applications necessary to manage large networks. It adopts object oriented techniques (via CORBA) and, although based on the OSI model, it also encompasses SNMP. Since UI and OSF, among others, were involved in OMNIPoint, it is reasonable to assume that their management products will be consistent with it.

Like DME, OMNIPoint uses X/Open's Management Protocol (XMP) to hide the differences between OSI and SNMP protocols. The OMNIPoint management model is illustrated in Figure 102.[7]

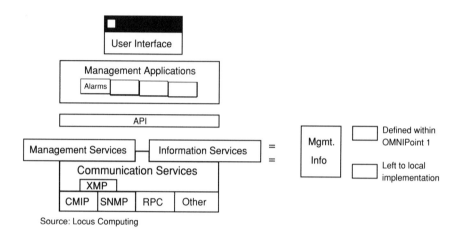

Source: Locus Computing

Figure 102. *The OMNIPoint Model*

18.2.9 Availability of DME

Due to the complexity of the DME technologies, they will be released in two phases:

Phase 1: Distributed Services release

- License management service
- Software installation and distribution management service
- Printing service based on ISO DIS 10175
- Event management service.

Phase 2: Framework, development tools and applications

- Management user interface
- Object services/development toolkit
- Development toolkit
- SNMP/CMIP support.

---

[7] From *Distributed Computing Review*, a Locus publication, January 1993.

In 1994, there will be work on code fixes, performance and some functional enhancements with a new release planned for 1995. This will include a C++ API and support for enhanced versions of SNMP and CMIP.

18.2.10 Conclusion

DME has set out to provide a significantly enhanced management environment for distributed systems. The idea of providing both a framework for management applications and some sample applications is new and may establish DME more quickly than would otherwise have happened. However, the success or failure of DME depends, as always in open systems, on its wide acceptance. This has yet to happen - though in fairness the significant improvements DME makes to traditional protocols means that on balance it is likely to succeed. In the meantime system and network administrators should select only those products which have a migration plan to DME.

In the interim, the major IT vendors are not being idle on the distributed management front and some of their pre-DME products are listed below:

- Openview from Hewlett-Packard
- Netview/Systemview from IBM
- Enterprise Management Architecture (EMA) from DEC with the DECmcc and Polycenter products
- SMS Framework from Unisys
- SuNet Manager from Sun
- Open Systems Management Centre from ICL
- Integrated Systems Management from Bull.

Claims to be DME compliant before the technology is delivered should be viewed with some disbelief.

Some of these offerings contain technology planned for use in DME and all aspire to a smooth migration to, or coexistence with, the delivered DME technology. Whether these proprietary products will converge happily to some common specification like DME or the UI-ATLAS equivalent is not clear. In the meantime, the Network Management Forum's OMNIPoint framework seeks to limit the variations in approach to the SNMP and CMIP protocols and is attempting to standardize the object management approach to distributed network management.

18.3 UI-ATLAS

18.3.1 Background

UNIX International, like the OSF, has recognized that the operating system is not the answer to most of the issues confronting open and distributed systems users today. The operating system has traditionally been concerned with a single machine and the peripherals and hosting other functions such as networking software. The complexity of using and managing a heterogeneous network of systems mandates other functions.

We have already discussed the OSF DCE and DME environments and here we cover the UI equivalent known as *UI-ATLAS*, a distributed computing model. After researching distributed computing requirements both inside and outside UI, it was concluded that the major business issues[8] were:

- ease of use
- standards-based environments
- protection of current investment
- broader access to, and integration of, information.

There can be little dispute between UI, OSF and X/Open over these needs, called by UI Stage 1 of the requirements. Stage 2 was drawn up, in September 1990, by a task force whose job was to define a distributed computing model which addressed the needs uncovered in Stage 1. The requirements laid down by the task force for such a model were that it must:

- have a lifetime greater than 10 years
- be based on existing and advanced technology
- be scalable to larger networks and enterprises
- be portable over a wide variety of architectures
- provide interoperability to existing systems
- provide compatibility with existing Unix systems
- be modular
- be easy to use and apply.

The Stage 2 implementation is expected to be delivered over two or three years (from 1991). The timescales can be found in the evolving issues of the *UI System V Roadmap* published at the start of each year.

---

[8] Compare these with the X/Open and other research in Chapter 2.

18.3.2 The UI-ATLAS Model

The words used by UI to set the scene for UI-ATLAS were 'Open Systems - beyond the operating system ... '.[9] This supports our thesis that the operating system is less important than what can be achieved by the functions it supports or hosts. Atlas is variously described as a framework, an integrated set of technologies, a long-range architecture and a distributed computing model. What it represents is UI's vision of the evolution of distributed computing systems based on its research on user requirements.

It is often difficult to read into UI documents whether UI-ATLAS is really an architecture, a set of software or both. It appears to us to be a specified set of enabling technologies and standards into which fit existing (and future) software-based technologies. Given this interpretation, it can be seen to be based on, and support:

- UNIX SVR4
- Tuxedo OLTP (integrated)
- X/Open DTP
- TCP/IP, OSI and OSI TP
- Open Network Computing (ONC) environment from Sun Microsystems, including NFS
- Elements of OSF's DCE and DME
- OSF/Motif and OpenLook
- Object technologies

In the 'Technical Overview', it explains 'UI-ATLAS is a five-layer framework for a complete software environment'. We will discuss these layers briefly now.

18.3.3 The UI-ATLAS Layers

In Figure 103 we have reproduced the standard UI-ATLAS model showing these five layers and their constituents. In the following pages we will describe the structure of the UI-ATLAS framework and then examine some SVR4 implementation details.

Base Operating Systems Services: These are provided by SVR4, but UI-ATLAS can be implemented on other Unix platforms.

Network Communication Services: The network services allow environments like DEC's NAS, IBM's SNA and PC LANs to interoperate within UI-ATLAS.

---

[9] Nick Price, 'UNIX SVR4 and UI-ATLAS Technical Overview', Nick Price, 1992.

The network services can use 'any reliable transport layer' - TCP/IP or OSI, for example - via the X/Open Transport Interface (XTI). The IDL compiler supports the ONS and DCE RPCs and will offer network access via the OSI RPC when available.

System Services: These are fundamental services that allow distributed computing system to function. They include:

- Object management, based on the work of the OMG to allow new services to be distributed as objects.

- Federated naming services. The UI-ATLAS naming services will include Internet Direct Name Service (DNS), X.500, OSF DCE Cell Directory Service (CDS), ONC Network Information Service (NIS), NFS and UFS.

- Time services are provided in two classes, the second class using the DCE Distributed Time Service.

- Systems management. In UI-ATLAS, this is an enabling framework rather than a set of tools. It supports a variety of user interfaces and allows the addition and customization of systems management applications.

Application Services: These services are for use in distributed applications and comprise:

- Transaction processing. The OLTP aspects of UI-ATLAS are covered by the Tuxedo System/T transaction monitor (described in Chapter 16). UI-ATLAS Tuxedo has X/Open XA compliant interfaces.

- File services. UI-ATLAS provides an enhanced version of the Network File System (NFS), referred to as Enhanced NFS. Features of the UI-ATLAS file services are:

  - Standard NFS features.

  - Data and directory caching at the client.

  - File replication for availability purposes.

  - Wide Area Network (WAN) support.

  - File service security via authentication. UI-ATLAS authentication mechanisms are Kerberos, the Challenge-Response[10] mechanism (CR/1) and a scheme based on public-key encryption.

  - File system stacking. This features a layered approach to file access and file caching, rather like the layered architectures we discussed in communications. Through such layers or stacks, file systems features can be implemented across different file system types. For example,

---

[10] 'Who goes there?'

caching can be a feature of the file system itself and is then applicable to many different file types.

■ POSIX compliance.

UI-ATLAS Cross Layer Features

There are two of these, *security* and *interoperability*.

Security: UI-ATLAS security services span every layer of the UI-ATLAS architecture and are based on SVR4 ES. SVR4 ES provides the B2 level of security based on the US National Computer Security Center (NCSC) and provides security services now familiar to to the dedicated reader:

● authentication

● authorization

● data integrity

● data confidentiality

● digital signature (proof of authenticity and origin of data).

It is an area for debate as to how consistent B2 security can be across a UI-ATLAS heterogeneous network.

Interoperability: UI-ATLAS provides interoperability between UNIX and the PC and mainframe worlds as follows:

● *MS-DOS and Macintosh Desktops* - via a variety of networking technologies including NetWare, LAN Manager, PC Interface and PC-NFS.

● *IBM Mainframes* - using the features of SNA, OSI and NFS.[11]

● *Departmental Systems* - using TCP/IP, OSI and NFS.

● *OSF DCE Compatible Systems* - UI-ATLAS will support the DCE technologies.

The UI-ATLAS 1993 Roadmap outlined two requirements for new building blocks with interoperability aspects:

● UNIX to NetWare interoperability

● Interapplication communications facility.

---

[11] IBM Mainframes also support TCP/IP, as a matter of interest.

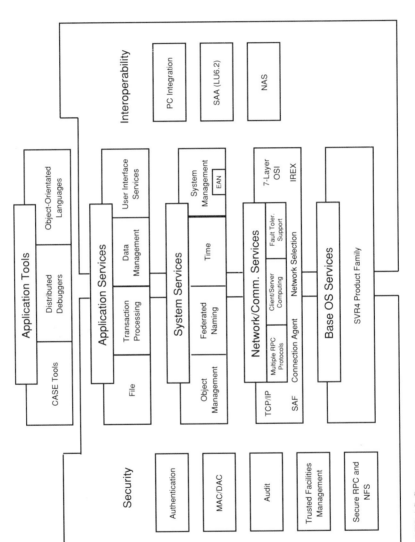

Figure 103. *UI-ATLAS Structure*

UI-ATLAS and DCE

In October 1992, USL announced its intention to ship early versions of the OSF Distributed Computing Environment (DCE) called DCE/SVR4. This version will contain:

- the DCE Remote Procedure Call (RPC 2.0)
- Kerberos security
- DCE Cell Directory Services (CDS)
- threads
- DCE Timing services
- X.500, added to DCE/SVR4 by USL and Siemens Nixdorf.[12]

In the future, UI will add the DCE Distributed File System (DFS) to complete the integration of DCE.

UI-ATLAS and DME

USL does not intend to deliver the OSF Distributed Management Environment (DME) in the form announced by OSF. It will contain much of the DME Gradient Technologies and Tivoli technologies but will also incorporate other technologies:

- user and group management from Pyramid
- software distribution and installation from Unisys
- print management from Siemens Nixdorf[13]
- OSF/Motif from the OSF as the user interface to DM (Distributed Management)/SVR4.

UI views the open computing world as comprising three environments and it is these that UI-ATLAS is to address as it evolves.

18.3.4 UI Computing Environments

Corporate Hub Computing

UI sees this as a mainframe type of centre employing large transaction processing servers and high-availability file systems. Like other elements of the UI-ATLAS

---

[12] It was Siemens Nixdorf which ported DCE to SVR4.

[13] DME uses Palladium.

framework, the core of this environment is SVR4[14] which, together with the planned functions in the UI Roadmap, aims to fulfil the following requirements:

- symmetric multiprocessing
- distributed OLTP
- security
- use of OSI and TCP/IP
- systems management
- support for multiple RDB types
- fault resiliency
- capacity planning.

The core technologies underpinning these goals are SVR4, Tuxedo/T,[15] and a variety of database systems such as Informix, Oracle and Sybase. There will also be links to existing systems in an enterprise, for example, DB2 on MVS mainframes.

Future enhancements in the Corporate Hub environment include administrative features like fault and performance management, all in an object oriented framework.

Distributed/Server Computing

To avoid the corporate hub becoming an 'island', UI has accommodated in the Roadmap features which will address the connectivity and server requirements of heterogeneous networks, for example:

- OSI
- distributed object management
- distributed systems management
- distributed OLTP
- network security
- DCE support.

Like the corporate environment described above, the distributed or server[16] environment uses existing technologies, such as SVR4 and NFS, as well as those in plan in the Roadmap. It is therefore an evolving picture that we are painting here and not a complete solution.

---

[14] SVR4 MP today, SVR4 ES/MP in the future.

[15] TopenD is also an OLTP option.

[16] UI documentation uses both terms.

Desktop Computing

This last environment focuses on the growing desktop computer population the majority of which, at least in the Unix world, is connected to other systems. The main objective of this environment is to integrate the user of personal productivity tools, like spreadsheets, into the enterprise IT network. The needs of the desktop systems user are catered for in this environment by features such as:

- ease of use, including the OpenLook and OSF/Motif GUIs and graphical systems administration
- interoperability via standards such as X Windows
- application development tools.

UNIX SVR4.2, the 'Destiny' product, is said to be the vehicle for driving the desktop environment towards its goals.[17]

The information handling aspects of the three environments we have examined are classified by UI literature as shown in Figure 104.

Figure 104. *Information Categories in UI Environments.*	
Scenario	*Environment*
Information Users	Desktop
Information Brokers	Distributed/Server
Information Providers	Corporate Hub

Conclusion

It is clear that the announcement of ATLAS took Unix International beyond the operating system, in the same way that DCE had done for the Open Software Foundation. By offering DCE on SVR4 we believe that Unix International has significantly improved the interoperability of SVR4. However, it has also significantly increased the chances of DCE gaining total acceptance. As DCE gains in acceptance so ATLAS, as a different product, seems increasingly irrelevant. So in performing a much needed service for one product (DCE) it seems that UI might have killed off its own.

---

[17] See the UI publication on SVR4.2 - 2-UXD13-0692 for more details.

18.4 Architecture Neutral Distribution Format (ANDF)

The Architecture Neutral Distribution Format (ANDF) was specified as an OSF Request for Technology (RFT) to enable the mass distribution of software in the open systems market. The reason for having a new method of distributing software via the usual methods of 'shrink wrapped' or source is that they have some disadvantages. In the first instance, the shipping of software in binary format limits the platforms on which it can run to those of with architectures compatible with that binary format. Secondly, the shipping of source code, although allowing more execution platforms, is open to theft of programming ideas or modules of the code itself.

The RFT said 'the OSF is soliciting technologies that will simplify the distribution of software by providing a single format for distribution that is hardware-independent. The architecture-neutral distribution format (ANDF) will provide an alternative to current techniques that require a separate format for each hardware architecture.'

ANDF, which offers a format between binary and source, gives obvious benefits to hardware and software vendors in the wider availability of application software and viable platforms respectively. ANDF opens up more platforms to software than the application binary interface (ABI) method but does not preclude it.

The successful submission for the adopted ANDF technology came from the UK Royal Signals and Radar Establishment[18] which had been doing research into application portability since about 1985. The technology it was developing was known as TDF (Ten15 Distribution Format).

What is ANDF?

ANDF is both a format and a translation mechanism and has several elements to it. These are illustrated schematically[19] in Figure 105. The actual mechanism is a little more complex than we have shown in the diagram but the principle is illustrated.

The issue of performance of ANDF delivered code was addressed at an early stage by OSF. The three reference platforms showed ANDF code in the first snapshot performed within 3% on average of the best native compilers for the reference platforms. Subsequent snapshots showed even better performance and increased robustness. The flow of the ANDF process is as follows:

---

[18] Now called the Defence Research Agency.

[19] The actual process has more stages than this.

- The source code is converted into the ANDF format. Initially it will handle C source code and others such as Fortran and Cobol. The code in this form is now non-executable and unreadable to humans.

- The ANDF code is transferred to a distribution medium and shipped to sites which require the software it represents.

- At the receiving site, the software installers translate the ANDF format into executable format for a particular hardware platform. Each target platform has a different translator but they all work from a single ANDF intermediate format.

At present, C is the only language with an ANDF format converter although ANDF translators have been written for VAX, MIPS, 80386, SPARC, 68000 and RISC System/6000 architectures. A revised ANDF specification from the DRA is capable of supporting C, C++, Fortran and Pascal. By the end of 1992, OSF had delivered three snapshots of the ANDF technology with a fourth due in first quarter of 1993.

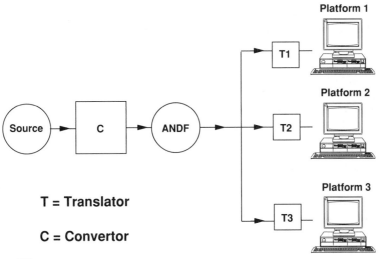

T = Translator

C = Convertor

Source: OSF

Figure 105. *Architecture Neutral Distribution Format*

There will be different converters for different languages and the target translators can be modified to handle the ANDF formats from these new languages. In theory, if a new hardware architecture is shipped, it only needs a new translator to be obtained for that platform to take advantage of existing applications in ANDF format.

The Status of ANDF

Despite our simple discussion, ANDF is complex underneath the usability features and will take some time before it is mature enough to gain widespread adoption. In May 1992, OSF changed the status of ANDF from an ***engineering*** program to an ***advanced technology*** program. This meant that its delivery was not imminent and was in reality still a research item needing further work on the underlying elements and ensuring universal usability. To this end, OSF is now cooperating with the European Esprit project and with USL, who are validating the ANDF technology and sponsoring development for their Destiny operating system (SVR4.2).

OSF and USL are committed to delivering a single ANDF specification to the marketplace, according to Ira Goldstein, Research Vice President of the OSF. ANDF will probably be complete by the end of 1993 and in productive use by 1994/95.

18.5 Conclusions

The picture we have painted about available functions and futures should be tempered with reality as to what can actually be delivered for use in any open systems planning. Much of the literature we consulted in drawing up this chapter was glowing with confidence about being able to do everything one might dream of in a distributed environment. In particular, examine the features and implementation details of any technology purveyed - it may involve you in an enormous amount of retraining and ongoing effort.

It must be said that the offerings of the OSF are more closely integrated than the components which comprise UI-ATLAS. The latter is essentially a 'shopping list', albeit a good one, of components for which 'some assembly is required'. UI-ATLAS has several components from DCE and DME which are complemented by other offerings. We feel that this must result in the loss of some of the synergy of the DCE/DME offerings which were selected and an integrable whole.

The next two to three years should see which of these technologies become accepted and which become effectively obsolete. It will prove an exciting time because the computer industry is undergoing another revolution. Whether the outcome is chaos or order will depend on how well these technologies live up to their claims. For all our sakes let us hope that they live up to them well.

Chapter 19 Final Thoughts

Afoot and light-hearted I take to the open road.
Healthy, free, the world before me.
The long brown path before me leading wherever I choose.[1]

The idea of forcing vendors into open price warfare may be attractive to users, but only adequate profit can provide the investment for research and innovation by those same vendors. It is a question of whether you believe that the supermarket philosophy of 'pile them high, sell them cheap' really applies to information technology. After all, little research or innovation is needed in the baked bean or saucepan industries.

Almost all innovative hardware and software products in the IT world today were either developed or funded by major proprietary vendors, often at considerable cost. Forcing profits margins to the very base may have the effect of destroying such work. Standards bodies, by their very nature, are slow, non-innovative and bureaucratic. The research and development sites of major vendors are usually the opposite and their survival is essential, in our opinion, to IT vitality.

Think for a moment about Xerox PARC (Ethernet, Smalltalk, Icon-based interfaces and early RPC models[2]), IBM (SQL, SNA, PC), and DEC (Clustering, Time Services, 4GB address spaces, etc.) and you will see that the Unix world is relatively sterile[3] and has inherent limitations even after 24 years of development. In fact, one of the best aspects of Unix workstations, the GUI, is based on Project Athena which was funded by DEC and IBM. Kerberos, the security system in OSF's DCE, came from the same stable.

---

[1] Walt Whitman, 'Song of the Open Road'.

[2] The Courier model, for example.

[3] C and Bjarne Stroustrup's C++ are exceptions.

If the profitability of open systems is low, then research projects will suffer to the detriment of the open systems movement. It is futile to argue that the OSF, UI/USL and X/Open will carry the flag since they are either funded to a great extent, or owned, by the major manufacturers which are hardest hit by low profit margins.

It is easy to imagine a scenario where research and delivery of open systems technology slows or even stops. This would almost certainly be the sign for major IT users to continue the technology route themselves, either individually or in concert. If they each look after their own needs, you can see the wheel turning full circle with proprietary systems once more the vogue but from the users' not the vendors' perspective. If they act in concert, they may take the place of vendors and consortia in open systems development. This will cost money, just as it did when vendors were the driving force, and savings on 'commodity' open systems hardware and software might well be swallowed up by their involvement. Whichever way you look at it, the cost of progress in open systems has to be borne by someone. It is not difficult to imagine the head of a business organization wondering why the company is developing IT technology instead of using it for competitive advantage as it used to.

To look at it from another perspective, take the car-computer analogy. People claim that the computer in the open systems era is simply a commodity like the car. Let us consider this analogy for a moment. Look at the range of cars available today in terms of price and function - it is a far cry from earlier times when Henry Ford said 'You can have any color as long as it's black'. Although today's cars are much more standard in the way one drives them, the range of added value and prices is literally staggering and innovation is still the order of the day for the major car manufacturers which are driven, metaphorically, by the driver. The computer industry today is also more market-driven but, like the car industry, needs profit to deliver what the market requires.

The desktop and deskside computer, be it OS/2, Windows, DOS or Unix, will have part to play in open systems if for no other reason than its all pervasive presence. It is often the only route a user has to access computer resources outside his own machine. It will not, as some people think, take over the IT world - not yet anyway. The idea of a single system image across an enterprise of desktop computers and servers is not a reality today, although technologies such as DCE and DME are approaching this. Time[4] is needed for a gradual, controlled and justified evolution in enterprise computing.

One reason for this is that the maturity of present-day IT installations did not occur overnight. Richard Nolan in the 1970s classified the phases of growth in IT as shown in Figure 106.

---

[4] Time is that property of the universe that ensures everything does not happen at once.

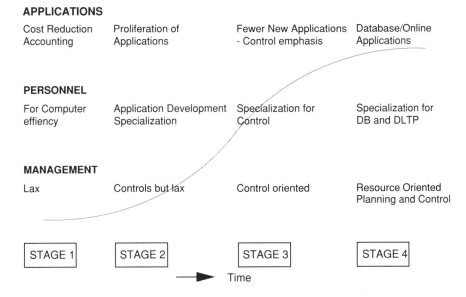

APPLICATIONS

| Cost Reduction Accounting | Proliferation of Applications | Fewer New Applications - Control emphasis | Database/Online Applications |

PERSONNEL

| For Computer effiency | Application Development Specialization | Specialization for Control | Specialization for DB and DLTP |

MANAGEMENT

| Lax | Controls but lax | Control oriented | Resource Oriented Planning and Control |

STAGE 1   STAGE 2 ➡   STAGE 3   STAGE 4

Time

Figure 106. *Nolan Phases of IT Development*

Where, in your view, do the Unix and PC worlds lie on the Nolan chart? Is the new open world of downsizing and rightsizing going to sidestep these phases or will it need to acquire such maturity by coexistence with the mainframe?

Conversely, the mainframe and midrange roles in IT must surely change as a result of changes to business requirements. Why don't they hand over their role entirely to 'open systems', one might ask? For one reason, there are a large number of these systems about and many businesses are totally dependent on them from day to day. The hint of business risk or scrapping the vast investment in them by the 'call to open systems' will antagonize many installations.

Legacy (or proprietary) systems are not suited to rapid change and the business they support may suffer the IT equivalent of the diver's 'bends' if they are forced to do so. Why not just move everything onto open systems which *are* suited to this rapid change? Firstly, there needs to be some tangible business benefit to do something on this scale at all. Secondly, nearly all 'mission critical' applications still run on legacy systems. There are an estimated 1,000,000,000,000 lines of code extant on these systems. Anyone reasonably conversant with coding rates for conversion or writing new applications, 4GLs notwithstanding, will tell you that such a migration represents the equivalent of thousand of years of effort. Existing packages can ease the burden but total replacement of an organization's software simply with packages is not realistic in all cases.

What then is the answer? Evolution of the roles of the legacy systems and the newer distributed systems into the cohesive whole that yields business benefit to the organization is our guess.

We have mentioned lack of responsiveness of large IT installations to change and in application take-on. A look at the strengths of both sides might indicate the new roles that they could usefully perform in the open systems world. Consider the following:

- Mature legacy systems and subsystems (like OLTP), outclass DOS and Unix systems in:
  - scale (power and memory)
  - reliability (operating system)
  - availability
  - recovery
  - security and integrity (not prone to virus attacks)
  - auditability[5]
  - system, data and network management
  - high-volume OLTP
  - batch job and transaction management, scheduling, prioritization
  - maturity
  - and many others.
- DOS and Unix systems, however, outclass legacy systems in:
  - adapting to change
  - ease of installation, use and support
  - package availability
  - ability to be terminal, client or server
  - GUIs
  - capital cost
  - and many others.

If, as many industry watchers predict, the mainframe evolves into an enterprise server and data 'warehouse', the systems programming and management workloads will be reduced considerably because of the stable nature of the mainframe's work pattern. The support cost argument levelled against legacy systems then loses some of its momentum, especially if they can make use of the emerging expert systems which might handle many of the actions normally taken by operators and systems programmers running an IT shop.

---

[5] Imagine your company totally dependent on a dispersed system you cannot audit.

There is a place for both and by capitalizing on the strengths of both, an organization can evolve an IT structure to meet the needs of the business, not just in times of recession, but in the future. It means for the legacy system an acceptance of the open systems world and developments, such as POSIX, X/Open, DCE, Atlas and so on. The new world, too, should harness the power and skills of the old proprietary warhorses to form a partnership whose objectives are in tune with those of the business they serve, not with those of the new technology gurus.

Two supporting quotes are appropriate here:

'Unless significant opportunities were envisaged, it would be a profligate organisation that could write off all proprietary equipment and provide a system which fully conforms to Open Systems standards from day one. Indeed, product availability may, for certain requirements, prohibit such a *big bang* approach.'[6]

'Computers have to integrate and work together and open systems provides the opportunity for new *open* and existing *proprietary* systems to coexist.'[7]

A practical example of this coexistence can be seen in the IT plans of Allied Dunbar, a financial services company. Over a period of three years (1992-95), it plans to replace non-intelligent terminals with 450 PCs, linked to its mainframe in client/server mode.

19.1.1 The Way Forward

Assuming the 'big bang' approach is not feasible for most medium to large IT infrastructures, how will they evolve into an open systems environment?

Firstly, there needs to be a change in the mental approach[8] to IT by both managers of mainframes and those who supply them. There is a certain fear that open systems and downsizing will reduce the manager's influence and the salesman's salary. If they adopt a 'mainframe only' approach, then these things will probably come to pass. In addition, a costly, stable mainframe site is a prime candidate for outsourcing[9] and possible job loss.

The solution is for the manager and salesman to adopt an 'open' mind in meeting computing needs, examining mainframe and non-mainframe options to address business needs. This 'business oriented' approach will very likely increase the influence and value of the IT manager in his organization. It will only increase

---

[6] *Open Systems - Exploring Key Issues*, DTI publication OT/KI/060.

[7] Keith Davies, 'Mix and Match the Old and New', *Open Systems* June 1991.

[8] Often called a paradigm shift by the cognoscenti.

[9] The operation of a company's computing by an outside agency.

the salesman's salary if he follows the same line of thinking - if he does not, some competitor will. This is one of the benefits to users of open systems technologies.

All is not lost for the salesman, however, since many people claim that the best person to help you to move into the area of open systems is the incumbent supplier. For their part, customer IT managers are probably happier to deal with that supplier than with a totally new one offering all the benefits of open systems tomorrow, or even that afternoon!

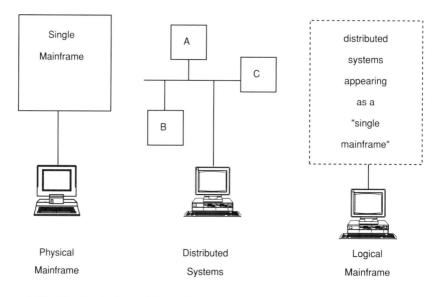

Figure 107. *The Evolution of Open Computing*

Secondly, people need to recognize the value of IT evolution against IT revolution. Most revolutions cost a lot of money and reputations and often achieve nothing. The technology of computing may be advancing at a revolutionary speed but its manageability is not. The gradual opening up of proprietary technology will allow it to participate in open, heterogeneous networks. In parallel, the networked environment will develop the necessary 'management'[10] skills over time. Eventually, the end users and IT staff will cease to treat their computing systems as a set of differing hardware and software components and consider the whole as a 'logical mainframe'.[11] This evolution is illustrated in Figure 107.

---

[10] See the list of mainframe advantages at the start of this Chapter.

[11] A term used by IDC, but in a slightly different context.

In the meantime, the distinction between proprietary mainframes and open minis will have probably vanished and the logical mainframe will consist many different systems, many with specialized roles.[12]

19.1.2 Postscript

Somehow, the idea of standard cars, beer, food, clothes and anything else that people buy from vendors, however many there are to choose from, does not quite appeal ... but then that is only *our* humble opinion!

We will bow out of the main part of this book with a judicial analogy. Proprietary vendors are the accused and you are the judge, jury and executioner. At the end of the day, only knowledge of the law and careful weighing of the evidence on your part can ensure you do not hang the wrong man. If you do, you may find yourself as the accused, with your company as judge and jury.

---

[12] Such as database engines, number crunchers, security systems and other servers.

Part 5
The World of Technical
Reference

Appendix A POSIX Standardization Details

The POSIX Standardization Process

The POSIX working groups and infrastructure are collectively known as the IEEE Technical Committee on Operating Systems (TCOS). Until 1993, the POSIX groups were Standards Subcommittees of TCOS, or TCOS-SS. They now comprise a Standards Committee which is organizationally a peer of TCOS. The TCOS development of the POSIX standards relies mainly on the voluntary efforts of experts from various IT vendors and users. For a POSIX standard to be initiated, a proposal needs to be made by an IEEE committee or member. A Project Authorization Report (PAR) is then submitted to the TCOS for approval. Once the PAR is approved, a working party is convened and drafting of the new standard can begin.

The steps in the life of a standard after PAR approval are:

- working group formed and mission statement assigned
- work on draft proposal over a period
- group consensus on completeness of the draft
- mock ballot via a Balloting Group, which often contains members outside the draft group
- official IEEE ballot to approve
- pass to ANSI for approval
- pass to ISO for consideration and approval as an international standard 9945-x.

These steps are not necessarily isolated since ANSI and ISO are aware of the status and content of the drafts before they are asked for approval. Approval is then not such a lengthy process as it would be if approached 'sight unseen'. It is also true that most vendors are aware of these developments when offering interim solutions to the issues addressed by the POSIX groups.

The POSIX 1003.xx Specifications

NOTE - As of November 1992, the POSIX 1003.3.x test suites have been renumbered 2003.3.x.

In this appendix, we explore the finer details of some of the more mature POSIX specifications and outline the contents and aspirations of emerging ones. Where they are available to us, we have quoted the original mission statements for the specifying groups. They are taken from 'IEEE Computer Society Standards Status' reports.

1003.0: 'An overview of POSIX and related standards that clarifies how they relate to each other, including languages, data base, graphics, user interface, etc. To provide information to persons evaluating systems and application software developers on the existence and inter relationships between application software standards, and as a guide for the development of Application Environment Profiles (AEPs)'.

This document is a management guide to open systems as defined by the POSIX 1003.0 committee. The definition of an 'open system' in this guide is the one we quoted in Chapter 2.

1003.1 System Interface: The 1003.1 Systems Interface Definition specifies the interface between application programs and the operating system and is based on the Unix operating system interface with the user or application. (see main text for an outline of POSIX 1003.1).

The POSIX specifications do not specify an operating system although the calls and terminology are obviously Unix-like. The basic specifications state how a function should operate and what error codes should

be returned by that function. POSIX 1003.1 also sets down minimum values for certain attributes supported by a conforming system.

The following list defines the areas to be covered in attempting conformance against the POSIX (1988) pre-numbered sections used below.

3. Process Primitives

- 3.1 Process creation & execution
- 3.2 Process termination
- 3.3 Signals

4. Process Environment

- 4.2 User identification
- 4.3 Process groups
- 4.4 System identification
- 4.5 Time
- 4.6 Environmental variables
- 4.7 Terminal identification

5. Files and Directories

- 5.1 Directories
- 5.3 General file creation
- 5.4 Special file creation
- 5.5 File removal
- 5.6 File characteristics
- 5.7 Configurable path name variables

6. Input and Output Primitives

- 6.4 Input and output
- 6.5 Control operations on Files

7. Device and Class Specific Functions

- 7.1 General terminal interface
- 7.2 General terminal interface control function

8. Language Specific Services for C

- 8.1 Referenced C language routines
- 8.2 FILE-Type C language functions
- 8.3 Other C language functions

9. System Databases

- 9.1 System databases
- 9.2 Database access
- 10. Data Interchange Format.

The breakdown of the POSIX 1003.1 calls is as follows. There are:

- 66 file system functions
- 21 control functions
- 34 character functions
- 25 mathematical functions
- 2 data manipulation functions
- 14 communications functions
- 42 other functions.

10. Data Interchange Format.

1003.1L: 'To develop a standard for POSIX system API extensions - C Language. This specific document is the draft that is in a language independent format. It has a sister document of IE1003.16'.

1003.2 Shells and Utilities (Tools): A shell is an interface between the user and the kernel which interprets commands and requests and passes them to the kernel or core of the Unix operating system. The kernel controls all the physical resources on a Unix system. The specifications use the System V shell as a base but add functions from the newer Korn shell.

In addition to this, there are some 70 utilities defined which can be invoked either from a shell script (a sequence of commands) or an application program. It is important to note that this standard does not concern itself with GUI aspects of interfacing with the end user. It deals with the basic shell programming language and a set of utilities to aid portability of shell scripts.

1003.2a User Portability Extension (UPE): This is further work done on enhancements and additional commands to the 1003.2 specifications. It standardizes commands (such as 'vi') that might not appear in scripts but are important to users.

1003.2b: 'Modifications and clarifications to 1003.2 and 1003.2a including support for symbolic links and a new archive / interchange format'.

This is the latest project in 1003.2 which will try to cater for extensions and requests from other groups, such as 1003.4 and 1003.6.

1003.3 Common Test Methods: 'To define test methods to measure conformance to IEEE 1003.1. To define test method requirements for implementations of test suites to verify conformance of an operating system product to POSIX.'

This is sometimes known as 'testing and verification' and the 1003.3 group are working on standard methodologies for testing POSIX conformance, initially for 1003.1 and latterly 1003.2:

- 1003.3.1 (2003.1) Test Methods for 1003.1 (system interface)
  'To define test methods to measure conformance to POSIX system interfaces'.

- 1003.3.2 (2003.2) Test Methods for 1003.2 (shell and utilities or tools).

The goal is: 'To define test methods for measuring conformance to POSIX shell and utilities interfaces'.

1003.4 Real-Time API: 'To determine a set of system interface extensions for POSIX to address portability of real time and other applications. To provide a specification for real time extensions to POSIX so that source level C-Language programs (later modified to be language independent programs) that require extensions to 1003.1 and can be written in a portable fashion, for conforming implementations'.

Real-time applications are generally those which need a guaranteed and predictable response time because of their important nature. These put different requirements on the operating system, and to maintain the ideal of portability, standards for

real-time functions are desirable. These 1003.4 real-time interfaces are syntactic and semantic changes to the 1003.1 specification covering areas such as timers, priority scheduling and interprocess communication (IPC).[1]

- 1003.4a Threads API

- 1003.4b System API Extensions
  'Part 1: Real Time System API Extension. To define a standard for real time system API extension. This is an extension of 1003.4 ...'.

- 1003.4c Language Independent (LI) Specification

1003.5 Ada Bindings: 'To determine the Ada environment interface and Ada required extensions to POSIX 1003.1. To provide a specification for the Ada environment interfaces and Ada required extensions so that Ada Application programs can be written to operate identically on all conforming POSIX/Ada environments'.

Because the UNIX operating system is closely linked with the C language (it is written in C!), access to system services understandably favoured C. In the period since UNIX was developed, other languages have become popular in the UNIX environment, especially Ada which is often mandatory for the development of military and government systems. To enable Ada to 'compete' on an even footing with C,

---

[1] See 'Real Time Extensions Need Standardization', *UNIXWORLD*, March 1990, Inder M. Singh.

the IEEE POSIX 1003.5 subgroup was set up because of the language structure and philosophy differences between the C and Ada languages. Its mission is defined in an IEEE Computer Society Standards Status Report as:

'To determine the Ada environment interface and Ada-required extensions to POSIX 1003.1. To provide a specification for the Ada environment interfaces and Ada required extensions so that Ada application programs can be written to operate identically on all conforming POSIX/Ada environments.'

1003.6 Security Extensions for 1003.1: 'To specify functional requirements and system interface standard for security, auditability, and control mechanisms in POSIX. Specifications will include minimum security-related functional mechanisms and system call interface specifications. Included within the scope of this effort are security aspects for all functional elements of POSIX, including the operating system interface, shell and tools, distributed environments, and real time. Of particular note is the fact that not all installations will have need for the full range of possible security mechanisms. However, existing POSIX security function is inadequate for an increasing number of situations and applications. There must be certain minimal functionality and interfaces built into POSIX so that security mechanisms can be implemented without adversely affecting applications portability'.

This group was formed from the Uniforum Security subcommittee and has as part of its brief to monitor the work of 1003.1 group to see if any of the specifications compromised attaining a 'trusted system' as defined by the U.S. Department of Defense TCSEC (Trusted Computer System Evaluation Criteria).

The working group is developing interfaces in four areas:

- Discretionary Access Control, or support for Access Control Lists (ACLs).

- Mandatory Access Control to meet the TCSEC requirements for mandatory access control rules.

- Privileges - interfaces for acquiring and altering process privilege and the administration of privileged users.

- Auditing - defining auditable events for 1003.1 and audit trail record formats and functions.

A special study group was formed in 1991 to look at standardization requirements in the area of distributed security, the Distributed Security Study Group (DSSG). In its early meetings, the DSSG attempted to:

- define a distributed security framework

- identify security services needed

- identify security APIs

- map existing and emerging implementations into the identified APIs and

- identify related standards and standards bodies.

The DSSG proposes to produce a 'Guide for Information Technology - Portable Operating Systems Interfaces (POSIX) Security within Distributed Systems'. The DSSG attained POSIX 'working group' status in January 1993 and it is estimated that the guide may take two years to produce.

1003.7 System Administration: 'Defines the utility program interfaces and, if needed, service interfaces and extensions for system administration. The utility programs may address the following functions but are not necessarily limited to: backup, recovery, system accounting, file system management, system startup and shutdown, clock daemons, print spooling and system wide messaging'. Another definition we came across, was similar but more specific.

'System Administration Interface Software for Computer Operating System Environments ... provide a common set of utility programs and service interfaces for software management of User ID information, consistent with that described in 9945-1, P1003.2, P1003.4, P1003.6 and P1003 Networking Groups'.

There are three small groups within 1003.7:

1. Printing with emphasis on distributed printing, which is to be based on the MIT

PALLADIUM 2.0 system (1003.7.1)

2. Software, primarily focusing on management of software installation, for example, *install, remove, packaging and audit utilities and mass install* (1003.7.2).

3. User Management with an object-oriented bias. This is the least well-defined of the three topics in 1003.7.

1003.8 Network Transparent File Access (TFA) API: 'This standard will outline network services for portable applications.'

Again, this group is pre-dated by Uniforum subcommittees and the initial mission was a networking one. However, the group split with 1003.8 concentrating on TFA, while 1003.12 deals with Protocol Independent Interfaces. The TFA group 'is working on a specification system services, including file system semantics which describe the behaviour which an application can expect when manipulating a file. TFA provides additional services so that application programs can access files in environments which may not be able to provide all of the functionality of 1003.1-1990.'[2]

1003.9 Fortran Bindings: 'To establish an interface for Fortran to POSIX, such that Fortran applications using POSIX functionality will be portable at the source code level'.

---

[2] From notes by an IBM member of 1003.8.

This group has a mission similar to that of the Ada group (1003.5) but for the Fortran language with a subtle difference in the type of binding ('thin' instead of 'thick'!). This need not worry most readers.

1003.10 Supercomputing Application Environment Profile (AEP): 'To develop a standard for a supercomputing Applications Environmental Profile'.

An AEP is a profile rather than a fundamental set of detailed standards and will invoke other existing standards. It defines the relationship between the components which will collectively make up that particular profile or 'working environment' for a particular subject.

This group was formed in 1989 and, although it does not define what is meant by a supercomputer, it is concerned with specifications about the work normally done on high performance computers, in either batch or interactive mode. It has connections with several other standards and standards groups, for example:

- POSIX 1003.4 (high performance I/O).

- POSIX 1003.7 (priority scheduling and checkpoint / restart in Sytems Administration).

- POSIX 1003.9 (Fortran binding) - Fortran is still the major language for numeric intensive applications.

- IEEE 754 (Floating Point specification) - many machines have their own standards for floating point representation, rounding

and so on, thus distributing calculations across a heterogeneous network requires some standardization if errors are not to be introduced when the results are combined in some way.

- ISO X3 Standards Groups including the Parallel Processing group.

1003.11 Transaction Processing AEP: 'To develop a standard for a transaction processing Applications Environment Profile (AEP)'.

The requirements of a good transaction processing system are many and varied and more often than not are being specified by a number of bodies and organizations. To produce a profile, and possibly APIs, this POSIX group must take cognisance of the following:

- POSIX 1003.2 (Tools)

- POSIX 1003.4 (Real Time)

- POSIX 1003.6 (Security)

- X/Open Online Transaction Processing Reference Model (XTP)

- The work of the OSI Distributed Transaction Processing Group (OSI TP)

- Existing OLTP systems.

The group decided to terminate its activities at the April 1993 meeting.

1003.12 Protocol Independent Network Interfaces: 'To define a programmatic interface for network process-to-process communications'.

In order to communicate effectively in heterogeneous environments, it is necessary to accommodate several protocols that exist in such a situation. In the search for true 'interoperability', some means of protocol-independent access is needed for use by applications and systems services, such as RPC. The 1003.12 group is working on two levels of interfaces to network protocols:

- Simple Network Interface (SNI). This is a totally protocol-independent interface that will guarantee application portability across different protocol stacks and POSIX compliant systems.

- Detailed Network Interface (DNI). This allows access to protocol-dependent options in a protocol-independent manner. Options being studied are BSD Sockets and X/Open's XTI.

At the July 1992 meeting of this group, it was decided to spin off a Real Time Distributed Computing Group (RTDC) to work on:

- a real time API to networking protocols

- an Ada binding.

1003.13 Real Time AEP: 'To determine a set of system interface extensions for POSIX to address portability of real time and other applications. To provide a specification for real time extensions to POSIX so that source level C-Language programs (later modified to be language independent programs) that require extensions to 1003.1 and can be written in a port-

able fashion, for conforming implementations.'

In 1991, three initial profiles were defined for consideration:

1. a single process with one or more threads and basic (synchronous) I/O but no file system.

2. as 1. but with a file system and asynchronous I/O

3. multiple processes with IPC, deterministic scheduling, clocks and timers and process memory locking.

1003.14 Multiprocessing AEP: 'To define a standard for POSIX multiprocessing application support'.

The work of this group is in the early stages but suffice it to say here that it seeks 'a multipart profile covering multiprocessors'. It has many several dependencies on other POSIX work not yet approved and this may delay its eventual completion.

1003.15 Supercomputing Batch System Administration: 'To define a standard for POSIX batch environment amendments, working in coordination with P1003.10'.

This group is working on a batch processing standard. The work was initiated by /usr/group, transferred to IEEE as 1003.10, then became a fully authorized POSIX project in its own right, 1003.15. The aim is to encompass all POSIX environments and not just supercomputing, as the title implies.

The work to date is based on:

- Networking Queueing System (NQS), a *de facto* standard for batch processing in the Unix environment, the major part of 1003.15

- H-Ps batch product called 'Taskbroker', broadening the standard beyond just what NQS offers.

The work has been broken into four parts

- user and operator command sets
- administrator command set
- application-level network protocol
- language independent 'programmatic' (library) interface.

This group has close ties with the 1003.10 group.

1003.16 C Language Binding: 'To define a standard for POSIX language bindings Part 1; C Language to system APL'.

The work of this group parallels that of the Ada and Fortran groups with the ANSI C language as its focus.

1003.17 Directory Service API: 'To define an application programming interface to a directory service, including but not necessarily limited to X.500 functionality. The standard will provide language independent specification and C-language binding'.

The standard will specify related name space(s), with naming rules schema, that are supported by POSIX systems'.

The standard will rely heavily on X/Open's XDS (X/Open Directory Services) and XOM (X/Open OSI Abstract-Data Manipulation API).[3] According to team members, XOM will be used by the IEEE 1224.1 (X.400 API) group, and possibly other POSIX groups.

In 1992, 1003.17 was renumbered and broken into the following parts:

- 1224.2 - Directory services API (LIS)
- 1326.2 - Test methods for 1224.2
- 1327.2 - C language binding to 1224.2
- 1328.2 - Test methods for 1327.2

1003.18 POSIX Platform Environment Profile: The responsibilities of this group are stated as:

'To establish a Platform Environment Profile (PEP) based on ISO9945-1 and ISO9945-2 (POSIX) work and related standards which describes a simple foundation for an interactive, often multiuser application environment. The environment specified is that appropriate to the development and execution of a mix of 'interactive' applications, using the services of interactive utilities provided by standards called out of this profile.'

---

[3] It used to be called the 'X/Open Object Management API'.

1003.19 Fortran 90 Binding: This mission is similar to that of 1003.9 but for Fortran 90.

1003.20 Real-Time Ada Bindings: 'Provide the Ada environment interfaces to the P1003.4/4a base work'.

This project is similar to 1003.5 but tackles the Ada binding (or access to system services) for the real-time extensions to POSIX 1003.1 (1003.4). The group was only formed in late 1991.

1003.20a Ada Bindings: to real time extensions of POSIX 1003.4a threads API.

1003.21 Real Time Distributed Communications Services: A group which was set up and approved in 1993. It is a spin off of 1003.12.

1003.22 Distributed Security Framework: (see 1003.6).

1201.1 Window Interface for User and Application Portability: 'Window Interface based on the X-Window Model'.

This group started by trying to produce a single standard for a toolkit API, based on OpenLook and Motif toolkits but this proved not to be feasible. The new plan is to develop a draft standard that allows a layered API that can be built onto existing toolkits but which does not explicitly use the components of the X Window system. It is thus possible for such an API to be implemented on other windowing systems.

1201.2 Graphical User Interfaces - Drivability: 'Window Interface - Recommended Practice on Drivability'.

The aim of this group is to lay out recommended practice for user interfaces so that users can move easily from one 'look and feel' interface to another. One major piece of work carried out was the examination and identification of common elements across the MOTIF, OpenLook, MAC, CUA (SAA), NEXT and Microsoft GUIs.

1224 OSI Abstract Data Manipulation API: This project will define an ASN.1 Object Management API to complement the X.400 and X.500 APIs. Related volumes in this work group will comprise:

- IEEE 1326 - Test methods for IEEE 1224
- IEEE 1327 - C-Language Binding to IEEE 1224
- IEEE 1328 - Test Methods for IEEE 1327

1224.1 X.400 Electronic Messaging API: This project will define an API to enable a message store or user agent to access a message transfer system. It will also define an X.400 gateway API. Related volumes in this work group will comprise:

- IEEE 1326.1 - Test methods for IEEE 1224.1
- IEEE 1327.1 - C-Language Binding to IEEE 1224.1
- IEEE 1328.1 - Test Methods for IEEE 1327.1

1224.2 Directory Services API Related volumes in this work group will comprise:

- IEEE 1326.2 - Test methods for IEEE 1224.2
- IEEE 1327.2 - C-Language Binding to IEEE 1224.2
- IEEE 1328.2 - Test Methods for IEEE 1327.2

1237 Remote Procedure Call (RPC definition): The IEEE P1237 group was disbanded before it actually produced any useful work. However, RPC work is currently under way via ANSI X3T5.5 and SC21/WG8. OSF, IBM, DEC are all actively involved in this work. The proposed standard is currently in its second CD (Committee Draft) ballot.

1238.0 OSI Connection Management API: 'A standard for OSI applications program interfaces - a common connection management and support functions'.

The aim of this group is to develop operating system independent APIs for OSI Layer 7 protocols. This will allow the building of applications in addition to the FTAM and Message Handling Services applications.

1238.1 OSI FTAM API: 'A standard for OSI applications program interfaces - a common connection management and support functions'.

'A standard for OSI applications program interfaces - a common connection management and support function'. The goal of the committee is to make these APIs operating system independent.

X3H6.6 X-Windows Library: This is a POSIX-related ANSI committee looking at window management.

A.1.1 POSIX Status, April 1993

P1003.0   Guide to POSIX Open Systems Environment
- first ballot completed 3Q92
- recirculation ballot planned 2Q93

P1003.1-LIS   Language Independent System API
- first ballot completed 4Q92
- recirculation ballot planned 2Q93

P1003.1a   System API Extensions
- first ballot planned 3Q93

P1003.2b   Extensions to P1003.2 and P1003.2a
- first ballot planned 3Q93

P1003.3.2 Test Methods for 1003.2
- first ballot completed 4Q92

P1003.4   Real Time and Related System API
- most recent recirculation ballot has achieved 80% approval
- expect IEEE Standards Board approval June '93

P1003.4a   Threads API
- third recirculation ballot planned 2Q93

P1003.4b   System API Extensions
- first ballot planned for 3Q93

P1003.4c   Language Independent Spec
- first ballot planned for 3Q93

P1003.6   Security
- first ballot completed 4Q91
- reballot completed 4Q92

P1003.7.1   Print Administration
- mock ballot completed 2Q92
- first ballot planned 2Q93

P1003.7.2   Software Administration
- mock ballot completed 1Q93

P1003.8   Transparent File Access
- first ballot completed 2Q92
- recirculation ballot planned 2Q93

P1003.10   Supercomputing Application Environment Profile
- first ballot completed 4Q92

P1003.11   Transaction Processing Application Environment Profile
- completed first ballot 2Q92, 75% negative
- balloting group has disbanded

P1003.12   Protocol Independent Interface
- first ballot planned 3Q93

P1003.13   Real Time Application Environment Profile
- completed mock ballot 4Q91
- completed first ballot 2Q92

P1003.14   Multiprocessing Application Environment Profile
- first ballot planned for 3Q93

P1003.15   Batch Environment Amendments
- mock ballot completed for 1Q92
- first ballot completed 4Q92

P1003.16   C Language Binding for P1003.1-LIS
- first ballot completed 4Q92
- recirculation ballot planned 2Q93

P1003.18   Platform Environment Profile
- first ballot planned 4Q93

P1003.19   Fortran 90 Binding
- ballot plans unspecified

P1003.20   Ada Bindings to 1003.4
- ballot planned for 4Q93

P1003.20a Ada Bindings to 1003.4a
- ballot plans unspecified

P1201.1   Window Interface for User and Application Portability
- ballot plans unspecified

P1201.2   Graphical User Interfaces - Drivability
- first ballot completed 3Q92
- recirculation ballot planned 2Q93

P1238.0   Connection Management API
- ballot planned for 3Q93

P1238.1   FTAM API
- ballot planned for 4Q93

P2003   Test Methods
- revision to IEEE Std 1003.3-1991
- ballot plans unspecified

Appendix B Open Systems Organizations

American National Standards Institute
1430 Broadway
New York
NY 10018
USA

ANSI Customer Service
11 West 42nd Street
New York
NY 10036
USA

Corporation for Open Systems (COS)
1750 Old Meadow Road
Suite 400
McLean
VA 22102-4306
USA

DDN Network Information Center
SRI International
333 Ravenswood Avenue
Menlo Park
CA 94025
USA

Display Industry Association
1007 Elwell Court, Suite B

Palo Alto
CA 94303
USA

European Committee for Standardization
CEN
Rue de Stassart
B-1050 Brussels
Belgium

European Computer Manufacturers Association (ECMA)
114 Rue de Rhône
CH-1204 Geneva
Switzerland

European Forum for Open Systems
Europen
Owles Hall
Buntingford
Hertfordshire SG9 9PL
UK

European Workshop on Open Systems
EWOS
Rue de Stassart 36
B-1050 Brussels
Belgium

Institute of Electrical & Electronic Engineers
IEEE
PO Box 1331
445 Hoes Lane
Piscataway
NJ 08855-1331
USA

IEEE (HQ)
345 East 47th Street
New York
NY10017-2394
USA

IEEE Computer Society (Europe)
13 Avenue de l'Aquilon
B-1200 Brussels
Belgium

International Organization for Standardization
ISO Central Secretariat
1 Rue de Varembe
Case Postale 56
CH-1211 Geneva 20
Switzerland

National Institute of Standards & Technology
NIST
Technology Building
Room B266
Gaithersburg
MD 20899
USA

Object Management Group
Framingham Corporate Center
492 Old Connecticut Path
Framingham

MA 01701
USA

Open Software Foundation (USA)
11 Cambridge Center
Cambridge
MA 02142
USA

Open Software Foundation (Europe)
Avenue des Pleiades-laan 15
B-1200 Brussels
Belgium

Open Systems in Manufacturing Interest Group
Institute for Industrial IT Ltd.
The Innovation Centre
Swansea SA2 8PP
UK

Open Systems Programme (DTI)
Information Point
Information Technology Division
Department of Trade and Industry
151 Buckingham Palace Road
London SW1W 9SS
UK

Petrotechnical Open Software Corporation
POSC
10777 Westheimer, Suite 275
Houston
TX 77042
USA

SPAG
Avenue Louise 149
Box 7
B-1050 Brussels
Belgium

UNIX International (Europe)
Avenue de Beaulieu 25
B-1160 Brussels
Belgium

UNIX International (USA)
20 Waterview Boulevard
Parsippany
NJ 07054
USA

Uniforum (UK)
9-11 EBC House
Richmond Station Buildings
Richmond-upon-Thames
Surrey TW9 2NA
UK

Uniforum (USA)
2910 Tasman Drive - Suite 201
Santa Clara
CA 95054
USA

**User Alliance for Open Systems
(Houston 30)**
Address as for COS above.

UNIX System Laboratories (Europe)
USLE
International House
Ealing Broadway
London W5 5DB
UK

UNIX System Laboratories (USA)
190 River Road
Summit
NJ 07901
USA

X Consortium
MIT X Consortium
545 Technology Square
Cambridge
MA 02139
USA

USENIX
P.O. Box 2299
Berkeley
CA 94710
USA

X/Open Company Ltd. (Europe)
Apex Plaza
Forbury Road
Reading
Berkshire RG1 1AX
UK

X/Open Publications
Oakwood House
St. John's Estate
Penn, High Wycombe
Bucks HP10 8HQ
UK

X/Open Company Ltd. (USA)
1010 El Camino Real, Suite 380
Menlo Park
CA 94025
USA

3141 Fairview Park Drive
Suite 760
Falls Church
VA 22042
USA

88Open Consortium
Marketing Dept.
100 Homeland Court, Suite 800

San Jose
CA 95112
USA

B.1.1 Reports on Open Systems

The following is a selection of the organizations whose reports we consulted
during research into this book. The inclusion of an organization does not imply
that we endorse their reports, only that they were consulted. For a full list of
reports you should write to the appropriate organization.

Nina G. Lytton (Open Systems Advisor)
268 Newbury Street
Boston
MA 02116
USA

Forrester Research
Harvard Square
P.O. Box 1091
Cambridge
MA 02238
USA

D.H. Brown Research
222 Grace Church Street
Port Chester
NY 10573
USA

Dataquest
PO Box 9324
550 Cochituate Road
Framingham
MA 01701
USA

Gartner Group Inc.
56 Top Gallant Road
PO Box 10212
Stamford
CT 06094
USA

Patricia Seybold
7th Floor
148 State Street
Boston
MA 02109
USA

Faulkner Technical Reports
114 Cooper Center
7905 Browning Road
Pennsauken
NJ 08109
USA

Butler Bloor
Challenge House
Sherwood Drive
Bletchley
Milton Keynes

MK3 6DP
UK

Xephon
PO Box 1059
Oviedo
FL 32765
USA

27-35 London Road
Newbury
Berkshire
RG13 1JL
UK

Technology Appraisals
Grove House
551 London Road
Isleworth TW7 4DS
UK

**UK IT Security Evaluation &
Certification Scheme**
PO Box 152
Cheltenham
GL52 5UF
UK

Appendix C Further Reading

R.C. Summers, *Local Area Distributed Systems*, *IBM Systems Journal*, Vol. 28, No. 2, pp. 227-240 (1989)

H. Lorin, *Limits to Distributed Computing*, *Computerworld*, 28 October, 1991, p. 83

R.J. Cypser, *Communications for Cooperating Systems*, OSI, SNA and TCP/IP, Addison Wesley (1991). ISBN 0-201-50775-7

Kurt Ziegler Jr., *Distributed Computing and the Mainframe*, John Wiley (1991). ISBN 0-471-51753-4

Pamela Gray, *Open Systems - a Business Strategy for the 1990s*, McGraw-Hill (1991). ISBN 0-07-707244-8

Ian Hugo, *Practical Open Systems, a Guide for Managers*, NCC/Blackwell (1991). ISBN 1-85554-079-7

The AS/400 in an Open World, January 1992, ADM Consulting Inc., 700 West Johnson Avenue, Cheshire CT 06410, USA

Peter Judge, *Guide to IT Standards makers and their standards*, Technology Appraisals (1991). ISBN 1-871802-17-2

C.1 Reference Sources

Many of the documents referred to in this section are in state of flux as standards work progresses. The list, however, should prove of use to people looking for specific information about the various standards, profiles and recommendations.

X/Open Publications

General

Publication & Branded Product Lists
Open Systems Directive - ISBN 1-872630-34-0

XPG3: Portability Guide, Issue 3 - ISBN 1-872630-43-X
XPG3: Portability Guide Overview, Issue 3 - ISBN 1-872630-44-8
X/Open Systems and Branded Products: XPG4 - ISBN 1-872630-52-9
XPG4 SET - ISBN 1-872630-59-6
Overview - ISBN 1-872630-52-9
Component Definitions - ISBN 1-872630-52-9
Profile Definitions - ISBN 1-872630-52-9
Guide to Branding - ISBN 1-872630-52-9
Trade Mark Licence Agreement (TMLA) - ISBN 1-872630-52-9
Conformance Statement Questionnaires (CSQs) - ISBN 1-872630-52-9
Branded Products - ISBN 1-873620-52-9
Publications - ISBN 1-872630-52-9

Data Interchange

CD-ROM Support Component (XCDR)
X Window System File Formats & Appln Conventions - ISBN 1-872630-15-4
OSI - Abstract - Data Manipulation API (XOM) - ISBN 1-872630-17-0
API to Electronic Mail (X.400) - ISBN 1-872630-19-7
Byte Stream File Transfer (BSFT) - ISBN 1-872630-27-8
EDI Messaging Package (XEDI) - ISBN 1-872630-25-1
Message Store API - ISBN 1-872630-26-X

Data Management

Indexed Sequential Access Method (ISAM) - ISBN 1-872630-03-0
SQL Remote Database Access
Structured Query Language (SQL)
Data Management, Issue 3 - ISBN 1-872630-40-5

Internationalization

COBOL Language - ISBN 1-872630-09-X
X/Open Transport Interface (XTI) - ISBN 1-872630-29-4
System Interface and Headers, Issue 3 - ISBN 1-872630-37-5
Supplementary Definitions, Issue 3 - ISBN 1-872630-38-3
Internationalization Guide - ISBN 1-872630-20-0
Commands and Utilities, Issue 4 - ISBN 1-872630-48-0
System Interfaces and Headers, Issue 4 - ISBN 1-872630-47-2
System Interface Definitions, Issue 4 - ISBN 1-872630-46-4

Interworking

Protocols for X/Open PC Interworking: (PC)NFS - ISBN 1-872630-00-6
Comparison Study of OSI Profiles
Interworking API Style Guide
Protocols for X/Open PC Interworking: SMB - ISBN 1-872630-01-4
Guide to the Internet Protocol Suite - ISBN 1-872630-08-1
Protocols for X/Open Interworking: XNFS - ISBN 1-872630-10-3
OSI - Abstract - Data Manipulation API (XOM) - ISBN 1-872630-17-0
API to Directory Services (XDS) - ISBN 1-872630-18-9
Guide to IPS - OSI Coexistence and Migration - ISBN 1-872630-22-7
Guide to Selected X.400 and Directory Services APIs - ISBN 1-872630-2
API to Electronic Mail (X.400) - ISBN 1-872630-19-7
Byte Stream File Transfer (BSFT) - ISBN 1-872630-27-8
EDI Messaging Package (XEDI) - ISBN 1-872630-25-1
Message Store API - ISBN 1-872630-26-X
X/Open Transport Interface (XTI) - ISBN 1-872630-29-4
IPC Mechanisms for SMB - ISBN 1-872630-28-6
X.400 (APIs and EDI Messaging) - Six Volume Set
Networking Services, Issue 3 - ISBN 1-872630-42-1
ACSE/Presentation Services API - ISBN 1-872630-53-7

Mainframe Data Access

CPI-C - ISBN 1-872630-35-9

Operating System Services

Supplementary Definitions, Issue 3 - ISBN 1-872630-38-3
System Interface and Headers, Issue 3 - ISBN 1-872630-37-5
Commands and Utilities, Issue 3 - ISBN 1-872630-36-7
System Interfaces and Headers, Issue 4 - ISBN 1-872630-47-2
XPG3 - XPG4 Base Migration Guide - ISBN 1-872630-49-9
System Interface Definitions, Issue 4 - ISBN 1-872630-46-4
Commands and Utilities, Issue 4 - ISBN 1-872630-48-0

Programming Languages

COBOL Language - ISBN 1-872630-09-X
Programming Languages, Issue 3 - ISBN 1-872630-39-1

Security

Security I'face Specs: Auditing & Authentication
Security Guide (Second Edition) - ISBN 1-872630-07-3

Systems Management

Systems Management: Problem Statement
Systems Management: Reference Model
Management Protocol Profiles (XMPP) - ISBN 1-872630-33-2
Managed Object Guide (XMOG) - ISBN 1-872630-31-6
Identification of Management Services (XIMS) - ISBN 1-872630-30-8
Management Protocols API (XMP) - ISBN 1-872630-32-4

Transaction Processing

Distributed TP: Reference Model - ISBN 1-872630-16-2
Distributed TP: The XA Specification - ISBN 1-872630-24-3

User Interface

X Window System Protocol - ISBN 1-872630-13-8
X Toolkit Intrinsics - ISBN 1-872630-14-6
X Window System File Formats & Appln Conventions - ISBN 1-872630-15-4
Window Management - Four Volume Set
Xlib - C Language Binding - ISBN 1-872630-11-1
Window Management, Issue 3 - ISBN 1-872630-41-3

Work Station Data Access

Protocols for X/Open PC Internetworking - ISBN 1-872630-00-6
Protocols for X/Open PC Interworking: SMB - ISBN 1-872630-01-4

Protocols for X/Open Interworking: XNFS - ISBN 1-872630-10-3
IPC Mechanisms for SMB - ISBN 1-872630-28-6

Open Systems in Practice

Open Systems in Practice   ISSN 0966-8063

X/Open in Action Series

X/Open and Interoperability (by Petr Janecek)   ISBN 1-872630-57-X
X/Open & Open Systems (by Colin Taylor)   ISBN 1-872630-55-3

Xtra-related Titles

Open Systems Directive   ISBN 1-872630-34-0
World Survey of Suppliers' Plans for Open Systems   ISBN 1-872630-70-7
World Survey of Suppliers' Plans for Open Systems: Overview
(ISBN 1-872630-74-X)

Business-related Titles

An Introduction to X/Open and XPG4 (by CCTA) ISBN 1-872630-68-5
An Introduction to X/Open and XPG4 (by CCTA) ISBN 1-872630-69-3
Open Systems: A Guide to Developing the Business Case ISBN 1-872630-72-3

XPG3-related Titles

XPG3: Portability Guide, Issue 3 (7 Vol. Set plus Overview)
(ISBN 1-872630-43-X)
XPG3: Portability Guide Overview, Issue 3 ISBN 1-872630-44-8

XPG4-related Titles

XPG4 Set:Binder (5 Vols) ISBN 1-872630-59-6
X/Open Systems and Branded Products: XPG4 ISBN 1-872630-52-9
Overview, Part 1 X/Open Systems & Branded Products: XPG4
(ISBN 1-872630-52-9)
Component Defns., Part 2 X/Open Systems & Branded Products
(ISBN 1-872630-52-9)
Guide to Branding, Part 4 X/Open Systems & Branded Products
(ISBN 1-872630-52-9)
TMLA, Part 5 X/Open Systems & Branded Products: XPG4
(ISBN 1-872630-52-9)

CSQs, Part 6 X/Open Systems & Branded Products: XPG4
(ISBN 1-872630-52-9)

Contact.

For all orders and ordering information, please contact:

X/Open Company Ltd (Publications)
P O Box 109
Penn
High Wycombe
Bucks HP10 8NP
UK

Tel: +44 (0)494 813844
Fax: +44 (0)494 814989

OSF Publications

AES

Application Environment Specification data sheet OSF-AES-DS-490-1

ANDF

ANDF, Application Portability and Open Systems O-ANDF-WP17-2
ANDF Q&A OSF-ANDF-QA1-0291-1
ANDF Rationale O-ANDF-RD-1

ANDF Technical Papers

From UNCOL to ANDF: Progress in Standard Intermediate Languages RI-ANDF-TB2-1
The Structure of ANDF: Principles and Examples RI-ANDF-TB1-1

ANDF Article Reprints

ANDF; Charting a Course OSA-8/21/89
OSF's ANDF - a Seybold report UNXOFFICE-ANDF1-1091

DCE

Overview OSF-DCE-PD-1090-4
DCE Rationale OSF-DCE-RD-590-1
The OSF Distributed Computing Environment: OSF-O-DCEVT-0191-1

DCE white papers

Directory Services in a DCE OSF-O-WP9-0990-2
File Systems in a DCE OSF-O-WP8-0990-2
Interoperability: A Key Criterion for Open Systems O-DCE-WP18-1
Remote Procedure Call in a DCE OSF-O-WP10-1090-2
Security in a DCE OSF-O-WP11-1090-2

DCE technical papers

Open Distributed Systems Architecture DEV-DCE-TP3-1
Towards a Worldwide Distributed File System DEV-DCE-TP4-1
RPC Technology Standardization and OSF's DCE DEV-DCE-TP5-1
Distributed Computing Environment Framework DEV-DCE-TP6-1

DCE article reprints

Client/Server computing OSF Catalyst OIS: E-096-727.2
Client/Server Computing An Explanation OIS: SPA-070-727.2
Interoperability: Cornerstone of Open Systems IDC-DCE-WP-1091

DME

Overview O-DME-PD-1
Rationale O-DME-RD-1

DME article reprints

OSF DME: The Final Selections - a Seybold report NETMON-DME1-1091
OSF DME - a Datapro report DATAPRO-DME2-0292

OSF/1

OSF/1 Operating System Overview OSF-OS-PD-1190-1
OSF/1 Advanced Software Development Features OSF-OSAD-1090-1
OSF/1 Kernel Services OSF-OSK-1090-1
OSF/1 Security Fact Sheet OSF-OSS-FS-1090-1

OSF/1 white papers

An Analysis of the OSF/1 Operating System & UNIX SVR4 OSF-O-WP16-0191-2
Security in the OSF/1 Operating System OSF-OSS-WP14-1190-1
Symmetrical Multiprocessing in OSF/1 OSF-OSMP-WP13-1190-1

OSF/Motif

OSF/Motif-The GUI for Open Systems white paper OSF-1-WP4-1090-2
OSF/Motif 1.1 data sheet OSF-M-DS-890-4
OSF/Motif 5 day programmers course OSF-ES-0890-1-E

General

A Look at Computing in the 1990s OSF-O-WP5-0890-1
Accelerating Open Systems Technology brochure OSF-O-B1-1090-1
OSF Founding video O-PROMO6VT-0291
OSF Open Systems Freedom video O-PROMO3VT-0291
Freedom by Design video O-PROMO18VT-1091
OSF Portability Lab brochure OSF-O-B2-0191-1
The Benefits of Membership brochure OSF-O-B3-0391-1

Article reprints

The OSF RFT process OSA-1/30/90

UNIX International Publications

General

UNIX International - Overview
UI-ATLAS - Overview
199x Roadmap - Executive Summary
199x System V Roadmap
Accreditation Application Guide
Accreditation User Guide
Financial Times Advertorial (from Open Systems '92)
SVR4 Product Catalogue

White Papers

Introduction to Distributed Computing
Online Transaction Processing (OLTP)
Desktop Computing in the 1990s
Vision 2000
SVR4 Background
UNIX International Overview
UNIX - Commercial Success Story
DCE Perspective
Systems Management

OSI Tutorial
OS/2 Compared with SVR4.2
NT Compared with SVR4.2
AIX vs SVR4.2
Tuxedo Compared with Transarc
UI-ATLAS Distributed Computing - Technical Overview
System V Security
ABIs (Application Binary Interfaces)

NOTE: There is a charge for some of these documents, which are available from:

UNIX International, Europe
Avenue de Beaulieu 25
B-1160 Brussels
Belgium

Fax: +32 (0)2 672 4415 for a 'Collaterals Order Form'.

There are many other technical manuals specific to SVR4 and other UNIX International products not reproduced here. A full publication list can be obtained from the address above.

C.1.1 88Open

The World of Standards (1991) : published by 88Open

Part 6
Glossary

Open Systems Terminology

There is no worse sight than ignorance in action.[1]

This section is a guide to terms and acronyms frequently encountered in open systems environments. Many of the topics are dealt with in the body of this book but are entered here for completeness and quick reference. We have confined the contents to terms which are relevant to open systems and which complement the book, particularly the notes on organizations. For this reason, some organizations and topics have been omitted.

Where a standard is of some importance, we have appended the relevant standard number or numbers to the description. Entries which appear in the text in ***bold italics*** have their own reference in the glossary.

ACE. Advanced Computing Environment: a consortium of hardware and software vendors aiming to define, for the UNIX world, common hardware (MIPS R4000 and Intel x86) and software (*OSF/1* and Microsoft Windows NT) platforms for application portability. Initial members included DEC, Microsoft and MIPS. The group is now defunct, although the products are still with us.

AEP. Application Environment Profile: a *POSIX* term defined in POSIX.0 as 'a profile, specifying a complete and coherent subset of the *OSE* (Open Systems Environment), in which the standards, options, and parameters chosen are necessary to support a class of applications'. This means a collection of standards including specified options and parameters, which define a prac-

tical environment for certain types of application environment.

AES. Application Environment Specification: a specification of the enabling technologies to support the Open Software Foundation's (*OSF*) implementation of the *UNIX* operating system - *OSF/1*. It includes *TCP/IP*, *NFS* and *DCE*.

AFS. Andrew File System: a network file system developed at the Carnegie-Mellon University (*CMU*) which has been adopted as part of the OSF's Distributed Computing Environment (*DCE*).

AIA. Aerospace Industry Association: an aerospace industry trade association whose members participate in the voluntary standards bodies where it is relevant to their business. AIA was instrumental in driving early acceptance of standards for electronic mail.

---

[1] Anonymous - at least to us.

AIM. A benchmark suite from the AIM Corporation. A major suite is the AIM III suite of multi-user benchmarks. It consists of a set of applications for testing systems on their all-round ability to do work. Examples are database operations, word processing and arithmetic in a set called the 'AIM Standard Mix.'

AIMS. Association for the Integration of Network Management Systems: a group formed in 1992 to feed vendor views into the relevant standards bodies.

AIX. Advanced Interactive eXecutive: IBM's implementation of the *UNIX* operating system. There are versions of AIX for the System/390 (AIX/ESA), the RISC System/6000 (AIX/6000) and the PS/2 (AIX PS/2).

Alpha. Digital's new 'classic super-scalar' 64-bit chip technology which runs DEC's proprietary operating system VMS and in the future DEC's implementation of *UNIX* - Ultrix.

ANDF. Architecture Neutral Distribution Format: the result of an *OSF* Request for Technology (*RFT*). The request was for a software format between source and binary, both of which have drawbacks in security and platform choice respectively.

ANSA. Advanced Network Systems Architecture: the label for both an evolving specification and software for supporting distributed applications. The project is funded by a consortium of European enterprises with initial support form UK government funds and, more recently, the EC *ESPRIT* programme.

ANSI. American National Standards Institute: the official standards making body of the US. It is a voluntary body which coordinates and approves a variety of standards, not all of them related to information technology. ANSI is particularly active in the areas of *OSI*, languages and graphics. Many ANSI standards have been adopted by other bodies such as *FIPS* and the US *DoD*.

ANSI-C. 'C' language standard defined by American National Standards Institute.

ANSI-SQL. Structured Query Language (*SQL*) standard defined by American National Standards Institute.

APACHE. An early sub-group of the *ACE* consortium, having similar aspirations but using the *SVR4* operating system. The group is now defunct.

API. Application Programming Interface: a set of programming functions and routines for applications to perform certain functions at a high level such that the API is not platform dependent. There are many APIs, e.g. for graphics, networking, transaction processing and so on.

APIA. X.400 API Association: a vendor group which aims to define *API*s for object management and *X.400*. The association works closely with the *X/Open* Company which covers similar areas.

APM. Architecture Projects Management: the name of the limited company set up to be the core team for the *ANSA* architecture work. For the first year or so of the Alvey ANSA project, the project was not a legal entity except as a consortium of participating companies which caused various adimistrative difficulties. APM Ltd was set up to solve this with two directors and about a dozen employees.

APP. Applications Portability Profile: an initial set of specifications for US government agencies to use in planning for the migration to Open Systems Environment (*OSE*).

ARPAnet. A *connectionless* network developed in the US as part of the *DARPA* project.

A/UX. The Apple Corporation implementation of *UNIX*.

ASCII. American Standard Code for Information Interchange : the *ANSI* standard for character representation as defined in ANSI

X3.4-1977. It defines ASCII as a 7 data bit coded character set (excluding parity) containing 33 control characters and 95 graphic characters.

ASC. Accredited Standards Committee: an *ANSI* accredited body which develops various standards. For example, ASC T1 deals with interoperability, X12 with information management and ASC X3 with general IT and office systems. X3 is well known in the areas of *OSI* and programming languages.

ASN.1. Abstract Syntax Notation 1: a language for describing data types and values. It is an *ISO* specification used in several *OSI* application layer standards.

ATLAS. See UI-ATLAS.

Binary portability. Binary executable code which can be moved from one machine to another and execute without change or recompilation.

BSD. Berkeley Software Distribution: a name given to the version of *UNIX* developed at the University of California. It was initially derived from the AT&T UNIX Version 7. BSD is popular in technical workstation environments. Development of BSD UNIX ceased in July 1992 on the issuing of BSD 4.4.

BSI. British Standards Institution: a UK body similar to the US *ANSI*. It deals with computing standards as well as non-computing standards, for example, unleaded petrol.

C. A general purpose programming language developed by Dennis Ritchie and Ken Thompson at AT&T Laboratories. In 1973 *UNIX* was rewritten in C hence its close connection with the UNIX world.

C++. An object oriented programming language developed at AT&T Bell Laboratories by Bjarne Stroustrup during the early 1980s. C++ is a hybrid in the sense that the object oriented features were grafted onto the existing *C* language. The name C++ is a play on words because in C the ++ operator increases a variable by one - so C++ represents the next step beyond C.

CAE. Common Applications Environment: a specification from *X/Open* modelled on the *UNIX* operating system. It is designed to define standards that can ensure portability of application programs at source code level. It complements the *POSIX* standards and is defined in the *X/Open* Portability Guides (XPG1, XPG2, XPG3 and XPG4).

CALS. Computer Aided Acquisition and Logistics Support: a US *DoD* initiative to help integrate and deliver technical information across systems, particularly its own.

CASE. Computer Aided Software Engineering: a structured methodology for application development.

CBEMA. Computer Business Equipment Manufacturers' Association: a standards-making body in the US whose members are producers of computers, business equipment, services and supplies. CBEMA acts as the secretariat for the Accredited Standards Committee (*ASC*) X3 (known as ASC X3) and the *JTC* Technical Advisory Group (TAG) to *ANSI*.

CCA. Character Content Architecture: an *ISO* architecture which is part of Office Document Architecture (*ODA*).

CCTA. UK Central Computer and Telecommunications Agency: the government agency which provides advice and guidance to UK government departments and public bodies to assist with the procurement of IT systems. It is now officially called the Government Centre for Information Systems - but it has kept the acronym CCTA.

CCITT. Comité Consultitif Télégraphique et Téléphonique: a sub-agency of the UN, the committee which produces recommendations for public telecommunication services, for example *X.25*, *X.400* and *X.500*. See *ITU-TS*.

CDIF. CASE Data Interchange Format: a standard format used in the exchange of information between *CASE* tools and repositories.

CEN. Comité Européen de Normalisation: the European Community's standardization body, it develops and publishes *EN*s - European Standards.

CENELEC. Comité Européen de Normalisation Electronique: the European Community's standardization body for electrotechnical matters.

CGI. Computer Graphics Interface: a 2D graphics standard emerging from *GKS*.

CGM. Computer Graphics Metafile: a standard for storing vector graphic data in a file for transmission to, and use on, another system supporting CGM. It is the interchange format for the *CALS* initiative within the US *DoD* ANSI X3.122-1986.

CIM-OSA. Computers for Integrated Manufacturing-Open Systems Architecture: one of the projects under the *ESPRIT* programme. As its name suggests, it is working on a architecture for computer integrated manufacturing.

CMIP. Common Management Information Protocols: the protocol used to exchange management information in *OSI*. ISO/IEC 9596.

CMIS. Common Management Information Service, an *OSI* standard specification for systems and network management. ISO/IEC 9595.

CMOT. *CMIP* over *TCP/IP*. RFC 1095.

CMU. Carnegie-Mellon University: major US university, originators of several UNIX innovations including the *MACH* kernel, LISP and the *Andrew File System* (after Andrew Carnegie).

Connectionless. When applied to a service, it refers to a transmission method where the data 'packets' have no relationship with each other and which has no sequencing or error checking or control. There is in fact no guarantee of delivery. See also *connection-oriented*.

Connection-oriented. When applied to a service it refers to a transmission method where there are a variety of control measures implemented such as 'packeting', sequencing and error checking. See also *connectionless*.

Conversation. A logical connection between two programs which interact with each other. The programs would typically reside on different systems in a network.

CORBA. Common Object Request Broker Architecture: model for communications in objected oriented environments from the Object Management Group (*OMG*). In particular, it deals with message passing between objects.

COS. Corporation for Open Systems: a membership-based non-profit research and development consortium. Made up of computer and communications vendors and major users. Dedicated to accelerating the introduction of *OSI* and *ISDN* products and developing conformance testing for networking standards.

COSE. Common Open Software Environment: a joint set of open specifications announcements made on 17 March 1993 by H-P, IBM, SCO, Sun (in the form of SunSoft), Univel and USL covering the following areas:

- Common Desktop Environment, to be submitted to X/Open when complete.
- Networking, covering the delivery and support of DCE, ONC and Novell/Univel NetWare products.
- Graphics, including Xlib and PEX.
- Multimedia, a submission to the Interactive Multimedia Association (IMA) request for technology.
- Object Technology, offering support for CORBA (from OMG) and assisting OMG in development and testing of products.

- Systems Management in the form of a working group to focus on software licensing and distribution, storage management, print spooling and distributed file system management.

CTS. Common Transport Semantics: a part of the IBM APPN (Advanced Peer to Peer Networking) specification of the Networking Blueprint. The ability to communicate over multiple stacks includes RFC1006 (*OSI* on *TCP/IP*) and *XTI*. XTI programs are stack-independent only if written to the inter-section of the semantics of the stacks. CTS is designed to operate with no semantic changes over SNA, OSI, TCP/IP and other layers.

CUA. Common User Access: part of IBM's Systems Application Architecture (SAA) dealing with the development of applications for programmable workstations (PWS) and non-programmable terminals. It is in essence a set of guidelines for the program and supporting services to interact with the end user. The GUI graphical model, introduced in 1989, is a *de facto* standard for GUI applications on Windows and OS/2. The OSF/*Motif* Style Guide is based on the CUA based OS/2 Presentation Manager (*PM*). CUA is a specification of a GUI whereas OSF/Motif and Presentation Manager (PM) are specifications and implementations.

CUE. Computer Users of Europe: an organization of over 300 of the largest IT users in Europe. Its aim is to ensure that the EC, governments and vendors continue to deliver open systems standards, products and services at a rapid and sustained rate.

DARPA. US Defense Advanced Research Project Agency: the originator and sponsor of a number of IT projects including *TCP/IP*.

DCE. Distributed Computing Environment: a software product from the *OSF*. It combines eight major technologies to provide a toolkit to enable distributed computing in a network of *heterogeneous* systems.

De facto standard. The term applied to a product that has been widely accepted and so becomes a 'standard' but is not controlled by an official standards body. An example is PostScript developed by Adobe Systems.

De jure standard. The term applied to a standard that has been officially approved by a recognized standards body, for example ISO 10021 - the X.400 standard.

DES. Data Encryption Standard: method of encrypting (or 'scrambling') data prior to transmission on a network. The data are decrypted by the receiver. DES was developed by IBM and adopted as a US Federal standard in 1977.

DIA. Display Industry Association: a group of major manufacturers of character display terminals formed in February 1991. Their aim is 'create and promote windowing standards for alphameric display terminals' and released the 'Alphanumeric Windows Specification' in September 1991. This specification defines support needed for concurrent windowing and a mouse interface for such terminals without impacting applications. Part of the standard is implemented in the terminal hardware, but *Motif*, *OpenLook* and other appearances can be added by vendor software.

DIS. Draft International Standard: the penultimate stage of an *ISO* standard before becoming a full International Standard.

DG/UX. Data General's implementation of *UNIX*.

Distributed Database. 'A distributed database is a database that is not stored in its entirety in a single physical location, but rather is spread across a network of dispersed, but interconnected computers. In principle, such systems could allow data to be physically stored close to the point where it is most frequently used - with obvious efficiency advantages - while at the same time permitting the same data to be shared by other, geographically remote users'.[2]

Distributed Processing. The sharing of data and/or processing tasks between computer systems, possibly in a *heterogeneous* network.

DME. Distributed Management Environment: the *OSF* software product which contains various technologies to help manage a network of *heterogeneous* systems.

DoD. Department of Defense: A US Government body that is not only a major IT procurer but also a key influencer of IT standards. It supplements US Government standards (*FIPS*) with its own MilSpecs.

Domain/OS. The implementation of *UNIX* for Apollo workstations.

Downsizing. A term used to denote the migration of one or more applications from a mainframe to a smaller system or systems. The term is often used, rightly or wrongly, in the same way as *rightsizing*. Often, a link is still maintained with the mainframe because of the need to access data or another application resident on the mainframe.

DRDA. Distributed Relational Database Architecture: IBM's architecture for distributed relational databases. The architecture has been offered to *ISO* for consideration as a part of its *RDA* standard.

DSIS. Distributed Support Information Standards: a standard for presenting network data. It is being defined by a group of major vendors who held their inaugural meeting in August 1992. Members include H-P, IBM, ICL, Microsoft, Olivetti and SUN.

DTP. Distributed Transaction Processing. See *XTP*.

EBCDIC. Extended Binary Coded Decimal Interchange Code: used to represent characters and numbers on IBM 370 architecture machines.

ECMA. European Computer Manufacturers' Association: a standards body, open to vendors developing, manufacturing or marketing in Europe. This body defined, for example, ECMA 3.-11, a standard for the shape of Optical Character Recognition (OCR) fonts. ECMA contributes to *ISO* standards activities and is a leading body in defining standards for *CASE* tools.

EDI. Electronic Data Interchange: a set of standard data and message formats for information exchange, often used by businesses to exchange documents and information.

EDIFACT. *EDI* for Administration, Commerce and Transport, an international standard for EDI syntax. It was the result of a United Nations initiative *ISO* 9735.

EIA. Electrical Industries Association: the body responsible for standards in the electrical industry, such as rack sizes for equipment. It is also responsible for the development of the *CDIF* (*CASE*) standard.

EISA. Extended Industry Standard Architecture: a bus (or data highway) specification allowing for 8, 16, and 32 bit transfer of data.

ENs. Européennes Normes: literally, European standards.

EPHOS. European Procurement Handbook for Open Systems: a document '... to provide those involved in European public administration procurement with definitive guidance on the standards and specifications to be used in the acquisition of *OSI* conformant goods and services in the field of Information Technology communications'.

---

[2] M. Stonebraker and E. Neuhold, Berkeley: University of California, Electronics Research Laboratory Memorandum ERL-M612 (September 1976).

Ethernet. Local area network (*LAN*) using CSMA/CD (carrier sense multiple access with collision detect) techniques. Very close to, but not exactly the same as, *ISO* 802.3.

ESPRIT. European Strategic Programme for Research in Information Technology: European Community sponsored IT research programme. The programme aims to increase international IT competitiveness.

ETSI. European Telecommunications Standards Institute: an organization founded in 1988 to handle standards for European customer equipment used on the Integrated Services Digital Network (*ISDN*).

EUUG. European *UNIX* Systems User Group: a non-profit organization bringing together 4000 members of national user groups in sixteen countries. It oversees the management of EUNET, the European segment of the UNIX mail network, and also provides joint funding for the monitoring of *ISO POSIX* standards projects. The organization is now called *European Forum for Open Systems* or Europen.

EWOS. European Workshop on Open Systems: a consortium of associations including *CEN*, *CENELEC*, *SPAG* and *ECMA*. It develops specifications of *OSI* profiles which, after approval, become European Standards (*EN*s)

FCS. Fibre Channel Standard: a networking standard for high speed, optical fibre based communications. It is faster than *FDDI*, supporting transmission speeds up to 1000 megabits per second. FCS is being developed, not necessarily to replace other protocols but to standardize the interfaces between senders and receivers of data. It aims at a standard interface which can encapsulate the command sets associated with existing interfacing protocols like *SCSI* and *HIPPI*.

FDDI. Fibre Distributed Data Interface: a standard for high speed, optical fibre based communications. It uses a token access protocol, similar to token passing in that stations wishing to transmit data must wait until a token arrives. On a *Token Ring* when the token is 'occupied', a bit is flipped in the token rendering it unusable as a token. The data from the station is then appended and transmitted. With FDDI, the token is removed by the transmitting station before sending the data. FDDI provides speeds up to 100 MB per second.

FFS. Fast File System: a feature of the *BSD* UNIX file system.

FIPS. Federal Information Processing Standard: US government standards defined by *NIST*.

FTAM. File Transfer Access and Management: the *OSI* application layer standard which allows files to be transferred to, and accessed from, remote systems. ISO 8571.

FTP. File Transfer Protocol: a part of the *TCP/IP* protocols. RFC 959.

Gateway. A link between two networking architectures which translates messages from one to the other by passing them through the application layer.

GGCA. Geometric Graphics Content Architecture: a part of Office Document Architecture (*ODA*) dealing with attributes that represent a vector graphic.

GKS. Graphical Kernel System: an *ANSI* standard for device-independent 2D graphics. GKS provides drawing capabilities for such things as lines, markers, text, and polygons filled with crosshatch patterns or colour. Interactive input from a variety of device types is also catered for. ISO 7942.

GKS-3D. A standard extension to *GKS* for three dimensions that covers similar areas to *PHIGS*. ISO 8805.

GL. Graphics Library: a set of routines from Silicon Graphics which helps development of 3D modelling and imaging applications.

GOSIP. Government OSI Profiles: a grouping of *OSI* standards defined by both

UK and US government agencies to simplify and standardize the purchasing of open systems by government departments. GOSIP 'compliance' means having the ability to meet these standards.

GPIB. General Purpose Interface Bus (also known as IEEE 488) it defines a bus interface between data collection and other instrumentation to a central processor.

GUI. Graphical User Interface: a graphics based way for a user to interact with a system or systems, often by menus, pointers, icons and a mouse.

Heterogeneous. 'Diverse in kind or nature' (OED). It is often used to describe a collection of unlike computer systems involving different hardware and/or software architectures. See also *Homogeneous*.

HIPPI. High Performance Parallel Interface - a communication standard supported by *ANSI* designed to run at 100 MBytes/sec.

HPPI. See *HIPPI*.

Homogeneous. Of similar nature. See also *Heterogeneous*.

HP-UX. The Hewlett Packard implementation of *UNIX*.

IAB. Internet Activity Board: a group formed in 1983 and commissioned by the US *DoD* to maintain the *RFC*s which make up the *TCP/IP* suite of protocols.

ICCCM. The Interclient Communications Conventions Manual: a standard published by the *X Consortium* at *MIT*, it provides a set of specifications to enable applications (clients) to communicate and interoperate consistently in a networked open systems environment.

IDL. Interface Definition Language: the *API* into the *Remote Procedure Call* from *NCS* - now also part of *DCE*. It is derived from the Apollo Network Interface Definition Language (NIDL).

IEC. International Electrotechnical Commission: the international body which deals with electrotechnical issues, like physical connections of IT equipment. It works closely with *ISO* on the Joint Technical Committee (JTC1).

IEEE. Institute of Electrical and Electronic Engineers: an accredited body in the US that creates standards for *ANSI*. It sets up and manages a number of working committees, including the *POSIX* groups.

IEEE 754. IEEE Standard 754 for floating point numbers. In computer hardware, implementations of floating point are often different and mixing results of calculations across architectures might sometimes leads to erroneous results. IEEE 754. is a standard for the representation of floating point numbers and their manipulation. Numeric tasks which run across a variety of machines will possibly need some accuracy checking routines if not all the hardware is IEEE 754 compliant.

IGES. Initial Graphics Exchange Specification: a graphics standard for exchanging CAD models from one system to another. See Chapter 13.

Interoperability. The ability to communicate between dissimilar systems in such a way that the characteristics of the systems providing the service to the user are transparent. It implies more than just the establishment of a physical or logical connection but useful, functional inter-operation, such as program to program communication or remote file access.

IP. Internet Protocol: the routing part of the *TCP/IP* protocol suite.

IPC. Inter-Process Communication: a protocol by which one process (or program) exchanges data with, or invokes functions in, another. Such communication can be achieved by *LU6.2* or *RPC* protocols, for example.

IPSIT. International Public Sector Information Technology: a group representing about 10 countries and the Commission of the European Community exploring ways of working together to encourage more cost-effective computing and communications procurements.

IPX. Novell's Internet Packet eXchange protocol: it is the connectionless datagram protocol on which all other NetWare protocols are built. It transports data (packet) between network devices such as workstations, file servers and routers, thus managing communications among network stations.

IRDS. Information Resource Dictionary System: a developing standard for the storage of data to support the application development process. It is an extension of the Data Dictionary concept and includes data for use by *CASE* tools.

IRIX. The Silicon Graphics implementation of *UNIX*.

ISDN. Integrated Services Digital Network: a high-bandwidth network and set of protocols designed to carry both digitized voice and data. ISDN networks can be used to carry protocols like *TCP/IP* and *X.25*.

ISEE. Integrated Software Engineering Environment: an ISEE working group started in 1989 to develop a reference model to support the goal's of the *NIST* Software Engineering Environment (*SEE*). The group adopted the *ECMA* Reference Model as a starting point for extensions and enhancements to the model.

ISO. International Standards Organization: an incorporated agency of the United Nations. ISO authorize international standards via industry organizations in each country.

ITSEC. Information Technology Security Evaluation Criteria: the functional equivalent of the US *DoD* Orange Books for the European Community. Procurers and vendors may need to seek certification for these

European standards in certain government, industrial and commercial procurements. In the UK, the IT Security Evaluation and Certification Scheme (initials ITSEC but known as the 'scheme') provides evaluation services leading to certification. This is done in conjunction with other bodies such as the UK DTI, the Communications-Electronics Security Group and third parties such as Logica, EDS-Scicon and Admiral Management Services. Areas covered by these criteria are:

- communications devices
- encryption devices
- multiple domain facilities
- operating systems
- PC Security devices
- virus protection software.

ITU. International Telecommunications Union.

ITU-TS. ITU Telecommunications Sector (formerly CCITT).

JTC1. Joint Technical Committee 1.

Kerberos. A security and authentication system for distributed environments developed as part of Project Athena at *MIT*.

LAN. Local Area Network: a system providing data communications over a short distance, e.g. within a building.

LIS. Language Independent Standard: a term used by *POSIX* groups when trying to make standards independent of the *C* language.

LVM. Logical Volume Manager: a feature of some modern *UNIX* systems such as *OSF/1* and *AIX* that enables file volumes within a UNIX file structure to be managed and manipulated more easily.

'Look and Feel'. General appearance and method of use characteristic of a particular graphical user interface (*GUI*).

LU6.2. SNA Logical Unit Type 6.2: an SNA defined interface providing peer-to-peer communications between transaction programs. A transaction program requests LU6.2 to schedule access to another program on a remote SNA node. A 'session' is then established on agreed rules or protocols and a conversation can then take place between the two programs.

MAP. Manufacturing Automation Protocols: an *OSI*-based functional standard set by the MAP Users Group. Originally specified by General Motors when it implemented an open systems policy. GM heads the MAP User Group.

MAC. Medium Access Control method: a sub-layer in the data link layer which controls access to the physical medium of a network.

MACH. A *UNIX* kernel, developed at *Carnegie-Mellon University* which forms the core of *OSF/1*. It has multiprocessing capability and supports multiple *threads*.

MIT. Massachusetts Institute of Technology: a leading US university. In 1983 it began Project Athena to create a campus-wide distributed network of workstations. The problems encountered led to the creation of a number of new products including *X Windows* and *Kerberos*.

MMS. The Manufacturers' Messaging Standard, a messaging system which forms part of *MAP*. It is an international standard which addresses the integration of shop floor devices and the computer systems controlling them.

Motif. The Open Software Foundation's graphical user interface, based on *MIT*'s *X Windows* and higher-level components from DEC and H-P. It has the *'look and feel'* of OS/2's Presentation Manager (*PM*).

MTA. Message Transfer Agent: the part of an electronic mail service which stores and forwards mail to other systems.

NCA. Network Computing Architecture: a network computing architecture from H-P/Apollo. A part of this architecture (the *RPC*) is emerging as *de facto* standard for

remote procedure calls. RPC 2.0, for example, forms part of the Open Software Foundation's (*OSF*) *DCE*.

NCC. National Computer Centre: 'a UK Centre for Information Technology. Backed by, and in cooperation with, government, the IT industry, and IT users, NCC directs technical programmes, administers national schemes, and develops products and services to promote the effective use of Information Technology'. The NCC has a range of *OSI* and *POSIX* conformance testing services and tools among the services it offers. NCC announced a European *POSIX* Conformance Testing System (CTS-2) on 6 May 1992. The NCC announced an 'NCC Open Link' programme in March 1993 to educate and assist companies in assessing and migrating to open systems.

NCS. Network Computing System: an architecture to enable users to access computer power across a network, originally developed by Apollo, which now has elements incorporated in the Open Software Foundation's (*OSF*) *DCE* offering.

NCSC. National Computer Security Commission: a US government department which is the driving force behind most of the recent developments on security in computer systems, the Rainbow series of documents.

NDR. Network Data Representation: a protocol, part of Network Computing System (*NCS*), by which machines of different architecture can exchange commands and data by using a uniform format called NDR (see also *XDR*).

NFS. Network File System: a file system developed by Sun Microsystems for distributed file access.

NIS. Network Information Service: the directory part of Network File System, (*NFS*) sometimes referred to, erroneously as 'yellow pages'.

NIST. National Institute of Standards and Technology: an agency of the US government which specifies US government procurement rules. NIST is responsible for the development of Federal Information Processing Standards (*FIPS*) and replaces the older National Bureau of Standards (NBS) in the USA.

NMF. Network Management Forum: an *OSI*-oriented group for promoting and accelerating the development of network management applications. The group, formed in 1988, consists of users, vendors and service providers.

NPA. Network Printing Alliance: a consortium of hardware manufacturers, led by the printer companies, that has developed a specification for communication between PCs and printers on a LAN.

NSFNet. National Science Foundation Network: a *TCP/IP* network for the interconnection of US supercomputing facilities.

NQS. Network Queueing System: a set of software developed by NASA, Sterling Software and latterly the Cummings Group designed to run batch jobs on different machines on a network. It permits the user to submit jobs which can then be queued and scheduled according to a load balancing algorithm. Such a setup is often referred to as a 'compute farm' and is in essence distributed computing for batch jobs. It is primarily a UNIX-based product but there is a version for MVS. NQS is used in *POSIX* 1003.15.

ODA. Open Document Architecture: the standard produced jointly by the *CCITT* and *ISO* which defines the basic structure of text in a document which may be transmitted between *OSI* systems. It is essentially a data stream architecture for revisable and non-revisable documents and provides for the description of a document in terms of contents, logical structure and layout. ODA also provides architectures for text, image and graphics. There are several standards which make up ODA. It is closely related to *ODIF*. ISO 8613.

ODIF. Open Document Interchange Format: a specification of document profiles, structure and content to enable the accurate interchange of documents between unlike systems. It is closely related to *ODA*.

OMG. Object Management Group: an international association of IT companies whose mission includes the production of an object-oriented environment to ease the portability and interoperability of software.

OLTP. OnLine Transaction Processing: the computer components needed to process discrete jobs or units of work (transactions), usually invoked from a terminal and involving database access of some kind. Tuxedo from AT&T, IBM's CICS and DEC's ACMS are examples of OLTP environments. There is considerable standards activity in OLTP. *IEEE* 1003.11, *ISO* 10026-1, 2, 3

ONA. Open Network Architecture: a generic term used to mean open systems.

ONC. Open Network Computing: Sun Microsystems networking architecture.

OpenGL. A vendor consortium formed to develop the Silicon Graphics Graphics Library (GL) via an open process. GL is essentially a *de facto* standard in graphics development (see also *PHIGS*).

OpenLook. Graphical User Interface (*GUI*) developed by Sun Microsystems and AT&T.

OSE. Open Systems Environment: a generic term used to denote open systems. It is also used in the *IEEE* 1003.0 definitions, although it is more closely defined there.

OSF. Open Software Foundation: a nonprofit organization whose aim is to provide the computer industry with a range of open system solutions including a modern implementation of UNIX (*OSF/1*), a toolkit for the creation of distributed environments (*DCE*), a product for the management of distributed environments (*DME*), a solution to the problem of application distribution across binary incompatible platforms (*ANDF*) and a graphical user interface (*Motif*). There are more than 150 members covering the spectrum from end users to manufacturers.

OSI. Open Systems Interconnection: a set of standard communication protocols, defined in the *OSI* Basic Reference Model to be independent of any one vendor, which will allow systems to be constructed which are guaranteed to be able to communicate easily.

OSI Basic Reference Model. The generic model by which open systems are constructed in *OSI*. Seven separate layers are defined to handle the communications process through the standard layer interfaces from an application on one machine, across a network to an application on another machine. It is also know as the *ISO* '7-layer model'. ISO 7498.

OURS. Open Users Resource Symposium: a forum established in 1992 for senior US IT executives to gather several times a year and discuss common issues involved in distributed systems, such as '*downsizing*' and client/server.

PARC. Palo Alto Research Center: Xerox Corporation's research establishment where several technologies used in UNIX were pioneered, including the development of *Ethernet* by Robert Metcalfe.

PCTE. Portable Common Tools Environment: an *ECMA* initiative aimed at specifying a common *CASE* environment (see also *SEE*). It is mainly aimed at *C*, *C++* and ADA programming environments. ECMA 149, 158.

PDES. Product Data Exchange Specification: the standard specified by PDES Inc., a consortium of US vendors and defense contractors using PDES to share data across systems.

PEX. PHIGS extensions to X: enables 3D drawings created using *PHIGS* to be distributed and displayed using the *X Windows* protocol.

PHIGS. Programmer's Hierarchical Interactive Graphics System: a standard (*ISO*, *FIPS* and *ANSI*) hardware independent high-function graphics programming specification. ISO 9592-1,2 and 3.

PHIGS+. Proposed extensions to *PHIGS* to provide enhanced function. ISO 9592-4.

PM. Presentation Manager: the graphical user interface (*GUI*) from Microsoft, designed for OS/2, the operating system for the IBM PS/2.

POSC. Petrotechnical Open Software Corporation: an open organization composed of members of the gas and oil industries in the areas of exploration and production.

POSIX. Portable Operating System Interface for Computer Environments: the name given to the *IEEE* 1003 committee and the related standards and functions which it is developing, e.g. 1003.1 which defines the low-level interface with the UNIX operating system. Other 1003.x committees deal with such things as systems management, security and transaction processing. IEEE 1003.1 to 20, ISO 9945-1.

PowerOpen Association. A group of vendors developing hardware and software based on the POWER PC *RISC* architecture developed jointly by Apple, IBM and Motorola.

Profile. In open systems terms, a grouping of *OSI* standards tailored to meet specific application requirements, for example, *GOSIP* (Government OSI Profiles) or the *POSIX* Application Environment Profile (*AEP*).

PSI. Process to Support Interoperability: a *SPAG* initiative, inaugurated in March 1992. PSI is a service, open to all suppliers of Open Communications Systems products. PSI provides vendors with a code of conduct for the development, implementation, testing and demonstration of such interoperable products.

PTT. A generic term for national Postal, Telegraphy and Telecommunications agencies.

RDA. Remote Database Access: an emerging International Standard for the access of data held on one system from another systems remote from it. It specifically addresses relational data but is not limited to it. It is for performance reasons that relational data is considered for the RDA standard since an *SQL* query can be shipped and executed in its entirety on a remote system. Hierarchical and network databases would need to retrieve records each time to navigate their way through a remote database. ISO DP 9759.

RDB. Relational DataBase: a generic term, for example, 'the Oracle RDB'.

RFC. Request For Comment: part of the process prior to *ISO* authorization of a standard. The RFC mechanism was the way that *TCP/IP* developed since it was not fully specified at the outset and much of its function was put in by users via RFCs.

RFT. Request For Technology: the *OSF* process for soliciting the submission of technology enhancements via an open process which are subsequently evaluated for inclusion in OSF's offerings.

RGCA. Raster Graphics Content Architecture: the part of *ODA* dealing with revisable and non-revisable raster image data.

Rightsizing. A term meaning the placement of applications on a system or systems best able to deliver the business benefits of those applications. It does not imply, as *downsizing* does, the removal of an application from a central site machine to somewhere else. It is often used to describe the placement of a new application on a system other than the host. (See also *downsizing*).

RISC. Reduced Instruction Set Computer: originally a computer with a small number of optimized instructions with the potential for high performance. The technology was

pioneered by Dr John Cocke of IBM and the term coined by Prof David Patterson and his students at Berkeley. IBM produced an experimental RISC machine, the *801*, in 1976.

Router. A device or method for choosing the best route for data packets based on knowledge of the network topology. Routers operate at level 3 of the *OSI* reference model and are independent of the physical layer (layer 1).

RPC. Remote Procedure Call: an architecture for requesting the execution of one or more processes on remote machines, as if they were local. The RPC architecture has several implementations, in particular those in Sun's *NFS* and H-P-Apollo's *NCS* - now part of the Open Software Foundation's (*OSF*) *DCE*. ECMA 127, ISO 10148, IEEE P1237, OSF DCE.

SAG. SQL Access Group: a vendor consortium with a mission to resolve some of compatibility problems among the different implementations of *SQL*. It also assists *ISO* in producing the *RDA* standard.

Scalability. The ability to run the same software without change while keeping acceptable performance on any size of machine.

SCO. Santa Cruz Operation: originally a distributor of Microsoft's *UNIX*-like operating system for the PC - *XENIX*. SCO is now the developer of XENIX which, through an agreement with AT&T, is now called SCO UNIX.

SCSI. Small Computer Systems Interface: an industry hardware standard protocol for attachment of I/O peripherals (disk, tape, etc.) to processor systems.

SEE. Software Engineering Environment: a *CASE* standard being developed by *ECMA* (cf. *PCTE*).

SMTP. Simple Mail Transfer Protocol: a part of the *TCP/IP* protocols. RFC 821.

SNMP. Simple Network Management Protocol, a set of evolving protocols and functions designed to manage *TCP/IP* networks (see also *CMIS*). RFC 1098.

S-SNMP. Secure SNMP: extensions to *SNMP* which will support Appletalk, Novell NetWare and *OSI* as well as *TCP/IP*.

SPAG. Standards Promotion and Applications Group: a group of European IT vendors and users whose aim is to promote interoperable products, especially *OSI*, which are based on international standards. (See also *PSI*.)

Solaris. Sun Microsystems Inc. restructured into a number of separate companies in the early 1990s. SunSoft, the software arm, renamed *SUN OS*, their *UNIX*-like operating system, Solaris. Solaris 2, the current version, is the version developed in conjunction with AT&T and is very close to *SVR4*.

SOS. Standards and Open Systems group: an informal group of IT executives which started to meet in 1991. Members include Du Pont, Kodak, General Motors, McDonnell Douglas, Merck, Motorola, 3M, Northrop, Unilever and American Airlines. These companies agreed 'that they had a common need to accelerate the commercial availability of Open Systems based on vendor neutral standards and enabling technologies in a proactive manner'. SOS has published a profile of standards it is pursuing, covering twenty five areas of IT activity, including graphics, networking, interoperability and CASE.

SPARC. Scalable Processor Architecture: a chip technology developed by Sun Microsystems and intended to become a *de facto* standard. It is licensed to a number of other vendors. Not to be confused with the ANSI X3 Standards Planning and Review Committee with the same initials.

SPARC. Standards Planning and Review Committee: an *ANSI* X3 committee.

SPEC. Standard Performance Evaluation Corporation (sometimes known as the Systems Performance Evaluation Cooper-

ative): a consortium of workstation and other vendors whose aim is to produce a series of consistent and agreed benchmarks and performance tests to assess the relative powers of different *UNIX*-based processors. SPEC 1.0 was the first benchmark produced by this body.

SPX. Novell's Sequenced Packet eXchange Protocol: its role is to monitor network transmissions to ensure successful delivery. It is the connection oriented protocol, based on *IPX*, and is needed for printing services.

SQL. Structured Query Language: a nonprocedural language for access to a database built according to the relational model. Access can be from within a program or via an interactive query. ISO 9075, ANSI X3.168.

STEP. Standard for the Exchange of Product Model Data: an *ISO* initiative for CAD model data exchange which seeks to eliminate some of the deficiencies of *IGES*. See Chapter 13.

Sun/OS. Sun Microsystems implementation of *UNIX*, based on *BSD*, and now called *Solaris*.

SVID. UNIX System V Interface Definition: the detailed specification of *UNIX* from which SVID compliant versions of UNIX implementations are derived. The interfaces are also used by System V programmers. SVID Issue 2 is based on System V Release 2 with some extensions from System V Release 3. SVID 3 is based on SVR4.

SVR4. System V Release 4: the latest (as of January 1993) *USL* implementation of *UNIX*.

TAPI. Trusted Application Programming Interface: the *API* for SecureWare's security products. It has been selected as part of *OSF/1*.

TCOS. Technical Committee on Operating Systems: the *IEEE* committee responsible for the development of the *POSIX* standards.

TCP/IP. the Transmission Control Protocol/Internet Protocol: a *de facto* standard approximating to layers 3 and 4 of *OSI*. It was developed the US *DoD* and later adopted by the UNIX community as the communications vehicle in *UNIX* networks.

TCSEC. Trusted Computer Systems Evaluation Criteria: the US *DoD* operating system security grading also known as the Orange Book. This is published by the *NCSC* and helps vendors and users in the specification of secure systems. The 'Orange Book' defines four levels of security:

- Level A - Verified Protection which uses formal security verification and extensive documentation. Sometimes known as the 'Shoot all the programmers' level of security.

- Level B - Mandatory Access protection which enforces mandatory access control rules for entities such as files, devices and processes.

- Level C - Discretionary Access protection which provides for discretionary protection and accountability of users and tasks and of the actions they initiate through the use of audit trails.

- Level D - Minimal protection. Such systems are those which have been evaluated but failed to meet the requirements of a higher level.

Each security level is subdivided using a numeric digit. For example, C level security is divided into C1 and C2. The higher the numeric digit, the higher is the security control within the level. For example, B3 represents greater security than B1 and any B level is higher than any C level security.

Telnet. The terminal emulation part of the *TCP/IP* protocols. It allows a user at a terminal attached to one system to access another system as if directly attached to it. RFC 793, 854.

TFTP. Trivial File Transfer Protocol: a part of the *TCP/IP* protocols. RFC 783.

Thread. A small unit of work or code into which a single process has been broken.

Such units allow the parallel execution of a process across several nodes in a network thereby increasing the speed of execution.

TNI. Trusted Network Interpretation: an *NCSC* document applying the specifications in *TCSEC* to network security.

Token Ring. A *LAN* in the form of a logical ring in which stations can only transmit messages when in receipt of a circulating token. A Token Ring can be configured so that it can survive a break at any station, which would not be possible with a physical ring topology. (See also *802.5*.)

TOP. Technical and Office Protocol: the functional standard promoted by Boeing Aircraft Corporation for the office systems environment. It is closely related, and complementary, to *MAP*.

TPPC. Transaction Processing Performance Council: an organization of vendors and others committed to developing controlled and auditable benchmarks for commercial transaction processing. TPC-A, TPC-B and TPC-C are well-known benchmarks from the TPPC.

UAOS. User Alliance for Open Systems: originally called the 'Atlanta 17', then the 'Houston 30', this organization of large companies and government agencies is 'vendor-free' and tries to specify users' open systems requirements and present them to the IT vendors.

UI-ATLAS. A distributed computing framework from *UNIX International* which provides a set of *API*s for accessing resources across the network. It allows the integration of *OSF DCE*, Sun *ONC*, DEC NAS and IBM SAA.

ULTRIX. Digital Equipment Corporation's implementation of *UNIX*.

UniForum. An organization of *UNIX* users which pioneered much of the work which led to the *POSIX* standards committees. It is a non-profit organization of systems professionals which disseminates information on open systems technologies through various activities such as conferences and trade shows e.g. annual UniForum Conference and Trade Show in the USA. UniForum has a strategic partnership with *X/Open*.

UNIX. An AT&T developed operating system widely adopted by most major hardware manufacturers which has become a *de facto* standard. The AT&T version is now marketed by UNIX System Laboratories (*USL*).

UNIX International. An open membership organization of users, vendors and developers of *UNIX* System V.

User interface. The part of the operating environment to which the user has direct access, allowing him to perform tasks by selecting an icon but which previously would have required lengthy commands. User interfaces usually support graphics and windowing facilities. This is then known as a *GUI*.

USENIX. An organization of AT&T licensees, sublicensees and other professional and technical persons, formed for the purpose of exchanging ideas about *UNIX* and similar operating systems and the *C* programming language.

USL. UNIX System Laboratories: the company which now owns the rights to AT&T *UNIX* As of January 1993 Novell had announced its intention to acquire USL and had already reached agreement with AT&T, the majority share holder. USL are developing UNIX System V and seeks to incorporate specifications developed by UNIX International (*UI*) into it. USL was previously known as UNIX Software Operation (USO).

UTS. Universal Timesharing System: a mainframe version of *UNIX*, running on IBM System/370 architecture machines and marketed by Amdahl Corporation.

VTP. Virtual Terminal Protocol: an *OSI* application layer specification for terminal access across networks. The real terminal is

mapped to a virtual terminal specification and mapped as a compatible terminal to the application at the other end.

X Consortium. A group of companies which, together with the Massachusetts Institute of Technology (*MIT*), control and support the development of the *X Windows* system. It delivers specifications, software and related documentation for each release.

X/Open. An international non-profit organization set up to define and promote open systems technologies. It is owned by a consortium of the world's largest computer manufacturers and, although it is not a standards-setting organization, it aims to combine existing and emerging standards to define a platform independent environment. It publishes its standards in the X Portability Guides (*XPG*).

WAN. Wide Area Network.

X Windows. A windowing system, full name the X Window System, developed as part of *MIT*'s Project Athena, which was funded by IBM and DEC. It is a set of low-level functions and libraries which are used to build higher-level tools like Widgets and Gadgets, which in turn can be used to produce sophisticated windowing environments like *OpenLook* and *OSF/Motif*. X Windows 11.5 is current at the time of writing.

XA. Transaction API. *X/Open*'s specification of the interface between a transaction processing program and associated databases - part of its *DTP* model. It is a protocol specified to enable different transaction processing systems to update multiple databases via 2PC (2-phase commit). In theory, it is independent of the *OLTP* or DB software.

XA+. The *X/Open* specification of the interface between transaction and communication managers in an OLTP system.

XDR. eXternal Data Representation: a data format, part of *NFS*, by which machines of different architecture exchange commands and data across a network via the *RPC* mechanism.

Xenix. An implementation of UNIX for Intel-based PCs. Originally developed by Microsoft, it is now developed and marketed by the Santa Cruz Operation (*SCO*).

XNS. Xerox Network Systems: a set of *LAN* communications software and a precursor of *TCP/IP*. It can be found on a number of proprietary LANs. XNS was documented in the famous 'grey book', 'Xerox Standards XNSS 028112', in 1981.

XPG. X/Open Portability Guide(s): specifications published by *X/Open*, they are an evolving set of specifications for application programming interfaces (*API*s) to make the applications portable across platforms which comply with XPG specifications. Products and systems can be submitted for conformance testing against the XPG specifications. If successful, they receive an *X/Open* Branding Certificate for the relevant XPG release. XPG4 became available in September 1992.

XTI. X/Open Transport Interface: an operating systems and transport layer independent interface. It defines a simple set of APIs to the networking services at layer 4 transport in the *ISO OSI* seven-layer model. These interfaces allow applications on different systems to link and exchange data using a variety of network services at layers 1,2 and 3.

XTP. X/Open Distributed Transaction Processing model: a software architecture that allows multiple application programs to share resources administered by multiple resource managers and allows their work to be coordinated into global transactions.

X.21. The *CCITT* standard for communication between user devices and a circuit-switched network.

X.25. The *CCITT* Interface standard for communication by user devices across a packet-switched network.

X.400. The *CCITT* standard service protocol for mail handling.

X.500. The *CCITT* standard directory services facility across interconnected computer systems. The directory allows applications on one system to locate and retrieve information about resources on another system. Examples of these resources are user name, address and routing information. ISO 9594.

X.700. A series of *CCITT* network management standards, equivalent to *OSI* standards: X.710, for example, is *CMIS* or *ISO* 9595; X.711 is *CMIP* or *ISO* 9596.

X.800. The *CCITT* security standard for authentication, access control and general security on networks. ISO 7498-2.

601. A *RISC* chip developed by Apple, IBM and Motorola from the IBM RISC System/6000 POWER architecture, the basis of the PowerPC.

801. The original IBM RISC project name and the number given to the experimental *RISC* machine produced in 1976 by Dr John Cocke.

802.3. A *LAN* protocol utilizing Carrier Sense Multiple Access with Collision Detect (CSMA/CD). It is more commonly known as *Ethernet* although there are header differences between the two.

802.5. The *Token Ring LAN* standard which avoids the collision situation of 802.3 by deterministic use of a 'token' to control traffic on the ring.

88Open. An organization of hardware and software vendors which has adopted the Motorola 88000 *RISC* architecture as their chosen platform for open systems implementations.

Index